# THE COMPLETE IDIOT'S GUIDE® TO

# Medical Tourism

*by Patrick W. Marsek and Frances Sharpe*

## ALPHA

A member of Penguin Group (USA) Inc.

## ALPHA BOOKS

Published by the Penguin Group

Penguin Group (USA) Inc., 375 Hudson Street, New York, New York 10014, USA

Penguin Group (Canada), 90 Eglinton Avenue East, Suite 700, Toronto, Ontario M4P 2Y3, Canada (a division of Pearson Penguin Canada Inc.)

Penguin Books Ltd., 80 Strand, London WC2R 0RL, England

Penguin Ireland, 25 St. Stephen's Green, Dublin 2, Ireland (a division of Penguin Books Ltd.)

Penguin Group (Australia), 250 Camberwell Road, Camberwell, Victoria 3124, Australia (a division of Pearson Australia Group Pty. Ltd.)

Penguin Books India Pvt. Ltd., 11 Community Centre, Panchsheel Park, New Delhi—110 017, India

Penguin Group (NZ), 67 Apollo Drive, Rosedale, North Shore, Auckland 1311, New Zealand (a division of Pearson New Zealand Ltd.)

Penguin Books (South Africa) (Pty.) Ltd., 24 Sturdee Avenue, Rosebank, Johannesburg 2196, South Africa

Penguin Books Ltd., Registered Offices: 80 Strand, London WC2R 0RL, England

## Copyright © 2009 by Patrick W. Marsek and Frances Sharpe

International Standard Book Number: 978-1-59257-808-5
Library of Congress Catalog Card Number: 2008935064

11   10   09      8   7   6   5   4   3   2   1

Interpretation of the printing code: The rightmost number of the first series of numbers is the year of the book's printing; the rightmost number of the second series of numbers is the number of the book's printing. For example, a printing code of 09-1 shows that the first printing occurred in 2009.

*Printed in the United States of America*

**Note:** This publication contains the opinions and ideas of its authors. It is intended to provide helpful and informative material on the subject matter covered. It is sold with the understanding that the authors and publisher are not engaged in rendering professional services in the book. If the reader requires personal assistance or advice, a competent professional should be consulted.

The authors and publisher specifically disclaim any responsibility for any liability, loss, or risk, personal or otherwise, which is incurred as a consequence, directly or indirectly, of the use and application of any of the contents of this book.

Most Alpha books are available at special quantity discounts for bulk purchases for sales promotions, premiums, fundraising, or educational use. Special books, or book excerpts, can also be created to fit specific needs.

For details, write: Special Markets, Alpha Books, 375 Hudson Street, New York, NY 10014.

**Publisher:** *Marie Butler-Knight*
**Editorial Director/Acquiring Editor:** *Mike Sanders*
**Senior Managing Editor:** *Billy Fields*
**Senior Development Editor:** *Phil Kitchel*
**Senior Production Editor:** *Janette Lynn*
**Copy Editor:** *Christine Hackerd*

**Cartoonist:** *Steve Barr*
**Cover Designer:** *Bill Thomas*
**Book Designer:** *Trina Wurst*
**Indexer:** *Heather McNeill*
**Layout:** *Ayanna Lacey*
**Proofreader:** *Mary Hunt*

# Contents at a Glance

# Contents

# Introduction

If you're looking for safe, affordable medical care provided in an exotic locale, this book is for you! This book is an easy-to-read, comprehensive guide to the fast-growing phenomenon of medical tourism—voyaging abroad in search of high-quality, low-cost medical care. The information in this book is based on years of experience helping people just like you find the quality medical care they want overseas. What you'll find is a book that's chock-full of the tools you'll need to plan a safe and successful medical voyage of your own.

## How This Book Is Organized

For your convenience, this book is divided into four step-by-step parts in addition to a section on the most popular medical tourism destination countries.

**Part 1, "What Is Medical Tourism?"** gives you the ABCs of medical tourism. Here you'll discover just how common medical tourism has become and why it's expected to explode in popularity in coming years. You'll also get the real deal on how much you actually can save by having surgery abroad, and you'll get the inside story on the procedures that are most popular among medical tourists. Not only that, you'll find out about quality and safety in foreign hospitals and whether you've got what it takes to become a medical tourist.

**Part 2, "Planning Your Health-Care Adventure,"** provides a blueprint to help you turn your medical tourism dreams into reality. This section gives you the inside scoop on how to choose a foreign doctor and fills you in on what to look for in an international hospital. In addition, you'll discover the best ways to research your Medical Tourism options. And you'll be introduced to a new kind of travel agency that can handle all the planning so you don't have to.

**Part 3, "Dollars and Sense,"** spells out everything you need to know about money matters and medical tourism. This section offers a breakdown of all the costs involved and includes handy budget worksheets to help you figure out the total cost for your overseas medical procedure. You'll also get the lowdown on loans and other financing options that can help you cover the costs of a health-care excursion. There also are helpful hints on deducting medical tourism expenses on your taxes. And there's a look at why medical tourism might be covered by insurance in the future.

**Part 4, "Globetrotting,"** provides you with the know-how to make your medical voyage a success. In this section, you'll discover the steps you can take before your trip to help ensure a safe procedure. You'll also get the 411 on international travel basics and a special packing guide specifically geared to health-care travelers. There also are a host of post-op do's and don'ts to help make your recovery as speedy and comfortable as possible. Finally, you'll get a crash course in what you can do to make your homecoming as easy and stress-free as possible.

A special Appendix A gives you a comprehensive overview of some of the most popular medical tourism destinations in the world. You'll get an inside look at what it's like to visit these exotic locations as a medical tourist, along with need-to-know info about the climate, vaccinations, cultural do's and don'ts, and much, much more. You'll also find briefings about the hospitals in each country that are the most amenable to North American medical tourists. And each country snapshot also includes a listing of average prices for some of the most popular medical tourism procedures.

## Extras

To help you get the most out of this book, we've included a healthy dose of valuable information in easy-to-spot boxes.

---

**CASE STUDY**

These boxes contain real-life stories from medical tourists who've already been there, done that.

---

**Doctor's Orders**

In these boxes, you'll find tips and strategies to make the most of your medical voyage. Think of them as an Rx for medical tourism success.

**Check-Up**

Intriguing facts and figures about the medical tourism scene.

**Code Blue!**

Keep these alerts in mind when planning an overseas health-care voyage. Remember, your health and well-being are on the line, so don't overlook these warnings.

**def•i•ni•tion**

You don't have to go to medical school to learn the lingo of medical tourism because these boxes will give you the definitions of terms you need to know.

## Acknowledgments

Patrick would like to thank Frances Sharpe for enthusiastically sharing her creative writing talents to develop this comprehensive guide to safe and affordable overseas health care. On a personal note, he offers his heartfelt appreciation to his wife, Lisa, and their sons, PJ and Joey, for sharing his passion to help others improve the quality of their lives. Patrick would also like to credit his business partner, Judson Anglin; his wife, Patty; and their two sons, Owen and Clark, for their roles in helping MedRetreat to become a truly wonderful resource for North Americans seeking surgery abroad.

He offers big thanks and praise to the entire staff and management at MedRetreat for their endless consideration and sincere compassion for the health and well-being of humanity. Through their daily interactions with patients in need, a safe and stress-free overseas health-care facilitation process was developed and proudly displayed within the pages of this book. A special acknowledgment goes out to the many MedRetreat clients who have allowed us to share their personal experiences in this book. He also wishes to extend his gratitude to his many colleagues in the medical tourism industry who graciously volunteered to lend their expertise to this project.

Frances is indebted to her co-author, Patrick Marsek, for sharing his tremendous expertise on Medical Tourism and for making the writing of this book such an enjoyable process. She extends great appreciation to all of the Medical Tourism trailblazers who agreed to share their personal stories with you, the reader. She offers profound thanks to Dr. Steven Tucker for his insights into the world of medical care overseas and for his sage advice for medical tourists. And, she is sincerely grateful to Dr. Art Schoenstadt for providing invaluable background health information.

She says "muchas gracias" to Carlos Zavala, "gamsa-hamnida" to Brad Brennan and Deokhyun Jo, "salamat" to Dr. Constantino Amores, and "terima kasih" to Tom Johnsrud for shedding light on the medical tourism scene in Mexico, South Korea, the Philippines, and Singapore, respectively. She extends tremendous thanks to Bruce Barwick, Dale Van Demark, David Boucher, Paul Laverty, Mark Argianas, and Adam Schwartz for lending their expertise on the financial, legal, and insurance implications of Medical Tourism. She offers a special thanks to Dr. Monica Silveira Cyrino who enlightened the authors on the practice of medical tourism throughout history.

She is grateful to agent Bob DiForio and to editors Mike Sanders, Phil Kitchel, and Christine Hackerd for their suggestions on polishing the manuscript.

Finally, she extends her warmest thanks to her amazing husband, Wil, for making life a whole lot more fun.

## Trademarks

All terms mentioned in this book that are known to be or are suspected of being trademarks or service marks have been appropriately capitalized. Alpha Books and Penguin Group (USA) Inc. cannot attest to the accuracy of this information. Use of a term in this book should not be regarded as affecting the validity of any trademark or service mark.

# Part 1

# What Is Medical Travel?

In this part, you'll learn the basics about medical travel. Find out why it's growing in popularity, how much you can save, and the types of medical procedures you can have overseas. In addition, you'll discover why going abroad for medical treatment can be just as safe as heading to your local hospital. And you'll find out if you fit the mold of the typical medical traveler.

# Medical Tourism at a Glance

## In This Chapter

- What is medical tourism?
- The history of traveling for health care
- Why medical tourism is gaining popularity
- Where health-care travelers are heading
- How insurance companies might get in on the act

Have you ever heard of "medical tourism"? That's a question I ask every person I meet. According to personal experience, most Americans have never heard the term and don't have any idea what it means. Although you may not be familiar with the concept now, chances are you'll be hearing a lot more about it in the coming years.

Medical tourism is a growing trend that has already been featured on national television programs, such as *60 Minutes*, and in dozens of major newspapers and magazines. Even so, the concept has yet to reach the mainstream. In this chapter, I spell out the basics of medical tourism, including how you may be able to benefit from it.

# What Is Medical Tourism?

Very simply, *medical tourism* is the practice of traveling abroad in search of high-quality, low-cost medical care. Over the past few decades, more and more Americans have ventured beyond our borders to seek out all kinds of medical treatment in foreign hospitals and clinics. The primary reason people are heading overseas is the potential for saving a bundle of money.

## def•i•ni•tion

**Medical tourism** refers to the concept of going abroad for the purpose of receiving health-care services.

Medical tourism also may be referred to by any of the following terms, which may be used interchangeably throughout this book:

- Medical travel
- Medical outsourcing
- Global health care

- Health tourism
- Health travel
- Health-care tourism
- Health-care travel
- Global outsourcing
- International health care

Whether you're interested in a face lift, a tummy tuck, a hip replacement, spinal surgery, or dental work, you can have it done in any one of dozens of countries offering first-class medical care at Third World prices.

For instance, a face lift that could cost upward of $20,000 in Beverly Hills might be as little as $6,000 in a U.S.-affiliated hospital in Malaysia, including airfare and resort-style accommodations. A bilateral hip replacement that could set you back as much as $90,000 in the United States could run you less than $20,000 in India, including five-star hotel accommodations and airfare.

If for any reason, you'd like to take advantage of more affordable medical treatment, you may want to look into medical tourism as an alternative. It's understandable, however, that the idea of going overseas for major surgery might be somewhat frightening to you, especially if you aren't a seasoned world traveler.

| | |
|---|---|
| Name: | Mary |
| Age at time of surgery: | Late 40s |
| Residence: | Alaska |
| Procedure: | Knee replacement |
| Destination country: | Malaysia |
| Cost in United States: | $90,000 (follow up therapy included) |
| Total cost abroad (travel included): | $17,000 |

"I needed to have my knee replaced by year's end, or I would be in a wheelchair," says Mary. With a $90,000 price tag and without insurance to cover the costs, Mary figured that a new knee might never be in her future.

That is, until her husband read an article about medical tourism in the newspaper and then heard a report about it on National Public Radio. Mary had never heard of such a thing, but was intrigued by the stories of people going to Singapore, Thailand, and India and saving thousands of dollars on medical procedures.

Not long after, Mary was on a plane heading to a foreign country for a knee replacement to be performed by a top-notch orthopedic specialist in a hospital with state-of-the-art equipment. "I found the medical staff, hospital, and doctor superb beyond words," she says. "Everyone spoke English and was extremely professional." All of this cost $70,000 less than what she would have had to shell out at home.

Just one month after her surgery, Mary was walking pain free and she was no longer taking pain pills—just two aspirin a day. "The quality of my life has improved," she says. "People say I look younger and taller. Having a new knee enables me to stand upright."

In this business, I find that people who are considering health-care travel often feel more confident about the concept after talking to former patients who've been there, done that. I can't do that in a book, but I can let you read what some people who've gone abroad for medical care are saying about their experiences.

K.H. in Texas: "My entire trip, including procedure, travel, and accommodations cost only $8,500 in Thailand, compared to $32,000 for the procedure alone here in America. And I was able to recuperate in peace and quiet in a beautiful paradise setting for about four weeks. I came back home feeling refreshed and ready to take on the world again."

S.L. in Washington: "My husband and I no longer think that the only outstanding medical care is found in the U.S."

J.S. in Missouri: "While overseas [for my hysterectomy], I was treated like a queen. I was impressed. Compared to the U.S., I felt there was much more doctor–patient contact, and, in the hospital, more nurses and staff per patient. I was visited by the hospital director at least every other day to be sure everything was OK, and the director of nurses visited me every day to be sure the nursing staff was taking care of me properly. The nursing staff was very attentive and made sure I was as comfortable as possible."

W.S. in Washington: "When I was told I needed a total hip replacement, I was devastated. I could never afford it, so I thought I would be disabled at fifty-five years [of age]. Then, one day in pain, I searched for 'hip replacement' on the Internet and discovered medical tourism. The entire cost was actually affordable. The hospital, doctor, accommodations, and everything were way beyond my expectations. I'm back to work and pain free."

B.B. in Arizona: "Of course, I was skeptical of medical tourism. But I can honestly say I had a wonderful experience. The hospital staff, my doctor, and everyone I came in contact with were very friendly and helpful. I traveled alone and was a little nervous about not only traveling to a foreign country alone, but facing surgery alone. I had a face and neck lift, eye lift, and upper arm lift. I could not be happier with the results and felt well enough only five days after my surgeries to start going on tours and shopping. I had a great vacation as well."

R.L. in Florida: "I had looked into the possibility of having a face lift here in the U.S., but simply could not afford it. So, I traveled to Malaysia to receive a full face and neck lift, liposuction in three areas of my midsection, and a couple of moles removed for less than half of what just the face lift would have cost me in the U.S. And, I got a vacation out of it, too!"

# Medical Tourism Through the Ages

Although the concept of medical tourism may be relatively new to Americans, it has been practiced for hundreds and even thousands of years. For instance, the ancient Greeks and Romans routinely hit the road in search of better health.

According to Dr. Monica Silveira Cyrino, a professor of classics at the University of New Mexico, the ancient Greeks traveled across borders to ancient healing shrines called Asklepeia. Dedicated to Asklepios, the god of medicine, these sacred hospitals were located throughout the Mediterranean.

**Check-Up**

"Ancient Greeks and Romans would actually travel across borders seeking out 'celebrity' doctors who were in high demand," says classics professor Dr. Monica Silveira Cyrino. "These doctors were almost always located in major urban areas, such as Athens, Rome, or Alexandria. And wealthy foreigners who could afford it would venture out on international journeys to seek care from them."

The ancient Romans traveled even further afield, according to Dr. Cyrino. Often called the world's first tourists, urban Romans traveled about 200 miles to the volcanic regions in Campania near Mount Vesuvius. The mountain's warm and sulfurous spas and hot springs were considered good for healing. As the Roman Empire expanded, so did the number of baths, spas, and healing shrines. People from all areas of the Roman world made long treks to experience the healing powers of these sites.

Historically, hospitals were few and far between. Medical facilities often were found in major metropolitan centers, so people living in outlying areas were forced to travel long distances to receive medical care.

For decades, modern Europeans have been traveling to nearby countries or to Africa, Asia, or South America for better or less expensive treatment. For many years, people from Third World countries have been coming to the United States in search of health care. The modern concept of medical tourism has become more popular in the last thirty to forty years thanks to the advent of the Internet and improvements in telecommunications and air travel. The overall ease of travel has made it far more convenient for people to journey to other countries for health care.

Only in the past few decades have Americans begun to venture outside our borders for medical treatment. At first, it was mainly major movie stars and the wealthy elite who sought out cosmetic surgery procedures abroad. By going overseas, these high-profile individuals can preserve their anonymity and dignity while recuperating in a foreign land where it is less likely that they will be recognized.

**Check-Up**

In the early days of American medical tourism, patients had to organize everything themselves and everything was conducted via word of mouth. A friend or acquaintance gave a referral to a foreign doctor, and the patient had to handle the rest. There weren't any organizations or websites to help them navigate the process. Today, a host of entities are simplifying medical tourism and making it as stress free as possible.

As the popularity of cosmetic surgery exploded, more and more Americans from all walks of life wanted to experience the benefits of a little nip/tuck, but couldn't necessarily afford it. These individuals began taking to the skies in search of cheaper prices for cosmetic procedures.

Now skyrocketing health-care costs have introduced a new segment of medical tourists—those in need of more affordable medically necessary treatments. This segment of the industry is expected to experience the most explosive growth over the next decade.

# Soaring Popularity of Medical Travel

According to the Medical Tourism Association (MTA), approximately 500,000 Americans traveled abroad for some type of health care in 2006. That figure is expected to jump into the millions as early as 2009, according to MTA projections. Add to that the widely reported 300,000 Canadians who go abroad each year for medical or dental procedures, and the numbers are impressive.

Other sources, however, differ wildly on the number of medical tourists jetting across the ocean for medical services. For instance, the McKinsley Quarterly places the current market at 60,000 to 85,000 inpatient medical tourists per year. These numbers don't include outpatients, expatriates seeking care in their current country of residence, and emergency medical care received while abroad.

Others swing to the opposite side of the spectrum and claim millions of U.S. citizens are already crossing borders for health care. I estimate that the actual numbers are somewhere in between these extremes.

The MTA estimates that by 2010, medical tourism will be a $40 billion industry. In India alone, medical tourism currently generates $2 billion per year and is growing at an annual rate of 25 to 30 percent. Studies report that Asia's medical tourism business is expected to reach $4.4 billion by 2012.

## The Numbers Game

Why are the statistics all over the map? Because most of the figures being thrown around are little more than guesstimates. There simply isn't a central organization that tracks the number of Americans going abroad.

**Code Blue!**

Be aware that some statistics about the medical tourism industry may be inflated. I don't claim to know exactly how many Americans are heading abroad for health care. I can truthfully say, however, that our business has doubled each year since we began in 2005. We currently receive more than 7,000 inquiries per year from people interested in medical tourism.

Renee-Marie Stephano, General Counsel for the MTA and editor of the association's *Medical Tourism* magazine, explains that the association's numbers are culled from a variety of reliable sources:

♦ Studies on medical tourism

♦ Immigration paperwork on which travelers can check the reason for their trip (for example, business, vacation, or health care)

♦ Foreign hospitals reporting numbers of international patients

♦ Foreign governments in countries that cater to medical tourists

However, Stephano adds that vast numbers of medical tourists may go unreported. "People going abroad for cosmetic surgery or cosmetic dentistry may go to clinics as opposed to hospitals, and clinics don't report to their national government," Stephano says. "Only hospitals report to the government, and our data comes from governments who get it from the hospitals and immigration paperwork."

The MTA is hoping to change all the guesswork. Stephano says the association is currently seeking funding to begin formally documenting medical tourism statistics. This would help give a clearer picture of the number of Americans heading overseas and the dollar figure being spent on medical and dental procedures abroad.

## What's Spurring the Growth?

Although it may be difficult to pin down statistics on the exact number of health-care travelers, there's no doubt that the industry is growing. Several things are helping stimulate that growth:

♦ Word of mouth

♦ The media

♦ The Internet

♦ Advertising

As rising numbers of Americans venture abroad for medical care, word spreads. When these patients return from their trips, they may share their experiences with friends, family, neighbors, and acquaintances. This helps build awareness about the industry.

The media also is largely credited with driving consumer interest in medical travel. In fact, the media directly influences which treatments people seek. How? When *60 Minutes* ran a story on patients going abroad for heart surgery and hip resurfacing, it caused a major spike in interest. Prior to that, many simply weren't aware that you could travel overseas to have those procedures at an affordable cost.

Each time there's a story on television or in *The New York Times* or *USA Today*, there's a surge in inquiries. As more people become aware of the myriad procedures available around the world, they are more likely to consider medical tourism as an option.

The advent of the Internet is another reason medical tourism is flourishing. With a simple Google search for "medical tourism" or "medical travel," you can find dozens and even hundreds of websites offering information on the industry. As Americans become more educated about the possibility of medical travel, they are more willing to give it a try.

As foreign countries attempt to tap into the growing medical tourism market, many have begun advertising directly to American consumers. Once again, these ads serve to make Americans more aware of health-care travel as an affordable alternative to pricey medical care in the United States.

# Popular Destinations for Medical Travelers

These days, nearly every country claims to be a destination for medical travelers. Some nations, however, have clearly emerged as leaders in the industry. Some of the most popular destination countries include: Thailand, Singapore, India, Malaysia, Costa Rica, Brazil, and Argentina.

Southeast Asia has become a destination of choice for many medical travelers. For the lowest prices, you can't beat India. Locations like Singapore, Thailand, and Malaysia, where English is widely spoken, boast helpful international patient centers, sophisticated infrastructures, and state-of-the-art hospitals with U.S. affiliations.

Mexico has become known for its many dental clinics, and Costa Rica has been a popular destination for cosmetic surgery and cosmetic dentistry since the 1980s. According to the Costa Rica Tourism Bureau, the number of visitors seeking out medical treatment has doubled since 2003.

**Check-Up** _____

According to a report by Abacus International, more than 1.6 million medical tourists each year head for Asia. Here's the breakdown of Asia's annual visitors:

- ◆ 1 million medical tourists head to Thailand
- ◆ 370,000 health-care travelers visit Singapore
- ◆ 150,000 international patients visit India
- ◆ 200,000 medical travelers opt for Malaysia

These countries are especially appealing to Americans because of their proximity to the United States. Individuals living in California, Arizona, or Texas can simply drive across the border into Mexico, and a flight from Miami to Costa Rica takes about three hours. That's far less than the travel time required for many other destination countries.

For similar reasons, Cuba has emerged as a popular choice for Canadians searching for access to health care. In 2006, 9,000 visitors from nearly 40 countries received medical treatments in orthopedics, general surgery, cosmetic surgery, cardiology, and pediatrics, according to Cubanacan Tourism and Health, which facilitates medical tourism to the Caribbean islands.

South America is another hot spot for health-care travel. In body-conscious Brazil, cosmetic plastic surgeons routinely sculpt the breasts, bellies, and behinds of medical travelers from around the world. Argentina, meanwhile, offers some of the lowest dental procedure prices of any destination.

Other countries are poised to make their mark in the medical tourism industry. Dubai, in the United Arab Emirates, is nearing completion of its highly anticipated Dubai Healthcare City. This facility will be the largest medical center between Europe and Southeast Asia, and it is being designed with international patients in mind.

**Check-Up** _____

Bumrungrad International Hospital in Bangkok, Thailand, is considered the most popular hospital for medical tourists worldwide. Each year, Bumrungrad serves more than 400,000 international patients, including expatriates and visitors from 190 countries.

**Code Blue!** _____

Be aware that travel time to many medical tourism destinations can take a total of 24 hours or even more.

# What About the "Tourism" Part?

Certainly, the idea of combining surgery with a vacation at a sunny beach resort sounds appealing. Many medical tourism destinations offer exquisite sightseeing opportunities. However, you may need to rethink the "vacation" portion of your trip.

Remember that your primary objective in traveling abroad is to receive high-quality medical treatment and to recuperate adequately until it's safe for you to return home. Tourism and vacation activities need to take a backseat to a safe procedure and recovery.

> **Doctor's Orders**
>
> Engaging in strenuous activities or heavy lifting following many surgical procedures can increase the risk for excessive bleeding and prolonged swelling. After many cosmetic procedures, you'll be advised to stay out of the sun. That means no lounging by the pool or tanning on the beach.

In general, many tourist activities aren't recommended after you've had surgery. Think about it. Going on a long, bumpy sightseeing bus tour while you're recovering from a hip replacement or a spinal procedure could be painfully uncomfortable, or worse, could land you back in the hospital for additional surgery or could cause severe or even potentially life-threatening consequences. Likewise, attempting a five-mile jungle trek on newly repaired knees could cause extreme pain and could seriously jeopardize your recovery.

Usually following an operation, you need to take it easy. After you're feeling better post-operatively, you might want to schedule a little sightseeing or window-shopping near your hotel, but don't overdo it.

# A Burgeoning Global Business

The medical tourism industry is expected to experience explosive growth in the next decade. Currently the industry is driven by individual consumers seeking treatment abroad. But in the future, that's expected to change as health insurance companies and *self-funded employers* try to get in on the savings, too.

## def•i•ni•tion

> The phrase **self-funded employers** refers to companies that pay out-of-pocket for their employees' health-care treatments. With a self-funded plan, the company doesn't pay monthly insurance premiums; it pays only for services the employees actually receive.

For several years, health insurance providers and self-funded employers have been investigating the possibility of making medical tourism an option for their members or their employees. In fact, some insurers have already created pilot programs in which Americans can opt to go abroad for more affordable medical services.

After insurers work out the liability issues and get systems in place to facilitate the process, medical tourism is expected to skyrocket. You can find out more about how these insurance programs can benefit both the provider and you in upcoming chapters.

## The Least You Need to Know

- ◆ Medical tourism isn't such a new concept.

- ◆ Each year, more Americans are going abroad for medical care.

- ◆ Medical tourism statistics can vary widely.

- ◆ Many countries are vying for your business.

- ◆ Insurance companies might be offering medical tourism as an option in the near future.

# 2

# Slashing the High Cost of Health Care

## In This Chapter

◆ How medical tourism can help you cut costs

◆ Why it's so hard to give precise figures for United States and overseas treatment costs

◆ Estimates of how much you can save on various procedures

◆ Why U.S. medical costs are soaring

◆ Why treatment overseas costs less

Those who look into medical tourism typically do so for one reason: to find affordable health care. As health-care costs in the United States skyrocket, you may find it impossible to cover the out-of-pocket expenses for a surgical procedure. In fact, trying to come up with the money for surgeon, hospital, anesthesiology, and lab fees could put you into serious debt for the rest of your life.

If a procedure in the United States is simply too expensive for you, medical tourism may be the solution. By heading overseas, you can slash costs and take advantage of substantial savings.

# How Much Can You Save?

Medical tourism potentially can shave thousands and even tens of thousands of dollars off your treatment costs. In some cases, you actually can save more than $100,000 by having your procedure performed abroad rather than in the United States. Sounds like a good deal, doesn't it? It can be. In general, you can trim about 50 to 80 percent off the price of your surgery by heading overseas. The amount you actually save depends on several factors: the type of treatment you're seeking, your individual needs, your destination country, your surgeon, and your travel preferences.

Yes, the savings are attractive, but don't let cost be the only factor you consider when seeking treatment abroad. I do not encourage you to travel abroad for surgery simply because it is cheaper. Surgery is risky regardless of where it is performed and should be taken very seriously. Of course, finding affordable health care may be the primary reason why you're seeking medical care overseas. However, you need to focus on finding the best international hospitals and doctors to perform your surgical procedure as opposed to identifying the cheapest price.

## Code Blue!

Answering the question "How much can you save?" can be very tricky. Consider that the United States price for a single procedure can vary widely depending on location, surgeon experience, surgical technique, and your particular needs. The same procedure abroad is subject to a similar set of variables. The price you end up paying for a procedure abroad could be vastly different from the "average prices."

Consider a rhinoplasty (nose reshaping) procedure. Depending on the source, the average cost for rhinoplasty in the United States is about $4,500 to $5,500. This price tag includes the surgeon, anesthesiology, and facility fees. Your actual costs could be lower or much, much higher.

Let's say you live in Alabama and all you require is the removal of a small hump on the bridge of your nose. If you go to a local surgeon who's fairly new in practice, your total cost (surgeon, anesthesiology, and facility fees) may be as low as $4,000.

On the other hand, imagine that you go to a highly sought-after surgeon in Beverly Hills or Manhattan. Assume that your crooked sniffer requires straightening, tip work, hump removal, shortening, narrowing, and more. That fee could jump to $12,000 or even higher.

Now consider that the same variables exist abroad. If you choose to fly to India, the cost of a simple nose job might be $1,800. In Singapore, Costa Rica, or Brazil, however, it could cost you closer to $2,700. If you go to the most renowned surgeon in the country, your costs might be higher. And, if you need a complex rhinoplasty procedure, you can be sure you'll have to pay more.

**Doctor's Orders**

When comparing U.S. costs to overseas prices, make sure you're comparing apples to apples. Many medical tourism websites offer comparisons of U.S. and overseas surgery costs, but they don't tell you what is and isn't included in each price. When you're researching fees, ask for details about what the price covers. Does the quote include only the surgeon's fee? Does it include anesthesiology and the operating room? Are follow-up visits included? What about the hospital stay?

With medical tourism, there's yet another factor that comes into play: the travel portion of your trip. You can choose a luxurious—and pricey—five-star voyage or a modest, low-budget trip. When comparing costs with U.S. procedures, you need to add these expenses to the total price of your treatment.

**CASE STUDY**

| | |
|---|---|
| Name: | Didi |
| Age at time of surgery: | 48 and 58 |
| Residence: | California |
| Procedure: | Face lift |
| Destination country: | Costa Rica |
| Cost in United States: | about $20,000 |
| Total cost abroad (travel included): | about $5,000 |

Back in 1997, Didi had never heard the term "medical tourism." At age 48, she wanted to turn back the clock with a face lift. The only problem was that she didn't have the $20,000 it would have cost her then to go to a top-notch Beverly Hills plastic surgeon.

What she did have was $4,000 in a face-lift savings account she had started three years earlier. One day, a bank teller asked her if she'd ever thought of having her face lift done in Costa Rica. Didi turned her nose up at the suggestion. "There's no way I'm going to a Third World country for major surgery," she thought.

*continues*

*continued*

Later that same night, she hit the Internet and started researching. She landed on a website that seemed legit and that listed a few plastic surgeons. Curious, Didi decided to send an e-mail and ask for referrals to former patients in the United States. One of the plastic surgeons referred her to a former face-lift patient who just happened to be a surgeon in New York City.

Didi immediately called the New York doctor, incredulous that a surgeon living and practicing in Manhattan would have a face lift in Costa Rica. The doctor explained that he'd been dating a woman who had the best face lift he'd ever seen, and it had been performed by a doctor in Costa Rica. The New York surgeon flew to the Central American country to get a tour of the plastic surgeon's facilities and was so impressed that he decided to book a surgery date right then.

That was all Didi needed to hear. With her $4,000 (and a little bit more), she headed to Costa Rica for her face lift. Her friends thought she was crazy, but they also were anxious to see the results. When Didi returned looking refreshed and more youthful, her friends wanted in on the action, and several of them made the trip to Costa Rica for cosmetic surgery. Ten years later, Didi returned to Costa Rica for her second face lift with the same surgeon.

## Average Procedure Costs in the United States

Finding out how much surgical procedures cost in the United States isn't easy. Resources that spell out the average fees involved in medically necessary procedures are few and far between.

You may think that all you have to do is ask your doctor for the total cost of the treatment he or she is recommending. Unfortunately, there's a good chance you'll be met with a blank stare. Yes, the surgeon can usually inform you about his or her own fee, but may not be able to give you anything more precise than a ballpark figure on hospital and anesthesiology fees.

Unfortunately, there's no consistency in what hospitals and anesthesiologists charge. Prices in hospitals in the same city might fall on opposite ends of the spectrum. The same goes for anesthesiology fees.

To get an estimate of what your procedure will cost, you may need to call the hospital; even then, it may be just that—an estimate. Actual costs can vary for a variety of reasons. For instance, if your surgery takes longer than anticipated, you may have to pay extra for the operating room and the anesthesiologist.

Fees for cosmetic procedures are easier to come by and are more widely available.

The American Society of Plastic Surgeons (www.plasticsurgery.org) and the American Society for Aesthetic Plastic Surgery (www.surgery.org) both publish annual statistics on the average surgeon fees for cosmetic plastic-surgery procedures. Their figures, however, don't include anesthesiology and operating-room fees. A variety of other sources, however, do factor in those costs.

The following average costs are culled from a number of sources and include surgeon, anesthesiology, and operating-room fees. Hospital stays are not included. As mentioned previously, your actual costs may differ.

## Average Procedure Costs in United States

| Procedures | Average Prices* |
| --- | --- |
| *Cosmetic* | |
| Face lift/neck lift | $6,000–$15,000 |
| Blepharoplasty (upper/lower eyelid) | $1,500–$7,000 |
| Rhinoplasty | $4,000–$12,000 |
| Brow or forehead lift | $2,000–8,000 |
| Otoplasty | $2,000–$5,000 |
| Liposuction (per area) | $2,000–$10,000 |
| Tummy tuck | $5,000–9,000 |
| Breast augmentation | $4,000–$10,000 |
| Breast lift | $4,000–$9,000 |
| Breast reduction | $5,000–$10,000 |
| Inner thigh lift | $5,000–$8,000 |
| Outer thigh lift | $5,000–$8,000 |
| Buttock lift | $5,000–$9,000 |
| Lower body lift (inner/outer thighs, buttocks) | $12,000–$50,000 |
| Arm lift | $5,000–$6,500 |
| *Orthopedics* | |
| Hip replacement (per hip) | $32,000–$45,000 |
| Hip resurfacing | $25,000 |
| Knee replacement (per knee) | $20,000–$35,000 |

*continues*

## Average Procedure Costs in United States (continued)

| Procedures | Average Prices* |
| --- | --- |
| Spinal fusion | $62,000 |
| Spinal disc replacement | $35,000–$50,000 |
| *Cardiology* | |
| Angiogram | $5,000–6,000 |
| CT angiography scan | $700–$1,000 |
| Bypass surgery CAB | $130,000 |
| Heart valve replacement | $50,000 |
| Coronary angioplasty (one stent and one balloon) | $57,000 |
| *Obstetrics and Gynecology* | |
| Hysterectomy | $20,000 |
| *Dentistry* | |
| Crowns | $500–$3,000 |
| Veneers | $500–2,500 |
| Implants | $1,000–$5,000 |
| Full mouth implants | $24,000–$100,000 |
| Bridges | $500–$900 |
| Bone grafts | $250–$25,000 |
| Root canal | $350–$860 |
| Extractions | $75–$650 |

*Keep in mind that these fees will vary depending on numerous factors.*

# Table of Average Procedure Costs Abroad

Although prices abroad can be all over the map, I've come up with some average costs based on my company's experience coordinating more than 1,200 medical trips.

The fees listed here include the following: surgeon, anesthesiologist, operating room, operating room nurse assistants, diagnostics, post-operative recovery, medications, supplies, equipment, all follow-up visits, and prosthesis (where applicable).

Not covered in these estimates are hospital stays, flights, accommodations, ground transportation, communications with family and friends back home, food and drinks, and miscellaneous expenses.

In the destinations listed in the following table, you can expect to pay the following:

- Malaysia: prices as shown

- India: about 10 percent less than prices shown

- Singapore: about 30 to 35 percent more than prices shown

- South America: about 30 percent more than prices shown

- Central America: about 35 percent more than prices shown

**Doctor's Orders**

There's only one way to get an accurate estimate of procedure costs abroad. You need to send your medical history, MRIs, x-rays, and any other diagnostic reports to an international surgeon, who will give you a quote based on your needs.

Remember that these estimates are only approximations. Within each destination country, different categories of treatment—that is, cosmetic, medical, or dental—may cost more or less than that region's average. For instance, in Argentina (like the rest of South America), cosmetic and medical procedures are usually about 30 percent higher than the overseas average. However, dental procedures in Argentina are among the least expensive of any destination country.

## Average Procedure Costs Abroad

| Procedures | Average Prices |
| --- | --- |
| *Cosmetic* | |
| Face lift/neck lift | $2,900 |
| Blepharoplasty (upper/ lower eyelids) | $1,600 |
| Rhinoplasty | $2,100 |
| Brow or forehead lift | $1,500 |
| Otoplasty | $1,200 |
| Liposuction (per area) | $1,000 |
| Tummy tuck | $4,200 |

## Average Procedure Costs Abroad    (continued)

| Procedures | Average Prices |
| --- | --- |
| Breast augmentation | $3,750 |
| Breast lift | $2,800 |
| Inner thigh lift | $2,900 |
| Outer thigh lift | $2,900 |
| Buttock lift | $2,000 |
| Lower body lift (inner/ outer thighs, buttock) | $6,250 |
| Arm lift | $2,700 |
| *Orthopedics* | |
| Hip replacement (per hip) | $9,900 |
| Hip resurfacing | $10,000 |
| Knee replacement (per knee) | $8,200 |
| Spinal fusion | $10,700 |
| Spinal disc replacement | $12,250 |
| *Cardiology* | |
| Angiogram | $1,250 |
| CT angiography scan | $450 |
| Bypass surgery CAB | $10,600 |
| Heart valve replacement (one valve) | $11,000 |
| Coronary angioplasty (one stent and one balloon) | $5,400 |
| *Gynecology* | |
| Hysterectomy | $4,400 |
| *Dentistry* | |
| Crowns | $170–$700 |
| Veneers | $45–$250 |
| Implants | $500–$2,200 |
| Bridges | $180 |
| Bone grafts | $300–$560 |

| Procedures | Average Prices |
|---|---|
| Root canal | $125–$190 |
| Extractions | $90–$115 |

# Why Is Medical Care Abroad So Cheap?

You may be wondering how the same procedure can cost so much less in another country. To some extent, it's due to the skyrocketing costs of health care in the United States. Other societies simply aren't facing many of the issues that are driving up costs at home.

On top of that, the general cost of living plays a major role in the overall prices you'll pay for medical care. As a rule, it costs more to live in the United States than in almost any other country in the world. That translates into higher costs for most goods and services, including medical care.

In this section, I examine a number of the reasons why health care in the United States is so shockingly expensive and why it's so much more affordable in other countries.

## Move Over, Medical Malpractice Insurance

In the United States, medical malpractice insurance premiums have escalated to an all-time high. American doctors routinely fork over at least $100,000 a year for malpractice insurance. For some physicians and surgeons, the annual premiums have jumped to more than $250,000. With rates like that, it's no wonder American surgeons need to charge exorbitant fees to cover their costs.

Other countries, however, aren't as litigious as the United States. People in foreign countries simply don't have that knee-jerk reaction to sue for medical malpractice like Americans do. To prevent costly lawsuits, many foreign hospitals have you sign forms stating that you agree not to sue under certain conditions.

Even so, foreign doctors still need to carry medical malpractice insurance. But the rates are minimal, sometimes as low as $4,000 a year. This results in lower out-of-pocket expenses for you.

## Bargain Real-Estate Values

Land and real-estate values in the United States are far higher than in most destination countries. To build a hospital in California, New York, or Connecticut, the cost of securing land can be astronomical. In India, Costa Rica, and other medical tourism destinations, land values are significantly lower. That means the fees for your hospital stay won't be going to pricey land acquisition.

## Cutting Hospital Construction Costs

The costs associated with building a hospital in foreign countries can be substantially less than in the 50 states. For instance, reduced material costs, architectural fees, engineering prices, and labor costs add up to lower overall expenditures. Again, this can cut hospital fees abroad.

## Lower Wages for Medical Workers

Wages paid to nurses, operating room assistants, physical therapists, and other hospital and medical personnel are far lower abroad than they are in the United States. In addition, U.S. employers often offer benefits packages that include things like health and dental insurance, 401(k) plans, and more. These additional benefits add to the employer's cost of doing business, which is then passed on to you, the patient.

In other countries, many of these extra costs are eliminated. For instance, health and dental insurance may not be necessary if the country provides some sort of government-subsidized medical care. Thanks to these cheaper labor costs, your costs go down, too.

## Saying Bye-Bye to Bad Debt

In our own country, many hospitals and doctors struggle to collect money that is owed to them. It's an unfortunate reality, but many Americans go to a doctor or hospital and receive care, but then are unable to pay their medical bills. Some may even declare bankruptcy because they can't keep up with their payments. The medical provider ends up having to cover the costs of bad debt, and those costs eventually trickle down to each and every patient in the guise of higher fees.

Many international destinations don't wrestle with collection issues. Most private hospitals in foreign countries require insurance authorization or a cash payment prior to treatment so they don't take on bad debt. These are the types of hospitals that cater to medical tourists.

**Code Blue!**

Medical tourism provides savings, but it isn't free. When you go abroad to a private hospital, you'll be required to plunk down a deposit before you actually have your operation. Some hospitals ask that you cover 100 percent of the cost of your procedure before being treated. I recommend that you reserve a portion of the payment, say 10 to 20 percent, until after your procedure to ensure that you are satisfied with the service and your outcome.

That doesn't mean that people abroad without financial means can't get medical care. In several overseas settings, low-income residents can visit government-subsidized hospitals for free or low-cost service. These institutions may not provide the same quality of care that is offered in private hospitals that cater to medical tourists.

## No More Paper Shuffle

Anyone who's ever had a surgical procedure in the United States knows that the paperwork can be overwhelming. "Sign here, sign there"—the signing never seems to stop. In part, the overflowing paperwork required is due to our litigious society. Hospitals need to ensure that they cover their bases in terms of liability.

There's even more paper shuffling behind the scenes. Expenditures on processing medical bills, claims processing, and bad debt collections are estimated to add up to $300 million. Think about it. Health insurance companies are in business to make a profit, and denying claims is one way they cut costs and pump up earnings. When claims are denied, doctors and hospitals don't get paid. Because of this, medical professionals employ teams of workers to negotiate with the insurance companies to overturn denials so they can get paid for services rendered. Hiring and paying all of these workers ends up costing you more money. In foreign countries, there's no need for these paper shufflers, which can cut your costs significantly.

## Low-Price Prescription Drugs

If you don't have insurance or prescription drug coverage, you may not be able to afford the medications you need. Some drugs easily can cost hundreds or even thousands of dollars each month. Blame research, advertising, and marketing costs for the high prices of prescription medications in the United States.

As a rule, you'll find that medications in medical tourism destinations are far less expensive than American pharmaceuticals. In many cases, pain pills and other medications are included in the cost of your treatment.

## Cheaper Cost of Living

Remember that most countries that cater to medical tourists have a much lower cost of living than the United States. In general, most goods and services are much cheaper in medical tourism destinations. So, it only makes sense that medical care is equally lower in cost.

# Is the Savings Worth the Hassle?

Only you can determine if the savings you will get from medical tourism is worth the extra work it takes to coordinate an overseas operation. Sometimes, it comes down to how much you can save.

Think about it. If you can shave $75,000 off the price of spinal surgery, it might be a no-brainer for you to decide to pack your bags. But, if your savings are more in the neighborhood of $500 after you include the costs of flights and accommodations, you may not be as inclined to hit the road.

Remember the $6,000 Rule. I came up with this rule to help you decide if medical tourism makes financial sense for you. If a procedure is going to cost more than $6,000 in the United States, then you can usually save money by going abroad for treatment even after you include flights and accommodations. If your procedure would cost $6,000 or less in the United States, you may not realize any financial savings by going overseas. Although the surgery would only cost about $1,500 abroad, by the time you add the airfare, post-op hotel accommodations, ground transportation, and other essentials of overseas travel, you may only break even.

That being said, many people still choose to travel abroad to achieve complete privacy and anonymity, peaceful recuperation, and the avoidance of daily hometown distractions.

## The Least You Need to Know

- The savings you can achieve with medical tourism depends on a wide variety of factors.
- When comparing costs of procedures in the United States and abroad, ask what's included in the quote.

◆ Remember that the price of a single procedure can vary widely overseas as well as in the United States.

◆ There are numerous reasons why health care is cheaper in foreign countries.

Chapter **3**

# Is It Safe?

## In This Chapter

- ◆ Why low prices don't equal low quality of care
- ◆ What stringent standards overseas medical facilities must meet
- ◆ Why international doctors are often just as qualified, if not more so, than their American counterparts
- ◆ What you can do to ensure a safe medical voyage

After "How much can I save?", the most common question asked about medical tourism is "Is it safe?" Although no surgical procedure is without risk, having your procedure abroad can be just as safe as having it at home. Rest assured that the United States is not the only country in the world that has rigorous health-care standards and strong patient rights.

You may be surprised to discover that many of the most advanced medical facilities in the world are outside the United States. You may be reassured to know that these technologically advanced medical institutions adhere to many of the same high standards that we in the United States have come to trust.

What may surprise you even more, however, is the fact that the United States doesn't boast the highest-ranked health system in the world, according to the World Health Organization (WHO). Global rankings released by the WHO in 2000 actually place the United States at #37, behind a number of medical tourism destinations, including Singapore (#6) and Costa Rica (#36).

# Quality Care

Foreign hospitals that cater to medical tourists are committed to providing the highest possible quality of care. In fact, many of these hospitals have dedicated vast resources over the past decade to prepare for the anticipated explosive growth of medical tourism.

> **Doctor's Orders**
>
> Look for hospitals that have on-site international patient centers to help you navigate the foreign medical experience. A growing number of institutions are adding such services to appeal to medical tourists.

To attract health-care travelers, many international institutions have created specific programs and processes carefully designed to ensure quality care and superior service. Hospitals also are working hard to develop better communication with American patients by enhancing the English-speaking skills of their doctors, nurses, and administrative staff. One hospital in India now requires all of its patient representatives, nurses, and head nurses to speak English.

In many destination countries, the government has made a commitment to promoting the medical tourism industry. In an effort to appeal to American patients, foreign governments are investing millions of dollars not only in their best hospitals and their medical systems, but also in their infrastructure. Upgrades and advances are being made to transportation and telecommunications systems to improve the overall experience for international patients.

Foreign hospital administrators understand that medical tourism is projected to be a $40 billion industry. They are working hard to get a foothold in the market. To satisfy demanding American consumers, they treat you and other international patients extremely well.

> **Check-Up**
>
> Foreign countries actually have been catering to medical tourists from Europe for more than a decade. But only within the last 10 years have they really started to focus on North American patients.

Part of the special treatment provided overseas is a longer and often more luxurious hospital stay. American hospitals and insurance companies are known for pushing patients out the door as soon after a surgical procedure as possible. Similarly, many cosmetic procedures performed in the United States are provided on an outpatient basis, in which you're sent home the same day to care for yourself.

Foreign providers, however, are so committed to providing quality care and ensuring your safety after surgery that they generally keep you in the hospital for up to a week or more following a procedure. This way, your progress can be monitored to help avoid complications or to treat minor complications before they become a problem.

For example, let's say you're having a hip replacement. Following your surgery, you might spend a couple of days in an American hospital before being sent home to recuperate on your own. In most of the foreign hospitals I work with, however, your hospital stay would probably last about 8 to 10 days.

> **Doctor's Orders**
>
> Look for hospitals that provide first-class aftercare for medical travelers. Ask if your surgeon will visit you every day during your hospital stay and find out if the hospital has English-speaking nurses.

## Doctor, Doctor

It's understandable that you might be concerned about a foreign doctor's education, training, and experience. You may feel more secure knowing that many international physicians have received some education or training in the United States, the United Kingdom, or Australia. Some overseas surgeons have even practiced medicine and maintain board certification in the United States.

### CASE STUDY

| | |
|---|---|
| Name: | Kathy |
| Age at time of surgeries: | 62, 63, and 64 |
| Residence: | North Carolina |
| Procedures: | Face and neck lift, eyelid surgery, dermabrasion, dental implant with crown, and liposuction |
| Destination countries: | Argentina, Thailand, and Malaysia |
| Cost in United States: | About $33,000 |
| Total cost abroad (travel included): | About $10,000 |

For Kathy, saving thousands of dollars on cosmetic surgery and cosmetic dentistry wasn't the only thing that sold her on the concept of medical travel. For this retired high school Latin teacher who has traveled to three different countries for procedures, the deciding factor was the credentials of her surgeon. Kathy's overseas surgeon was American-born and board certified, and had practiced in the United States for 30 years before moving abroad.

*continues*

*continued*

On her first surgical excursion, Kathy discovered that the hospitals where she was treated were just like those she'd visited in the United States. But that's where the similarities ended. According to Kathy, the quality of care she received overseas was infinitely better than what she would have expected back home.

The three or four nurses who tended to her every need all held Master's degrees. Her doctor visited her every day, and she was encouraged to call him directly at any time of day or night. "I had total access to my surgeon," she says. "In the U.S., I probably would have seen the doctor once a week, and he would have been in and out in a matter of minutes. There's just no access to doctors at home."

Even if an international doctor doesn't boast U.S. training, he or she may still have as much or even more experience than U.S. doctors. For instance, some foreign physicians begin their careers working in government-subsidized hospitals where they typically perform extremely high volumes of procedures. Doctors in foreign countries may also gain experience working for the military.

**Doctor's Orders**

Look for foreign doctors who are board certified M.D.s and who are trained according to international standards and practices comparable to those operating in the United States. Facilities throughout the world are accredited by the same organization that audits American medical institutions, and a host of international hospitals that cater to medical tourists have affiliations with some of the most renowned U.S. medical institutions.

Often, a doctor must pay his or her dues in government-subsidized and/or military facilities before being considered for a post in a foreign private hospital. Since surgeons typically perform such a high volume of procedures in these facilities, they are able to hone their skills. Because of this, the surgeons typically have ample experience by the time they begin practicing in private hospitals,.

Another advantage of going to a physician in a foreign country is that you get to choose your doctor based on the strength of his or her *curriculum vitae (CV)*, or resumé. As a medical tourist, you can select the surgeon with the best credentials and the most experience performing the procedure that interests you.

In the United States, that isn't always the case. How many times have you actually seen a U.S. doctor's CV or resumé? Probably never. Most of us simply assume that our doctors have the proper qualifications.

In addition, a health maintenance organization (HMO) will likely dictate which doctors you can see if you want your treatment to be covered. This means your choice of physicians may be severely limited. Sometimes, the medical providers in an HMO network may not be the most qualified physicians. Instead, they may be those with newer practices or simply those who are willing to accept the lower payments offered by an HMO.

## def•i•ni•tion

A physician's **curriculum vitae (CV)** is similar to a resumé and should include information on his or her education, residency, employment history, board certification, specialties, publications, and membership in professional associations.

## Hospital Accreditation

Whether you're going to a medical facility across town or across the Pacific Ocean, knowing that the hospital is accredited can give you peace of mind. *Accreditation* indicates that the hospital has met certain standards for quality care. In the United States, you may not even think about verifying whether your local hospital is accredited.

When going abroad, however, you may be a little more apprehensive about what to expect from a medical facility. Rest assured that many private international hospitals either meet or exceed the high standards of quality care, technological innovation, and accreditation for which American medicine is known.

## def•i•ni•tion

**Accreditation** means that a medical facility has been evaluated by a third-party agency and that it has met rigorous standards regarding the safety and quality of patient care.

As a health-care facilitator, I've spent several years visiting dozens of medical facilities around the world. My colleagues and I have performed site inspections at hospitals and we have interviewed surgeons and medical staff to determine which institutions truly deserve to be called world-class establishments.

Based on this research, I've discovered that not all international hospitals are alike. In every medical tourism destination, there are dozens of public and private hospitals serving their own domestic population. Many of these hospitals have opted to jump on the bandwagon of the emerging medical tourism trend by promoting their facilities to medical tourists. That doesn't mean that they offer the kind of quality service you're looking for.

> **Code Blue!**
>
> Buyer beware! Not every international hospital that is catering to medical tourists meets the standards you deserve. Because you can't possibly visit dozens of foreign medical facilities yourself, you may want to enlist the services of a medical tourism service agency that has personally inspected international institutions.

I've found that in every medical tourism destination, there are at least three to five elite hospitals. These institutions serve the most important citizens, dignitaries, and government officials in their respective countries. Typically, these foreign facilities are on a par with international medical standards. Such leading health-care institutions are equipped with the latest, state-of-the-art medical technology and are staffed by board certified surgeons.

In fact, elite institutions usually use the same equipment and instruments as those utilized in the most advanced U.S. hospitals. A growing number of these facilities have also developed safety programs, patient rights programs, and medication distribution systems similar to what you'll find in the United States. Any foreign hospital you're considering should meet the following standards:

- ◆ Offer comprehensive English speaking, American-friendly staff
- ◆ Offer a diverse group of trained and certified physicians, many of whom have long-term experience working in American hospitals and facilities
- ◆ Provide the most advanced medical and communications technology available
- ◆ Maintain regularly inspected, clean, and sterile environments for all medical and nonmedical areas

> **Check-Up**
>
> The last thing that any of these elite health-care providers would ever want is for you to have a complication resulting from their error. They understand that such a story could end up on *CNN Headline News* the next day and negatively impact their future in the medical tourism industry. That's why hospitals catering to American medical tourists typically go the extra mile and offer superior service.

# Staying Safe Overseas

In addition to wondering how safe the medical care is overseas, you may be concerned about your general safety when traveling abroad. If you aren't a seasoned traveler, you might be worried about being robbed, getting food poisoning, or worse—contracting bird flu, dying in a plane crash, or getting caught in a terrorist attack. Certainly, there's no shortage of cautionary tales about the scary possibilities associated with foreign travel.

Remember, however, that the most frightening travel scenarios are exceptionally rare. For instance, take a look at your chances of dying from the following causes:

◆ Terrorist attack: 1 in 9,270,000

◆ Airline crash: 1 in 8,450,000

◆ Car accident: 1 in 18,800

◆ Heart disease: 1 in 300

Based on these statistics, you're far more likely to die from a lifetime of eating too much fried food or from driving your car to the airport than from a plane crash or a terrorist attack. However, when a plane crashes or terrorists target innocent people in foreign countries, images are splashed across television screens for weeks. Sure, that's scary stuff, but remember: each year, millions of Americans travel overseas for business or pleasure without incident.

The chances of being caught in a major catastrophe are infinitesimally small. But more minor things, such as being the target of a pickpocket or coming down with diarrhea, are more likely possibilities you do need to consider.

To ensure your safety overseas, use common sense. For instance, be aware that some medical tourism destination countries don't have the same sophisticated infrastructure we're used to in the United States. They may not have the same safety standards for drinking water or food preparation, so stick to bottled water and avoid eating from food vendors on the street.

> **Doctor's Orders**
>
> Be aware that you or your traveling companion may face some minor ailments while abroad. Diarrhea is one of the most common troubles tourists encounter. Other problems you may experience include motion sickness, insect bites, and heatstroke.

In general, you should approach your destination country just as you would any major city in America. Realize that there may be good and bad areas of town. Regardless of the destination country you choose, a few basic travel do's and don'ts apply:

- Don't walk alone.

- Do avoid dark alleys at night.

- Do stay alert to your surroundings.

- Don't carry lots of cash.

- Don't wear jewelry.

- Don't carry a purse from the strap.

- Do keep your purse close to your body.

- Do consider using a concealable "interior wallet."

For more general travel tips, consult reputable travel websites, such as Travellerspoint Travel Community (www.travellerspoint.com), Fodor's (www.fodors.com), Lonely Planet (www.lonelyplanet.com), and Frommer's (www.frommers.com).

# Playing It Safe as a Patient and a Traveler

You, too, play a critical role in ensuring your own safety before, during, and after your procedure. Of course, your surgeon oversees your safety during your surgery, but the way you treat yourself before and after your procedure can affect your chances of developing complications and can make a big difference in how quickly you recover.

Your surgical journey begins long before you ever set foot in your destination country. In fact, your international surgeon likely will give you a list of pre-operative do's and don'ts for you to follow for several weeks or even a month or more before the procedure. These directions are specifically designed to reduce the risk of complications during and after surgery. Carefully follow your doctor's instructions.

Your surgeon also will present you with post-surgical guidelines to speed your recovery and help prevent complications. Again, it's to your benefit to comply with your surgeon's advice.

In general, you need to remember that recovering from a surgical procedure requires rest and relaxation. Although you may be in a beautiful destination you would like to explore, you need to avoid overdoing it. You may not need to sit in your hotel room all day (depending on the procedure), but don't expect to be going on a five-mile trek in the jungle either.

## The Least You Need to Know

♦ Quality of care should be your primary goal in seeking treatment abroad.

♦ International medical institutions may be accredited by national and/or international agencies.

♦ Medical travelers often are treated by a medical facility's best and most experienced physicians.

♦ Medical tourists often get the VIP treatment from foreign hospitals.

♦ Longer hospital stays and greater patient–doctor contact is common in medical destination countries.

♦ Do your part to stay safe and sound.

# Chapter 4

# Cosmetic Procedures and Popular Destinations

## In This Chapter

◆ The most popular cosmetic procedures abroad

◆ The ABCs of various cosmetic treatments

◆ The most popular locales for cosmetic procedures

◆ The noninvasive cosmetic treatments to add to your trip

The current notion of medical tourism first emerged when Americans started heading overseas more than a decade ago in search of cheaper alternatives for cosmetic surgery. Today, cosmetic surgery remains by far the most popular type of treatment being sought in international locations.

Here, I take a look at the various cosmetic procedures available, which treatments rank highest with medical travelers, and where you can find them.

# Cosmetic Nips and Tucks

Within the United States, cosmetic surgery has soared in popularity in the last few decades. According to the American Society of Plastic Surgeons, nearly two million cosmetic surgical procedures were performed in the United States in 2006, compared to fewer than 400,000 a decade earlier. Aesthetic surgery is no longer reserved for the rich and famous. People from all walks of life and at all income levels are opting for a little nip/tuck to enhance their looks.

> **Doctor's Orders**
>
> If you're considering cosmetic surgery, make sure your expectations are realistic. Remember that improvement—not perfection—is the goal of any cosmetic surgery.

Because insurance doesn't cover cosmetic procedures, you must foot the entire bill. Those bills can be pretty hefty. Many common cosmetic treatments can set you back $10,000, $20,000, or more. Paying that kind of fee isn't easy when you aren't one of those rich and famous types, which is a big reason why many Americans are globetrotting for cosmetic surgery.

Some cosmetic procedures, however, don't make as much sense for the medical tourist. For instance, medical tourism isn't recommended if your primary purpose is a procedure that provides only a temporary fix—think Botox, collagen, or Restylane injections. These procedures require repeat treatments, which makes medical tourism less of a viable option.

Although medical tourism doesn't make sense if your main objective is to have a temporary cosmetic procedure, you can get greater value from your trip by lining up such services in addition to a major procedure. Say you're going to Brazil for breast augmentation. You can pump up your savings if you also schedule Botox injections, a chemical peel, dermabrasion, or laser hair removal.

# Facial Cosmetic Surgery

For more than a decade, facial cosmetic surgery has ranked as one of the most requested procedure types among medical tourists. Considering that a huge number of baby boomers is entering that time of life when wrinkles start to become more noticeable and skin starts to head unmercifully south, this trend is expected to continue.

Based on my company's experience coordinating medical tourism for more than 1,200 patients, the top five facial cosmetic procedures among medical travelers are as follows:

1. Face lift (rhytidectomy)

2. Eyelid surgery (blepharoplasty)

3. Nose reshaping (rhinoplasty)

4. Brow or forehead lift

5. Ear surgery (otoplasty)

Not sure what's involved with these procedures? Here's a quick look at the top facial cosmetic surgery procedures and what they can do for you.

## Face Lift

A face lift, which is usually performed with a neck lift, can turn back the clock by restoring a more youthful appearance to the face and neck. By minimizing fine lines and sagging, a face lift can make you look up to 10 years younger. Several types of face lifts can be performed using a wide variety of techniques and incisions:

◆ **Standard face lift**   This surgery addresses the lower two-thirds of the face and neck.

◆ **Mid-face lift**   This targets the area between the eyes and mouth.

◆ **Deep-plane face lift**   This treats severe sagging in the mid-face and lower face.

◆ **Mini face lift**   This generally focuses on the lower portion of the face but not the neck.

◆ **Minimally invasive face lift**   This treats minimal sagging in the forehead, eye area, and nasal folds.

The most commonly performed face lift is the standard face lift, often referred to as a *subcutaneous musculoaponeurotic system (SMAS)* face lift. SMAS refers to the layer of facial muscles located below the surface of the skin. With an SMAS face lift, these muscles

## def•i•ni•tion

**SMAS** stands for subcutaneous musculoaponeurotic system, which is the curtain of facial muscles found beneath the skin.

are tightened to create longer-lasting results. The neck muscles also may be tightened for internal support and to make your results last longer.

For a standard face lift, incisions extend from the temple to the front of the ear, around the bottom of the ear, and into the hairline behind the ear. Most of these incisions are well-hidden within the hairline. A small incision also may be placed under the chin.

Another variation of the standard face lift is the deep-plane face lift. With this technique, a thicker layer of underlying muscles and tissues are lifted and repositioned to improve the contours of your face.

Mid-face lifts, mini face lifts (also called "S-lifts"), and minimally invasive face lifts (also called "thread lifts" or "feather lifts") typically don't involve tightening of the underlying facial muscles, and produce more subtle refinements in your appearance. These face lifts usually involve fewer or smaller incisions, and the results may not be as long-lasting as those produced with a standard face lift.

Considering the many different types of face lifts and surgical techniques available to perform face lifts, be sure you understand what your overseas plastic surgeon recommends. Ask your plastic surgeon which areas of your face will be addressed, where the incisions will be placed, and what techniques will be used.

## Eyelid Surgery

As you age, your eyelids may start to droop, or you may develop puffy bags under your eyes. With eyelid surgery, you can minimize sagging on the upper eyelids and puffiness or hollowness under the eyes. Depending on your needs, you may elect to have surgery on either the upper or lower eyelids or both.

With eyelid surgery, skin, fat, and muscle may be removed or repositioned to create a more youthful look. Incisions for upper eyelid surgery are typically well-hidden within the creases of the eyelids. For lower eyelid procedures, incisions may be placed on the inside of the eyelids or may go through the skin. Eyelid surgery is commonly performed with a face lift, so you may want to inquire about a combined procedure.

## Nose Reshaping

If you think your nose is too big, too wide, too long, or too anything, you might be thinking about nose reshaping. A "nose job" can smooth out a hump on the bridge of the nose, straighten a crooked sniffer, or soften a pinched tip.

In addition to enhancing the appearance of your nose, this surgery also may improve your breathing. During your surgery, your surgeon may correct airway obstructions or blockages to enable you to breathe more freely.

> **Code Blue!**
>
> Rhinoplasty is considered the most complex of all facial plastic surgery procedures. It's very important to make sure that your international surgeon has vast experience in performing this specific operation. Just because your best friend got a fantastic face lift from a plastic surgeon in Brazil doesn't mean that same surgeon also will be good at nose reshaping.

There are two types of nose surgery. Open rhinoplasty involves internal incisions placed within the nose as well as an external incision made across the *columella*, the tissue that separates the nostrils. This external incision will leave a very small, but often unnoticeable, scar. Open rhinoplasty is commonly performed for more complex procedures.

With closed rhinoplasty procedures, there are no external incisions. All of the incisions are placed within the nose, so there are no visible scars. If you require only minimal changes to your nose, a closed procedure may be recommended.

## Brow or Forehead Lift

A brow lift, also referred to as a forehead lift, treats visible signs of aging, such as lines on the forehead and sagging eyebrows. To perform a brow lift, a surgeon can choose from a variety of techniques involving incisions that can be placed within or at the hairline, in the mid-forehead, or directly above the eyebrows.

A common technique is the *endoscopic* brow lift. With this technique, small incisions are placed along the scalp, and a tiny camera is inserted to allow the surgeon to visualize the muscles and tissues of the forehead. Next, the forehead skin and eyebrows are lifted and secured in a more pleasing position.

> **def•i•ni•tion**
>
> The **columella** is referred to in plastic surgery as the narrow strip of nasal tissue that divides the nostrils.
>
> When a surgery involves the use of a miniature camera inserted through small incisions, it is called **endoscopic** surgery.

Brow lifts often are performed in conjunction with a face lift or with eyelid surgery. To get the most value out of your medical overseas voyage, you may want to consider combining several such procedures.

## Ear Surgery

Otoplasty is most commonly performed to correct ears that stick out too far or to reduce the size of large ears. The procedure can also improve the appearance of several other minor ear deformities. Procedures to make the ears lie flatter against the head usually involve an incision on the back of the ear. Although this does produce a visible scar, it usually fades significantly with time.

Ear surgery can be performed on children or adults. Although it isn't nearly as popular as the other facial cosmetic surgery procedures, otoplasty can be performed overseas at a substantial cost savings.

# Body Contouring

Body contouring procedures can trim, tone, and enhance your figure. These treatments account for three of the top five cosmetic surgery procedures currently performed in the United States, so it's no surprise that many Americans are seeking these treatments abroad.

Based on my experience planning health-care trips, the top five body contouring procedures among medical travelers are as follows:

1. Liposuction (lipoplasty)

2. Tummy tuck (abdominoplasty)

3. Breast augmentation (augmentation mammoplasty)

4. Breast lift (mastopexy)

5. Thigh and/or buttock lift or lower body lift (belt lipectomy)

Here's a quick look at what's involved with these procedures and what kind of results you might expect.

## Liposuction

If you've got stubborn pockets of fat that simply won't go away no matter how much you starve yourself or hit the gym, liposuction may be the answer. This surgical procedure permanently removes fat from your body. Areas that can be treated with liposuction include the following:

- Abdomen
- Flanks (love handles)
- Outer thighs
- Inner thighs
- Buttocks
- Knees

- Calves and ankles
- Breasts
- Face and neck
- Upper back
- Lower back
- Upper arms

Liposuction ranks first among medical tourists for a few reasons. Small incisions and a relatively quick recovery period make it an attractive option for travelers. In addition, liposuction is commonly performed in combination with other body contouring procedures. For instance, if you want a tummy tuck or a thigh lift, your surgeon may also recommend liposuction as a way to fine-tune your results.

Different types of liposuction are available. Tumescent liposuction, which uses *tumescent fluids* to prepare fat cells for removal, is considered the industry standard. Ultrasound-assisted liposuction, which uses tumescent fluids and an ultrasonic probe to prep fat cells for easier removal, may be advised in some situations. Find out which liposuction techniques are being offered in your destination country.

Note that the cost of liposuction depends on the number of areas being treated, and surgeons may charge separately for body parts that you consider a single area. For instance, the outer and inner thighs may count as two separate areas. Similarly, the abdomen and love handles may be charged individually. Make sure you understand the fees for the areas you wish to have treated.

## def•i•ni•tion

**Tumescent fluids** usually consist of saline, a local anesthetic, and epinephrine to constrict blood vessels. Used in liposuction, these fluids cause fat cells to swell, making them easier to remove and making it easier for the surgeon to sculpt the area in a more precise manner.

## Tummy Tuck

Pregnancy, major weight loss, and the natural aging process can do a real number on your tummy, leaving it looking flabby. A tummy tuck permanently removes saggy skin and fat to smooth out bulging bellies and also can tighten underlying abdominal muscles to help redefine the contours of the waist.

Depending on the amount and location of loose, saggy skin, different types of tummy tucks may be advised:

- Standard tummy tuck

- Extended tummy tuck

- Mini tummy tuck

The standard tummy tuck involves a horizontal incision that extends from hip bone to hip bone. This incision is usually just above the pubic hairline and can be hidden in underpants or a bikini. Excess skin and fat are removed, and the abdominal muscles are tightened to create a smoother, more defined waistline. Note that your belly button may require repositioning.

An extended tummy tuck is virtually identical to the standard version, except the incision extends beyond the hip bones. The extended variation is generally recommended when excess skin is also present on the sides of your abdomen.

If you have a minimal amount of saggy skin on your belly, you may be a candidate for a mini tummy tuck. This procedure involves a shorter horizontal incision and may or may not include tightening the abdominal muscles. Although a mini tummy tuck may seem appealing because of the shorter scar, it is limited in its achievable results. In general, only a small percentage of people can benefit from this tummy tuck variation.

## Breast Augmentation

Currently the most popular cosmetic surgery procedure in the United States, breast augmentation also is highly sought after in foreign countries. Breast augmentation involves the placement of saline or silicone gel implants in the breasts to add volume and fullness.

Many women and surgeons think that silicone gel implants produce a more natural look and feel than saline. Outside the United States, silicone gel implants have long been the most widely used type of implant. The vast majority of women in the United States, however, have opted for saline implants. In fact, a 2005 survey by the American Society for Aesthetic Plastic Surgery showed that more than 83 percent of American women chose saline implants.

The overwhelming popularity of saline implants is largely due to the fact that for many years, saline was the only implant option available for the majority of American women. Following controversy surrounding the safety of silicone gel implants in the 1990s, the Food and Drug Administration (FDA) severely restricted their use in the United States. In 2006, after years of clinical trials investigating the safety of silicone gel implants, the FDA approved the implants for widespread use.

Breast implants come in a variety of shapes, textures, and sizes. Shapes include round and anatomical, also called teardrop or contoured. Anatomical implants are more full on the bottom and mimic the natural slope of a woman's breast. The outer surface of the implant can be smooth or textured with a sandpaper feel. Do your homework to determine what types of implants are available in your destination country and what might be right for you.

> **Check-Up**
>
> U.S. surgeons are reporting that since 2006, when silicone gel implants gained FDA approval, a growing number of U.S. women are opting for this type of breast implant.

Incision placement for breast augmentation can vary, and is often a matter of your surgeon's preference. Incisions may be located in the crease below the breast, around the nipple, in the underarm, or in the belly button.

Something else you must consider is the placement of implants within the breast. Implants can be either placed partially below the pectoral muscle (*submuscular*) or above the muscle and below the breast tissue (*subglandular*). The vast majority of U.S. plastic surgeons recommend submuscular placement for aesthetic reasons and because it helps prevent some of the risks associated with breast augmentation surgery.

> **def•i•ni•tion**
>
> **Subglandular placement** means that breast implants are placed above the chest muscle but below the breast tissue. When breast implants are placed partially below the chest muscle, it is called **submuscular placement**.

Be aware that breast implant manufacturers note that breast implants are not lifetime devices. You likely will require unplanned follow-up surgical procedures at some point, possibly including the removal or replacement of your breast implants.

# Breast Lift

When breasts start to sag, pregnancy and breastfeeding are often to blame. The natural aging process and major weight loss can also rob breasts of their fullness and make them droop. A breast lift is designed to reduce sagging and create a perkier and more youthful look.

A breast lift removes extra skin from the breasts, lifts your breasts higher on the chest wall, and repositions nipples to the center of the breasts. A variety of surgical techniques can be used, all of which leave visible scars on the breast.

   ◆ Anchor lift (also called an "inverted T lift")

   ◆ Vertical lift (also called a "lollipop lift")

   ◆ Donut lift (also called a "purse string lift")

With an anchor lift, three incisions are made on the breast: a circular incision around the areola, a vertical incision from the areola to the crease below the breast, and a horizontal incision across the crease. Of all the breast lift techniques, anchor lifts can remove the greatest amount of extra skin and are often recommended when sagging is severe.

**Code Blue!**

If you require follow-up surgery, you may have to make a return trip to your destination country for treatment, which will add to your overall costs.

Vertical breast lifts involve only two incisions on each breast. One incision is made around the areola and another is made vertically from the areola to the crease below the breast. Some surgeons may refer to this technique as a "short-scar" breast lift.

A donut lift requires incisions only around the areola area. This technique can only offer slight improvement and may not provide adequate lifting if you have more than minimal sagging.

Usually, the method chosen depends on the amount of sagging you have. Some international surgeons may specialize in short-scar techniques that limit the amount of scarring on the breast.

# Thigh Lift/Buttock Lift/Lower Body Lift

If you have a lot of loose, saggy skin on your body, it may be due to massive weight loss, pregnancy, or the aging process. The hips, thighs, and rear end are areas where sagging can be at its worst. Unfortunately, no diet or exercise program can rid you of all that extra skin. However, a thigh lift, buttock lift, or lower body lift may be the answer.

Thigh lifts can improve the appearance of your legs, and buttock lifts can remove excess skin from your behind. A newer procedure called a lower body lift can address problem thighs and buttocks—as well as a bulging tummy—in a single operation.

Thigh lifts may trim the outer thighs, inner thighs, or both, and may involve incisions in the groin area, the inner thigh area, and/or the area above the buttock crease on your backside. A buttock lift typically requires a horizontal incision that extends from hip bone to hip bone above the buttock crease. A lower body lift involves an incision that encircles the entire torso. Surgeons typically try to place this type of incision so it can be hidden by underwear or a bikini bottom.

Thigh lifts, buttock lifts, and lower body lifts are soaring in popularity in the United States. In fact, from 2000 to 2006, the lower body lift was the fastest-growing plastic surgery procedure, according to the American Society of Plastic Surgeons. The increasing popularity of these procedures is due in large part to the rising number of people undergoing *bariatric surgery* for weight loss. With bariatric surgery, weight loss can occur very quickly, leaving behind folds of unsightly, stretched-out skin.

These procedures generally involve long incisions that will leave visible scarring. It's up to you to determine if you can live comfortably with visible scars.

> **Doctor's Orders**
>
> A lower body lift is a major surgery involving an incision that goes all the way around the torso. If you're considering this procedure, plan on spending at least two to three weeks recovering in your destination country before going home.

**def•i•ni•tion**

> **Bariatric surgery,** also referred to as weight-loss surgery, reduces the size of the stomach and may also alter the digestion process to reduce the absorption of calories and nutrients. The two main types of bariatric surgery are gastric bypass and adjustable gastric banding surgery.

# Popular Destinations for Cosmetic Procedures

Because cosmetic surgery procedures are so popular with Americans going abroad, they are offered in nearly every destination country. Some of the most popular destinations for beautification treatments include Brazil, Costa Rica, Malaysia, Singapore, and Thailand. In each of these locations, you can find high-quality facilities, top-notch surgeons, and excellent aftercare.

So which country is the best for cosmetic surgery? Unfortunately, it's impossible to say. The best country for you depends on numerous factors, including your budget, your individual needs, your travel preferences, and more.

To help you narrow down your choices, we've come up with a rating system that covers some of the things that may be important to you:

◆ The amount of savings you might expect in each of these countries

◆ The amount of time required to travel to each destination

◆ How sophisticated or underdeveloped the infrastructure is (such as transportation systems, roads, and telecommunications)

◆ Whether English is widely spoken

## Cosmetic Surgery's Most Popular Destinations

| Country | Savings | Travel Time | Infrastructure | English |
|---------|---------|-------------|----------------|---------|
| Brazil | ** | ** | *** | * |
| Costa Rica | ** | *** | *** | ** |
| Malaysia | *** | * | *** | *** |
| Singapore | ** | * | *** | *** |
| Thailand | ** | * | *** | ** |

| Savings | Travel time (flight only from Los Angeles) | Infrastructure | English |
|---------|------------------------------|----------------|---------|
| *** *Highest savings* | *** *Under 10 hours* | *** *1st world* | *** *Widely spoken* |
| ** *Great savings* | ** *10–20 hours* | ** *Developing* | ** *Spoken only in metropolitan areas* |
| * *Good savings* | * *20+ hours* | * *3rd world* | * *Not widely spoken* |

## The Least You Need to Know

- ◆ The types of procedures most medical travelers want.

- ◆ Procedures can be performed using a variety of techniques.

- ◆ The type of procedure determines the recovery time necessary in the destination country.

- ◆ Add-on cosmetic services and treatments can increase the value of your trip.

- ◆ Some treatments might require a repeat trip to the destination country.

# 5

# Medical Procedures and Popular Destinations

## In This Chapter

◆ Medical procedures popular with health travelers

◆ Medical treatments available abroad

◆ Countries where medical procedures are being performed

◆ Wellness screening and other extras that can add value to your trip

Although Americans have been seeking cosmetic surgery overseas for more than a decade, the search for medically necessary treatments has more recently emerged. According to the Medical Tourism Association, the number of people booking trips for medical purposes started rising dramatically around 2004.

Increased awareness about medical tourism gets some of the credit for the bump in numbers. Soaring health-care costs also are playing a major role in the rise in individuals seeking noncosmetic procedures outside the United States. As both awareness and health-care costs continue to go up, the pursuit of medically necessary procedures provided in the global community is expected to continue climbing rapidly.

# Medically Necessary Procedures

You may have heard stories about people going abroad for a face lift or breast augmentation, but a growing number of Americans also are venturing overseas for heart surgery, hip procedures, spinal treatments, and more. In fact, all types of advanced medical procedures are being performed in hospitals around the world for a fraction of what they would cost in the United States. In general, if it's being performed in the United States, it's probably being offered abroad, too.

> **Code Blue!**
>
> If you have an acute medical condition that needs attention now, medical tourism may not be the answer. It takes time to organize an international health-care trip. Your condition may require a more immediate intervention, or render international travel unsafe for you.

Based on my company's experience coordinating overseas medical trips, the top five types of medical procedures among medical tourists are as follows:

1. Orthopedic surgery

2. Spinal procedures

3. Limited cardiac procedures

4. Gynecological surgery

5. General surgery

# Orthopedic Surgery

Medical tourists seek out orthopedic surgery more than any other type of medical procedure. It's no wonder, considering that some orthopedic surgery procedures can cost $80,000 or $90,000 in the United States. Orthopedic procedures are intended to treat injuries and disorders of the musculoskeletal system. The most commonly sought-after orthopedic procedures among health travelers are as follows:

- Hip replacement

- Knee replacement

- Hip resurfacing

Hip or knee replacement often is sought as a last resort when pain, stiffness, or swelling severely limits activities or mobility. These conditions are commonly associated with arthritis and other degenerative diseases.

## Hip Replacement

With hip replacement, damaged bone and cartilage are removed and replaced with an artificial joint that allows the patient to move more freely and without pain. Two parts of the hip joint are removed and replaced: the hip socket and the ball of the hip. Depending on your needs, you can have one hip or both hips replaced in the same operation.

### Doctor's Orders

Recovering from hip or knee replacement often requires extensive physical therapy. Although your physical therapist abroad must provide you with a comprehensive recovery program, you also may want to arrange for post-operative therapy after you return home. This can be arranged before you leave for your procedure. Once safely back home, however, most people simply continue the program they were given abroad.

## Knee Replacement

Knee replacement involves removing damaged bone and cartilage from the kneecap, shin bone, and thigh bone, and replacing it with an artificial joint. A variety of knee joints are available. The best one for you depends on several factors, including your activity level, age, weight, and overall health.

## Hip Resurfacing

An alternative to hip replacement is a newer procedure, which was pioneered outside the United States, called hip resurfacing. This procedure is similar to hip replacement, but it doesn't require that the "ball" of the hip be removed. Instead, this area is reshaped to allow for better mobility.

Many Americans originally were in search of hip resurfacing overseas because the Food and Drug Administration (FDA) did not approve the procedure in the United States until 2007. Although it's now available stateside, its price continues to make it a popular procedure for medical tourists.

**Check-Up**

Did you know that hip replacements may not last more than 15 or 20 years? Replacing artificial joints is difficult and requires additional surgery. That's why hip replacement is typically recommended for older patients. If you're middle-aged or younger, hip resurfacing, which has been offered internationally for many years, may be a good interim solution.

# Spinal Procedures

If for any reason you have debilitating back pain that limits your ability to take part in normal, everyday activities, you may be advised to consider spinal surgery. Costs for spinal surgery in the United States can sometimes top $100,000, which is why seeking lower prices elsewhere is becoming increasingly popular. Most medical tourists seeking spinal surgery are interested in spinal fusion or spinal disc replacement.

## Spinal Fusion

Spinal fusion may provide some relief for lower back pain when all other treatment options have failed. The procedure permanently fuses or welds together two or more vertebrae to prevent motion between discs that can cause pain. During the procedure, spaces between the discs are filled with small pieces of bone that may be grafted from another area of your body, such as the pelvis, or may come from a bone bank.

Surgeons use a variety of techniques to perform spinal fusion, and the surgery may require a large incision or several small incisions. Spinal fusion typically involves a lengthy recovery period, so you may need to stay in your destination country for several weeks after your surgery.

**Check-Up**

Don't expect to emerge from spinal surgery pain free. Typically, the goal of spinal procedures is to reduce pain, not eliminate it.

Spinal fusion is associated with a few disadvantages. For instance, fusing the discs may cause stiffness or limit back mobility. In addition, it may add stress to the adjacent discs, eventually leading to problems with those discs.

## Spinal Disc Replacement

Spinal disc replacement has emerged as an alternative to spinal fusion, and may alleviate some types of lower back pain. Also called lumbar disc replacement or artificial disc replacement, this procedure may be recommended if you have degenerative disc disease, which wears away the cushion that lies between the spinal vertebrae.

Similar to knee or hip replacement, disc replacement involves replacing a disc with an artificial implant. Made of metal and plastic, artificial discs are designed to move the same way a real disc does. Disc replacement also may reduce the risk of creating additional stress on the adjacent discs.

# Limited Cardiac Procedures

Cardiac procedures can be some of the most expensive treatments available in the United States. That's why so many Americans are checking into medical tourism for their cardiac care needs.

Major heart procedures (such as bypass surgery and heart valve replacement) are an option for the medical tourist, but these procedures may be considered emergencies, which means you need surgery immediately. In some cases, it's simply too difficult to coordinate an overseas health-care trip that quickly.

In general, limited cardiac procedures (such as angioplasty and stent placement that help open clogged arteries) often make the most sense for the medical tourist. That's because they usually can be planned in advance and aren't considered emergencies.

> **Code Blue!**
>
> If you need immediate cardiac surgery, you may not have enough time to properly plan a medical trip. Also if your heart condition is severe, your doctor may decide that you aren't healthy enough for international travel.

## Angioplasty

Angioplasty, which also may be called coronary balloon angioplasty or percutaneous coronary intervention (PCI), is a minimally invasive procedure that can improve blood flow to the heart. When an artery has blockages due to plaque build up, blood flow to the heart is restricted, which can cause chest pain and can eventually lead to a heart attack.

An angioplasty procedure involves the placement of a tiny balloon within the artery to open it and increase blood flow. A *stent*, or tiny mesh tube, may be placed in the artery to help keep it open.

## def•i•ni•tion _____

> A **stent** is a tiny mesh tube that is inserted into an artery to keep it open. More than 90 percent of angioplasty procedures involve the use of stents.

Angioplasty is considered a minimally invasive procedure because it does not require the chest to be surgically opened. Instead, the procedure involves catheterization, which means a long, narrow tube is inserted through a small incision in your leg or groin. The tube is then guided through the artery until it reaches the area of blockage. An x-ray dye is injected to allow the physician to see the problem area.

## Cardiac Diagnostic Procedures

While you are abroad, you may want to take advantage of price savings on cardiac diagnostic procedures, such as an angiogram or CT angiography scan. An angiogram is a diagnostic test that can detect blockages and other blood flow problems in the coronary arteries. This procedure involves a catheterization process similar to an angioplasty procedure. The long, narrow tube may be inserted through your leg or arm for this procedure, and x-ray dye is used to reveal any irregularities.

A CT angiography scan delivers images of the heart and arteries in motion. A CT scanner quickly and painlessly detects blockages in the coronary arteries. An x-ray dye may be injected through an intravenous (IV) site in your arm, and you may be asked to hold your breath for a short time while the machine captures the images of your heart.

# Gynecological Surgery

Medical tourists routinely seek out gynecological procedures, especially hysterectomies. In addition, fertility treatments, which can cost tens of thousands of dollars less than in the United States, are gaining popularity.

More than 600,000 women have a hysterectomy each year in the United States, making it one of the most common surgical procedures performed. In fact, studies show that one out of three women in the United States will have a hysterectomy by age 60. Because it is such a commonly performed procedure, a hysterectomy often is the reason for an overseas medical trip.

Depending on your needs, several types of hysterectomies can be performed, including:

◆ Partial hysterectomy (removal of uterus)

◆ Total hysterectomy (removal of uterus and cervix)

◆ Radical hysterectomy (removal of uterus, cervix, upper portion of the vagina, surrounding tissue, and lymph nodes)

◆ Bilateral salpingo oophorectomy (removal of the ovaries and fallopian tubes; may be performed in addition to hysterectomy)

Typically, the more extensive hysterectomy required, the more expensive it will be.

A variety of surgical techniques are available for hysterectomies. The majority are "open" procedures that involve a horizontal incision above the pubic hairline. Other options include vaginal incisions that don't leave visible scars or laparoscopic techniques that use only small incisions. All of these techniques are usually available abroad.

# General Surgery

General surgery covers a wide range of treatments in the following categories:

◆ Vascular

◆ Stomach and bowel

◆ Kidney and urinary

◆ Ear, nose, and throat

◆ Opthalmology

Procedures that are considered general surgery are typically offered in every destination country. A few of the many procedures that may fall under the heading of general surgery include:

◆ Gallbladder removal

◆ Hernia repair

◆ Cataract surgery

◆ LASIK surgery

◆ Hemorrhoid removal

◆ Endo laser vein surgery

By itself, the savings on LASIK surgery may not be great enough to warrant a trip abroad, but if you add LASIK as an ancillary treatment to another surgical procedure, it may be worthwhile.

# Other Medical Procedures

If you need a medical procedure that doesn't rank among the most popular, that doesn't mean you're out of luck. A wide variety of additional medical treatments can be carried out in first-class hospitals around the world.

## Bariatric Surgery

More than 15 million people in the United States are considered morbidly obese, and there's no end in sight to the obesity epidemic. That explains why more and more Americans are turning to bariatric surgery, which restricts food intake and in some cases alters the digestive system to reduce calorie absorption.

The American Society for Metabolic & Bariatric Surgery estimates that more than 200,000 Americans had bariatric surgery in 2007. That number is expected to sky-rocket. There are two main types of bariatric surgery:

◆ Roux-en-Y gastric bypass: The stomach pouch is decreased in size, and the small intestine is shortened to reduce the absorption of calories and nutrients.

◆ Adjustable gastric banding: An adjustable band is placed around the stomach pouch to limit the amount of food that can be consumed.

> **Check-Up**
>
> With bariatric surgery, you will need to make lifelong changes in your eating habits, and you may have to take nutritional supplements on an ongoing basis.

Finding a bariatric surgeon in a foreign country may not be as easy as locating an orthopedic or heart surgeon. Why? Many international destinations don't have the same problems with obesity that we're facing in the United States., so hospitals and surgeons may not have as much experience performing bariatric surgery. However, many foreign hospitals that are actively catering to Americans are beefing up their bariatric surgery departments.

# Fertility Treatments

Some couples who aren't able to conceive naturally are turning to in vitro fertilization (IVF). IVF is typically a last-resort option reserved for couples who already have tried other fertility treatments, such as artificial insemination and fertility drugs, which have failed. But the treatment, which often isn't covered by insurance, is so expensive—$12,400 is the national average, but prices can near $30,000—that many couples can't afford the procedure.

IVF is a complex process that requires several steps. A woman typically undergoes a few weeks of hormone therapy commonly referred to as "fertility drugs" and then her eggs are retrieved in a short procedure that usually involves anesthesia or mild sedation.

On that same day, the man donates a sperm sample, and the sperm is combined with the eggs in a laboratory. When an embryo or embryos form, they are placed in the woman's uterus in a relatively quick and painless office procedure. A pregnancy test is usually given a few weeks later to see if IVF has been successful.

IVF is a staged procedure that takes several weeks or even months. Are you able to remain in a foreign country for that length of time? If not, you may need to make more than one trip to your destination country for IVF treatment.

# Oncology

If you've been diagnosed with breast cancer and need surgery, you may want to check into options outside the United States. Surgical options for breast cancer include the following:

- Lumpectomy
- Mastectomy
- Breast reconstruction

With a lumpectomy, only the cancerous tumor and some of the surrounding healthy tissue is removed. A lumpectomy is a procedure in which the breast is spared, but there will be a visible scar. On the other hand, a mastectomy is a procedure in which the entire breast—in addition to the tumor—is removed. A mastectomy also may be referred to as a total mastectomy. The best procedure for you depends on a wide variety of factors.

Breast reconstruction is a surgical procedure in which the surgeon can restore the shape of a breast that has been removed during a mastectomy. You can choose from several surgical options for reconstruction, including reconstruction with breast implants or with your own tissue.

Reconstruction with implants usually requires two separate surgeries and several appointments with your plastic surgeon in between. In the first surgery, a tissue expander is placed within the breast. Then, over the next two to four months, fluid is injected into the expander to stretch the skin of the breast. After the desired size has been attained, a second surgery is performed in which the expander is removed and replaced with a breast implant.

### Code Blue!

Breast reconstruction with implants is a long process that requires two surgical procedures months apart and several appointments in between. If you're considering medical tourism for this type of procedure, you need to make more than one trip abroad and you may have to coordinate care with a local plastic surgeon.

Reconstruction using your own tissue is another option in which tissue from another area of your body is moved to the breast area. Such procedures include the following:

- TRAM flap: skin, fat, and muscle from the abdomen are moved to form a breast.

- Free DIEP flap: skin and fat (but no muscle) from the abdomen are transferred to the breast area.

- Latissimus dorsi flap: skin and muscle from the back are shifted to create a breast.

- Gluteal flap: skin, fat, and muscle from the buttocks are transferred to shape a breast.

Each of these methods has advantages and disadvantages. Be sure you understand each technique before making a decision about surgery.

## Transplants

There's no doubt that transplant surgery in the United States is hugely expensive. But, coordinating transplant operations abroad can be extra complicated because you're dealing with two travelers: the organ donor and the organ recipient.

> **Code Blue!**
>
> Note that in many foreign countries, it is illegal to transplant organs from cadavers due to a very disturbing practice in some countries. Impoverished and desperate individuals will actually commit suicide to make their organs available for sale, with proceeds from the sale going to their family.

## Stem Cell Treatments

Stem cell treatments hold great promise and eventually things like cancer or spinal cord injuries may be successfully treated or even cured. Several stem cell treatments are currently available in the United States, such as bone marrow transplants. But many other treatments, such as those using umbilical cord blood stem cells, may be considered experimental, which typically means that insurance doesn't cover them. Stem cell treatments also can be very expensive, which is why overseas treatment may be an attractive option.

Although some controversial stem cell treatments also may be available abroad, most reputable medical tourism facilitators steer clear of coordinating procedures involving embryonic stem cells.

## Sex Reassignment

Surgery to transform from a male to a female or vice versa can be performed overseas at substantial savings over U.S. costs. Thailand has emerged as the worldwide destination of choice for this procedure. The world's most renowned gender reassignment surgeon is Dr. Preecha Tiewtranon. According to his website, patients must undergo hormone therapy and live in the cross-gender role for at least one year before being considered for surgery. Approval from a psychiatrist or clinical psychologist is also a prerequisite.

The female-to-male process is a staged procedure involving four separate surgeries. It takes approximately one to two years to complete the process. The male-to-female transition may be completed in one surgical procedure.

## Addiction Treatments

Numerous addiction-recovery centers can be found around the world. Addiction treatment programs often take a month or more, which would require you to stay abroad for a lengthy time period.

## Wellness Screenings

MRIs, bloodwork, colonoscopies, and other routine screening exams can be done for a fraction of the cost in the United States, and many international hospitals and clinics can schedule same-day or next-day appointments for your convenience. It doesn't make economic sense to fly overseas just to have some screening exams, but if you're going abroad for a procedure anyway, it makes a lot of sense to schedule additional testing.

> **Check-Up**
>
> Many foreign hospitals offer day-long "Executive Screening" or "Wellness Screening" packages that include a vast array of diagnostic tests. You and your traveling companion may benefit from taking advantage of the low prices offered for such screenings.

# Popular Destinations for Medical Treatment

You can have most medical procedures performed in hospitals throughout the world. However, many medical tourists head to Southeast Asia for big savings in addition to first-rate hospitals, highly trained surgeons, and cutting edge surgical techniques.

For instance, India has earned a reputation for its mastery and innovation with cardiac procedures, as well as joint-replacement surgery and the newer hip resurfacing procedures. Medical tourists also are flocking to Singapore, Thailand, and Malaysia for everything from hysterectomies to spinal surgeries. As mentioned earlier, more sex reassignment surgeries have been performed in Thailand than in any other country. In the coming years, Dubai is expected to become a major international hub for a wide selection of medical procedures.

Choosing which location is the best for the medical treatment you need depends on your individual diagnosis, the recommended procedure, your budget, and more. Using the rating system described in Chapter 4, here's a chart to help you narrow your choices.

## Most Popular Destinations for Medical Procedures

| Country | Savings | Travel Time | Infrastructure | English |
|---|---|---|---|---|
| India | *** | * | * | *** |
| Malaysia | *** | * | *** | *** |
| Singapore | ** | * | *** | *** |
| Thailand | ** | * | *** | ** |
| Dubai | ** | * | *** | ** |

**Savings**
*** *Highest savings*
** *Great savings*
* *Good savings*

**Travel time**
**(flight only from Los Angeles)**
*** *Under 10 hours*
** *10–20 hours*
* *20+ hours*

**Infrastructure**
*** *1st world*
** *Developing*
* *3rd world*

**English**
*** *Widely spoken*
** *Spoken only in metropolitan areas*
* *Not widely spoken*

## The Least You Need to Know

◆ All types of advanced medical procedures are being performed in hospitals around the world. If it's being performed in the United States, it's probably being offered abroad.

◆ Medical procedures can be performed using a wide variety of surgical techniques.

◆ Some types of medical procedures require more than a single surgical procedure.

◆ Adding low-cost wellness screenings can increase the value of your health-care voyage.

# Dental Procedures and Popular Destinations

## In This Chapter

- ◆ Popular dental procedures among health-care travelers
- ◆ Various dental procedures
- ◆ Popular destinations if you're looking for dental work
- ◆ Extra treatments to maximize cost benefits

If your smile needs a little TLC, medical travel gives you a lot of options. For more than a decade, people have been crossing borders in search of affordable dental work. Because of this, thousands of qualified dental professionals worldwide have begun catering to an international clientele, and a staggering number of dental procedures are being offered around the globe.

## Dental Work

Going to the dentist can be painful—for your wallet, that is. It's estimated that more than 100 million adults and children have no dental insurance, so every check-up, filling, and root canal must be paid for out-of-pocket. Even if you do have a dental plan, your co-pays might add up to thousands of dollars for certain procedures. That's why having dental work in a foreign country can make a lot of sense.

Based on my company's experience in helping coordinate hundreds of trips for dental services, the top three types of dental work among medical tourists are cosmetic dentistry; dental implants and bridges; and bone grafts, root canals, and tooth extractions.

# Cosmetic Dentistry

Cosmetic dentistry is a booming $2.75 billion market in the United States, with nearly 2.7 million Americans opting for procedures to enhance their smile. But giving your pearly whites a makeover comes with a hefty price tag in the United States. By heading overseas, you can slash costs for in-demand services such as crowns, veneers, bonding, and whitening.

## Crowns

Dental crowns are tooth-shaped "caps" used to repair and beautify cracked, damaged, or discolored teeth. Your dentist will make a molded impression of the tooth or teeth to be treated and will send it to a dental lab. There, a custom-fitted crown will be created.

Dental crowns can be fabricated using a variety of materials, including:

- Metal
- Porcelain fused to metal
- All-resin
- All-ceramic or all-porcelain

Each material comes with its own set of advantages and disadvantages. Metal crowns are the most durable, but they don't match the color of your natural teeth. Porcelain fused to metal, all-porcelain, and all-ceramic crowns can be color-matched to your natural teeth, but are more prone to wear down the adjacent teeth. All-resin crowns are more likely to wear down or fracture over time.

While your crown is being crafted, you will be fitted with a temporary crown that will protect the cracked or damaged tooth. After the final crown is ready, the temporary crown will be removed and replaced with the final product. Crowns last an average of 5 to 15 years before needing replacement.

Because crowns involve a two-step process, it may mean a return trip to your destination country. You'll have to factor that into the total cost of your trip.

## Bonding

If you have chipped, cracked, or broken teeth, bonding can improve their appearance. Bonding also can let you say bye-bye to stained teeth or gaps in your smile. For minimal flaws, bonding may be all you need to beautify your smile. In other cases, bonding may be used in addition to crowns and other procedures to create a more gorgeous grin.

With bonding, a dental material that looks like tooth enamel is affixed to the surface of a tooth. The dentist then shapes and polishes the material to make the crack, chip, or imperfection invisible. Dentists can employ any number of techniques to perform bonding. Some of the more advanced techniques may cost more. One advantage of bonding is that it is a one-step procedure that can be accomplished in a single visit to the dentist.

> **Code Blue!**
>
> Some dental work is performed in stages, requiring more than one visit to the dentist's office. This means another trip abroad, which will add to your costs.

## Veneers

Veneers are thin shells made of a ceramic material that looks like real teeth. Each veneer is custom designed to cover a wide variety of problems, including chipped, stained, cracked, crooked, or otherwise unsightly teeth.

Veneers are typically fashioned from either porcelain or composite resin. Porcelain veneers typically last 10 to 15 years, which is longer than composite resin veneers that last about five to seven years. That explains why porcelain veneers come with a much higher price tag.

Before either type of veneer can be fitted onto teeth, the existing teeth must be contoured, a process that permanently alters the shape of your teeth. A small device called a *bur* is used to gently shape the teeth so the veneer can fit over them.

> **def•i•ni•tion**
>
> A **bur** is a small, handheld dental tool that has a rotating cutting device. It is used to shape and hone teeth to prepare them for a variety of dental devices, such as veneers.

After your teeth have been prepped, your dentist will take an impression of your teeth. The impression will be sent out to a dental lab where the veneers will be fabricated, or your dentist may have an in-house lab. The time length required for your veneers to be ready varies depending on your dentist. Temporary veneers may be placed in the meantime.

> **Code Blue!**
>
> Veneer placement is often a two-step process that may require a return visit to your destination country. Some international dentists, however, can complete the process in a single visit.

Some dentists boast advanced technology that allows them to create the veneers in their own office during your visit. With this technique, you don't have to come back a second time to have your veneers placed.

## Whitening

Teeth whitening is the most popular cosmetic dentistry procedure performed in the United States. It can be an ideal way to brighten your smile if you have mildly discolored teeth. Although teeth whitening can be performed at home with store-bought products, having it done in a dentist's office produces more immediate and often more dramatic results.

When performed in a dentist's office, a whitening gel is applied to the teeth, and a special lamp is used to activate the gel. To protect your lips and gums from the potent gel, a guard is placed in your mouth.

> **Check-Up**
>
> Teeth whitening is one of those inexpensive add-on services that can increase the value of your medical trip.

Going abroad solely to have your teeth whitened doesn't make much financial sense. Sure, you can save $100 or more on the cost of the simple procedure, but that certainly doesn't cover the cost of overseas airfare and hotels. It can be worthwhile, however, to have it done if you're having other treatments done as well.

# Dental Implants and Bridges

When missing teeth are a problem, implants or bridges may be the solution. These dental devices can be used to replace teeth lost due to all kinds of problems, including:

- ◆ Gum disease
- ◆ Injury to the mouth

- ◆ Tooth decay
- ◆ Wear and tear
- ◆ Root canal failure

In addition to being a cosmetic imperfection, missing teeth can lead to other problems inside the mouth. For instance, missing teeth can cause other teeth to shift and can heighten the risk for tooth decay or gum disease. That's why it's advisable to replace lost teeth.

## Implants

A dental implant is a titanium screw that is implanted into the jawbone and then covered with a crown to replace a lost tooth. This method is touted as being the most effective and long-lasting remedy for missing teeth. In fact, implants are considered to be a permanent solution for missing teeth. In some cases, implants may be used in conjunction with bridges or crowns.

Dental implants are usually performed as a two-step procedure. The first step is a surgical procedure to insert the implant into the jawbone. During this procedure, a small hole is drilled into the area of the missing tooth. The implant is placed into the hole and sealed with a protective covering.

After the implant is inserted, you need to wait approximately three to six months for *osseointegration*, in which the implant root anchors to the jaw bone. After successful osseointegration, a second procedure takes place in which a permanent crown is attached to the implant.

For medical travelers, the two-step dental implant process requires two trips abroad. However, you don't have to go to the same country twice. If you'd prefer to see more of the world, you can visit one country for the implant placement and another down the road when you have the crown attached to the implant.

## def•i•ni•tion

**Osseointegration** occurs when bone in the jaw grows around a dental implant and secures it in place. Osseointegration must occur before a crown can be placed over the implant.

# Bridges

Bridges are dental devices used to replace missing teeth. Unlike implants, which typically treat only the missing tooth, bridges involve the use of crowns on the adjacent teeth as well. These crowns are connected to a central replica tooth, or false tooth, that replaces the missing one. The false tooth can be made from porcelain, gold, alloys, or some combination thereof.

Several types of bridges are available, including:

◆ Conventional or traditional bridges, used when teeth are present on both sides of the missing tooth.

◆ Cantilever bridges, used when teeth are present on only one side of the missing tooth.

◆ Resin-bonded bridges, made of plastic teeth and gums with a metal framework attached to existing teeth.

Your dentist will determine which type of bridge is right for you, but often it depends on the location of the missing tooth. For instance, resin-bonded bridges are more likely to be used to replace missing front teeth.

Like many dental procedures, bridge placement is a staged procedure. During your first visit, the teeth adjacent to the missing tooth are prepared. This usually involves gently shaving them down with a bur. After the neighboring teeth have been prepared, a putty-like material is used to create an impression of your teeth. The impression is sent off to a dental lab where the bridge is made. In the meantime, you are fitted with a temporary bridge.

Several visits to the dentist's office may be necessary to achieve the ideal fit for a bridge. This process can take several weeks, which means you'll have to remain in your destination country for an extended time period, or you'll have to make a return trip. When the permanent bridge is ready, you will return to the dentist office for a second visit. This typically means a second trip abroad for health-care travelers. At this time, the temporary bridge is removed and replaced with the permanent one. The final bridge is then cemented into place.

**Check-Up**

Bridges are not considered to be as durable as implants, and they usually last about 5 to 15 years.

# Bone Grafts, Root Canals, and Tooth Extractions

Medically necessary procedures such as bone grafts, root canals, and tooth extractions can be performed in other countries at a cost savings.

## Bone Grafts

In some cases, you may not have enough jaw bone to accommodate a dental implant. When this occurs, a bone graft may be necessary before the implant can be inserted.

Bone grafts usually involve one of the following materials:

- Bone from another area of the patient's body
- Cadaver bone
- Bovine bone
- Synthetic bone

Bone that comes from the patient's own body is the preferred technique and boasts the highest success rate. This type of bone graft involves a surgical procedure in which small pieces of bone, commonly taken from another part of the jaw, are placed in the jaw. This way, the surgical procedure and all of the incisions are confined to the mouth. When bone is taken from a different area of the body, such as the pelvis, it requires an additional surgical incision and leaves a visible scar.

When bone grafting is necessary, it significantly lengthens the amount of time it takes to complete the implant procedure because it can take four to six months for the jaw to heal following bone grafting. Only after you're healed can the implant be inserted, and then you need to wait for osseointegration before the final crown is secured in place. That means it might take up to a year before the entire process is completed, and it may require up to three trips abroad.

## Root Canals

A root canal may be recommended to treat a tooth that has become infected or that is decayed, usually because tissue or the nerve inside the tooth has become damaged or diseased, causing bacteria to grow within the tooth and causing infection. In the past, an infected tooth would have been pulled, but a root canal may save a tooth from extraction.

**def•i•ni•tion**

The soft area within a tooth is called **dental pulp.**

During a root canal, the dentist will drill a hole into the tooth and then use special instruments to clean out the interior of the tooth. The dentist will remove the tooth's nerve along with the *dental pulp* and any bacteria from inside the tooth.

The next step involves filling the interior of the tooth with special dental materials and closing the access hole with a filling. This portion of the process may take place on the same day as your root canal or may occur during a follow-up appointment within a few weeks.

It's common to have a toothache or to experience tooth sensitivity when you need a root canal. Because of this, you may want immediate care and may not have adequate time to plan an overseas trip. Let's say you're in Costa Rica for cosmetic dental work, and your dentist discovers that you also need a root canal. Usually, this procedure can be performed as an extra service during your overseas stay.

## Tooth Extractions

Teeth may need to be extracted for a variety of reasons:

- Injury
- Severe decay
- Severe infection
- Severe gum disease
- Extra teeth blocking others from coming in
- In preparation for orthodontic work

Wisdom teeth usually come in when you're in your late teens or early twenties. Reasons why you may need your wisdom teeth removed include the following:

- **Impacted wisdom teeth**—Occur when the teeth are unable to break through the gums because the jaw is too small.

- **Partially impacted wisdom teeth**—Occur when only a portion of the teeth breaks through the gums.

- **Angled wisdom teeth**—Occur when the teeth grow in at abnormal angles.

Tooth extractions usually are categorized as either a simple extraction or a surgical extraction. A simple extraction is usually performed when a tooth is visible in the mouth. For this procedure, forceps are used to grasp and loosen the tooth until it can be gently removed. When this technique is used, the area is numbed with a local anesthetic.

Surgical extraction is advised when teeth are impacted or aren't easily visible in the mouth. For surgical extraction of a single tooth, a local anesthetic may be used to numb the area. If several teeth are being surgically removed, the patient will likely be given some form of anesthesia to prevent the patient from feeling pain and to make him or her sleep through the procedure.

For surgical extractions, the dentist or oral surgeon makes an incision in the gum tissue and removes the tooth. In some cases, the tooth may need to be broken into smaller pieces to facilitate removal. Stitches may be required to close the incision. These may be absorbable and will dissolve, or they may require removal in your dentist office. Your dentist will let you know if you need to come into the office for stitch removal.

# Other Dental Procedures

Of course, you also can save some dough on routine dental services, such as cleanings, fillings, and x-rays. Although these services alone don't merit a health-care voyage abroad, they make ideal add-on services that can pump up your overall savings.

Not all dental procedures make sense for medical tourists. Orthodontic work, for instance, isn't advised. Yes, braces can put a serious dent in your wallet, and they cost a lot less overseas, but braces require regular follow-up visits for adjustments over a period of several years. You probably can't afford to be flying off to a foreign country every few weeks or months for appointments.

# Popular Destinations for Dental Work

Countries that are particularly well-known for their dentistry offerings include Mexico, Costa Rica, Argentina, Brazil, and Malaysia. Many other nations provide a full slate of high-quality dental services as well. Choosing which nation to visit depends on your personal travel preferences, your budget, and more. Using the rating system described in Chapter 4, here's a chart to help you zero in on a location.

## Most Popular Destinations for Dental Work

| Country | Savings | Travel Time | Infrastructure | English |
|---------|---------|-------------|----------------|---------|
| Argentina | *** | ** | *** | * |
| Brazil | ** | ** | *** | * |
| Costa Rica | ** | *** | *** | ** |
| Mexico | ** | *** | *** | ** |
| Malaysia | *** | * | *** | *** |

| Savings | Travel time | Infrastructure | English |
|---------|-------------|----------------|---------|
| *** *Highest savings* | **(flight only from** | *** *1st world* | *** *Widely spoken* |
| ** *Great savings* | **Los Angeles)** | ** *Developing* | ** *Spoken only in metropolitan areas* |
| * *Good savings* | *** *Under 10 hours* | * *3rd world* | * *Not widely spoken* |
| | ** *10–20 hours* | | |
| | * *20+ hours* | | |

## The Least You Need to Know

◆ Some types of dental work make more sense for health-care travelers than others.

◆ What's involved in various dental procedures.

◆ Some dental work is staged and might require a repeat trip to the destination country.

◆ Adding minor treatments like teeth whitening can give you more bang for your buck (or your baht or your rupee).

# Are You a Good Candidate for Medical Tourism?

## In This Chapter

◆ Who fits the medical tourist model

◆ How your overall health plays a role

◆ Why a good attitude is essential

◆ Why you have to go with the flow while abroad

◆ Facing up to some uncomfortable feelings

Medical tourism is a fascinating concept that can potentially save you thousands of dollars. But is it right for you? That depends. Shaving a substantial amount off the price of a procedure definitely is the primary reason why you might benefit from medical tourism. But wanting affordable health care is only part of what makes a good candidate for medical tourism.

Several other factors come into play to determine whether medical tourism makes sense for you. In this chapter, I examine whether you've got what it takes to be considered a good candidate for a medical retreat.

# Are You Uninsured?

If you're uninsured, you're stuck paying the bills for all your medical care. Although you may be able to handle the costs of routine screenings and other minor medical treatments, you may not be able to cover the costs of a major surgery. Being uninsured makes you a prime candidate for medical tourism. In my experience, uninsured individuals make up the vast majority of people seeking medical procedures abroad.

If you don't have insurance, you aren't alone. In fact, the number of uninsured Americans is rising at a dangerous rate. According to the U.S. Census Bureau, the number of Americans without health insurance coverage has jumped to 47 million, and uninsured children account for nearly 9 million of that figure.

You might think that this insurance crisis affects only unemployed individuals, but that isn't so. Sure, unemployed people whose insurance coverage has lapsed do make up a portion of the uninsured group. But the lack of insurance also affects many employed Americans. It used to be that if you had a job, you automatically received insurance through your employer as part of a benefits package, but those days are gone. In the current economy, having a job—even a high-paying gig—is no guarantee that you'll receive health insurance as a benefit.

Many employers simply can no longer afford the escalating costs of offering health insurance to their employees. Because of this, employers are requiring employees to pony up for higher deductibles, pricier premiums, and larger co-pays. Or, they're no longer offering health insurance at all.

Small businesses, for example, are especially hard hit by rising insurance costs. To stay afloat in a competitive market, many smaller ventures have stopped offering health insurance altogether. This means employees must search out private insurance, which can be difficult to obtain, is more expensive, and may provide less coverage.

**Check-Up**

If you're older or you have a medical condition, acquiring individual health insurance may be extremely difficult due to the practice of underwriting. With this practice, insurance companies may charge higher premiums or may refuse coverage for individuals with pre-existing conditions or for older adults who may incur higher health-care costs. Insurance companies also may exclude coverage for pre-existing conditions.

There's no doubt the insurance crisis is taking a toll on people's health. According to the Centers for Disease Control and Prevention (CDC), almost 6 percent of the population doesn't receive necessary medical care due to the high costs. In addition to foregoing needed care, uninsured individuals are less likely to obtain routine preventive screenings and treatments, according to the Institute of Medicine.

If you fall into the category of uninsured Americans, you may be a candidate for seeking health care abroad. As awareness of the concept increases, more and more uninsured Americans are turning to medical tourism for a solution to the high cost of health care.

# Are You Underinsured?

Unfortunately, having health insurance doesn't mean you're protected from having to shell out big sums of cash for medical care. In fact, approximately 16 million insured Americans are considered underinsured. Being underinsured means that your health-care coverage doesn't adequately cover major medical expenses. This is why medical tourism has emerged as a very attractive option if you're underinsured.

In many cases, you may be woefully unprepared to pay the deductibles or co-pays should you require a major surgical procedure. A study that appeared in *Consumer Reports* magazine reported that 43 percent of people who have insurance categorize themselves as somewhat to completely financially unprepared to handle an expensive medical emergency.

**Check-Up**

Many underinsured individuals have restricted health-care coverage due to pre-existing conditions. This can result in huge out-of-pocket expenses if you need a pricey procedure related to that pre-existing condition.

According to the study, underinsured people aren't only those at the bottom of the income scale. Even some households earning more than $100,000 a year are among the ranks of the underinsured. No matter where you fall on the income scale, if you're underinsured, you may be a candidate for medical tourism.

# Do You Want a Cosmetic Procedure?

If you're one of the millions of people who are lining up for a cosmetic procedure, you may be an ideal candidate for medical tourism. Cosmetic treatments (such as facial surgery, body contouring, and cosmetic dentistry) aren't covered by even the best insurance plans. That means you have to shell out the funds to cover all the costs associated with these procedures. Because cosmetic surgery and cosmetic dental procedures can cost tens of thousands of dollars in the United States, you may have trouble coming up with that kind of cash.

In my business, people seeking cosmetic procedures make up about 70 percent of the clientele. That's because medical tourism can easily shave 50 to 80 percent off the price of a face lift, tummy tuck, or new smile. If you're looking for any type of cosmetic procedure, you fit into the main category of medical tourists.

# Do You Want Quicker Access to a Procedure?

A desire to cut costs isn't the only thing that might make you a good candidate for medical tourism. If you live in Canada, where health care is largely provided free of charge, you might think you have no reason to look into medical tourism. But even though you don't have to pay an arm and a leg for medical care, you still might have the makings of a medical tourist.

In Canada, you might experience lengthy delays when seeking medical care. In some cases, you might have to wait as much as one to two years for a surgical procedure.

A 2006 study of Canadian health care by the Fraser Institute reported that the waiting period for treatment after referral to a specialist averages about 18 weeks. If you need to see an orthopedic surgeon, the delays are even longer. According to the study, it takes an average of 16.2 weeks just to get an initial visit with an orthopedic surgeon. Then, you have to tack on an additional 24.2 weeks for the treatment to be performed. That's more than 10 months of total waiting time for an orthopedic procedure. That's just the average; some delays are even longer.

Playing the waiting game can be frustrating, especially if you have a condition that causes pain. For instance, if you need a procedure that can provide pain relief—think knee or hip replacement, spinal fusion, or spinal disc replacement—you may not be able to endure such a long waiting period. In these cases, medical tourism might be looking like an attractive option.

**Doctor's Orders**

If you're considering medical tourism as an option to gain quicker access to medical care, remember that medical tourism also takes some time to plan. On average, it takes about 45 to 60 days to coordinate a trip. But in some cases, when you want a procedure as soon as possible, it's feasible that a trip may be planned in about 30 days.

# Do You Want a Procedure Not Offered in the United States?

If you're seeking treatments unavailable in the United States, you may fit the medical tourist profile. Although this scenario is relatively rare, it is possible that you might want a procedure, treatment, or medical device that isn't currently offered in the United States. Or, if your doctors deem that you don't qualify for a procedure that you think you need, you may want to seek treatment abroad.

## CASE STUDY

| | |
|---|---|
| Name: | Nicole |
| Age at time of surgery: | 22 |
| Residence: | Klamath Falls, Oregon |
| Procedure: | Hysterectomy |
| Destination country: | Malaysia |
| Cost in United States: | With insurance coverage, about $10,000 out-of-pocket |
| Total cost abroad (travel included): | $8,000 |

Hysterectomies are one of the most common surgical procedures performed in the United States. That doesn't mean you can actually have one, even if you need one and even if you have health insurance. Just check out what happened to Nicole.

By the age of 17, Nicole had already had two ovarian cysts removed and was suffering from severe endometriosis. Endometriosis, in which tissue similar to the lining of the uterus spreads outside the uterus, is one of the most common causes of pelvic pain and infertility in women. It also can cause extremely heavy menstrual bleeding.

To try to control Nicole's endometriosis, her gynecologist put her on birth control pills and kept increasing the dosage because it wasn't working. When she was 21, Nicole began hemorrhaging and had to go to the hospital to stop the bleeding.

Nicole's mother, a nurse, encouraged her to find a new gynecologist. This doctor put Nicole on a drug that is intended to basically induce menopause, but that has some nasty side effects, such as increased facial hair and weight gain. This drug also causes bone deterioration, a real problem for Nicole, who also suffers from degenerative joint disease in her knees and hips.

Getting desperate for help, Nicole headed to Portland to see a specialist. For more than a year, Nicole tried different kinds of birth control pills and injections, to no avail. She bled almost continuously and again experienced hemorrhaging. She also experienced six major bladder infections during her ordeal.

*continues*

*continued*

In most cases, doctors would recommend a hysterectomy for a woman with symptoms this severe. But because of Nicole's age, none of her gynecologists would agree to perform the procedure. They were fearful of getting slapped with a medical malpractice lawsuit for sterilizing someone that young. Her doctors said "come back when you're 30 and you've had two kids."

Due to her condition, Nicole couldn't even get pregnant if she wanted to. Because severe endometriosis and ovarian cysts have been linked to cancer, she might have developed cancer and died before age 30.

Nicole certainly couldn't keep living the way she was. Due to the tremendous amount of blood loss, she was severely anemic and was sleeping 12 to 14 hours a day. She had to eat almost constantly to make up for the loss of nutrients.

When a family friend mentioned that Nicole might want to look into medical tourism, Nicole and her mom didn't hesitate and booked a trip. They were stunned when they discovered that a medical voyage would actually cost less than what Nicole would have to pay in the United States *with* her insurance coverage. A $5,000 deductible and 20 percent of the procedure cost would have been more than her entire trip overseas.

Soon, Nicole was on her way to Malaysia for the hysterectomy she couldn't get in the United States. There, her surgeon was shocked by how advanced her endometriosis was and feared that Nicole might already have cancer because of it. He ordered a slate of screening tests that, fortunately, came back negative.

During her operation, the surgeon also removed three endometrial lesions from her bladder—the cause of those painful bladder infections. Nicole's mom is certain that if those lesions hadn't been removed, it eventually could have damaged Nicole's kidneys and required her to be on dialysis for the rest of her life.

Since Nicole's surgery, she feels like she has a new life. Her pelvic pain and bleeding are gone, allowing her to enjoy her daily activities. She was so pleased with her experience overseas that when the time comes for her to have knee replacement surgery to fix her degenerative joint disease, she plans to go abroad again.

For example, silicone gel breast implants weren't approved for widespread use in the United States until 2006. This spurred some breast augmentation patients to travel to foreign countries where silicone gel implants have been available for years.

Similarly, some procedures and medical devices are developed overseas and may not be approved for use in the United States until years later. One example is the BIRMINGHAM HIP Resurfacing System, a medical device that originated in

England in 1997 and that has been implanted more than 70,000 times worldwide. Although it was being used throughout most of the world, this hip-resurfacing device only recently became available in the United States.

Other procedures that are considered experimental may inspire you to venture out of the country for treatment. For example, certain nonembryonic stem cell therapies that involve processing your own blood are currently available outside the United States and may offer hope for individuals suffering from a wide array of conditions.

# Are You Healthy Enough to Travel?

To be considered a good candidate for medical tourism, you need to be healthy enough to travel. A health-care trip may require up to 24 hours (or even more) of travel time. If you have certain medical conditions, a long journey may not be recommended. Some conditions that might make traveling a concern include the following:

- ◆ Advanced heart disease
- ◆ Daily dialysis needs
- ◆ Oxygen therapy requirements

Having one of these conditions doesn't automatically exclude you from medical tourism. Your doctor at home or an international physician can make that decision based on your medical history, your current condition, and the procedure you want.

# Do You Have the Right Attitude?

When it comes to medical tourism, attitude counts … a lot. In fact, your mindset could be the determining factor in whether you'll make a good candidate for a medical retreat. Having a good attitude is essential if you want to have a good experience.

## Be Prepared

If you're thinking about a possible health-care voyage, you've got to be willing to put in some legwork. Being prepared for your trip and understanding what to expect will greatly improve your chances of having a good experience. It's crucial that you take the time to learn about your procedure, your destination country, and the travel process.

Even if you hire someone to help you coordinate your trip, you'll still need to do some homework on your own. If you aren't willing to make the effort, you may not be cut out for medical tourism.

# Be Flexible

If you're an experienced traveler, you know that you've got to be flexible whenever you go on a trip. Air travel lines, delays, and cancellations can put a kink in the best-laid plans. After you land in your destination country, you may encounter tangled traffic, communication breakdowns, or other common travel snafus.

Add to that the potential pitfalls that go with having a major surgical or dental procedure. Even in hospitals, surgery centers, and dental clinics in the United States, you can run into roadblocks when seeking care. Misplaced medical files, appointment delays, and scheduling conflicts can arise. When these mishaps occur in a foreign country, they can seem even more frustrating.

> **Doctor's Orders**
>
> If you can adopt a go-with-the-flow mind-set, you can avoid getting upset by unforeseen changes in plans. If you're the type of person who gets completely bent out of shape if things don't go as planned, you might find medical tourism too frustrating.

No matter how carefully you plan, you can generally expect something to go awry at some point during your trip. In general, the vast majority of travel and medical glitches are only minor things that shouldn't impact the quality of care you receive or your overall experience.

# Be Compliant

To have a successful surgery and a positive medical tourism experience, you have to be willing to listen to your doctor and to comply with any pre- and post-operative instructions. These orders are intended for your own safety and can help speed up your recovery, so it's vital that you do as you're told.

If you aren't willing to follow your surgeon's directions, you put yourself at greater risk for developing complications either during your surgery or during your recovery. In addition, it will likely lengthen the amount of time you need to fully recuperate.

# Be Respectful

One of the best things you can do to improve your chances of having a good medical retreat is to be respectful to everyone you meet. Even the simplest things, like saying "please" and "thank you," can make a huge difference in the overall treatment you receive from doctors, nurses, hospital staff, hotel workers, and drivers.

As a rule, Americans tend to be very demanding consumers. We expect a certain level of service and we may make a stink if our expectations aren't met. This behavior is considered normal and perfectly acceptable in the United States but in many overseas destinations, that attitude can be misinterpreted as rude or condescending. If your caretakers think you're being rude, they may not be inclined to provide you with the best treatment possible. In the end, you're the one who loses if you're too demanding because you can end up with poorer service.

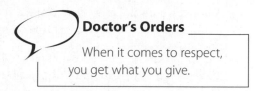

**Doctor's Orders**

When it comes to respect, you get what you give.

On the other hand, adopting a more gracious demeanor can pay off big time. By making an effort to treat people kindly, you're more likely to receive outstanding treatment. That can greatly enhance your overall health-care adventure.

---

**CASE STUDY**

| | |
|---|---|
| Name: | Wayne |
| Age at time of surgery: | 35 |
| Residence: | Sacramento, California |
| Procedure: | Two-level spinal disc replacement |
| Destination country: | Penang, Malaysia |
| Cost in United States: | $105,000 |
| Total cost abroad (travel included): | $27,500 |

Wayne had been suffering from major spinal disc degeneration in his lower back for years. The painful condition dated back to high school when he was in a car accident. By the time he was 31, his condition had worsened so much that he couldn't stand for more than 20 minutes at a time. The pain was so bad, he admits he was "popping pain pills like candy all day."

That's when his quest for pain-relieving back surgery began. Three different orthopedists recommended a relatively new surgery called artificial disc replacement, which promised increased mobility and reduced pain. But, when Wayne tried to gain approval for the surgery from his insurance company, he got nothing but denials. According to the insurance company, artificial disc replacement was still considered an experimental procedure, and they wouldn't cover it.

*continues*

*continued*

Instead, the insurance provider offered to cover a spinal fusion procedure. In Wayne's case, spinal fusion was more likely to leave his back rigid and immobile and could eventually lead to the degeneration of other discs in his back. Wayne fought hard to get the insurers to sway their decision, but they refused to budge.

Desperate for the operation, Wayne decided he would just go ahead and have the $100,000+ procedure and then declare bankruptcy. He figured the shame of declaring bankruptcy was worth the relief he would get from the operation. But the hospital informed him that he would have to put down $50,000 on the day of his surgery, something he couldn't possibly afford.

Wayne was starting to believe that his situation was hopeless until he caught an episode of *Dateline* featuring a segment on medical tourism. Intrigued, he decided to check into the possibility of having his surgery in a foreign country. When he discovered that he could have a foreign specialist who was experienced in performing spinal disc replacement do his surgery for about one-fourth the U.S. cost, he jumped at the chance.

Before long, he was on a plane to Malaysia. Wayne's surgery was a success, and he says his entire medical tourism experience was phenomenal. He's certain that his attitude played a major role in making his health-care journey so positive.

From the beginning, Wayne was determined not to be one of those "ugly Americans" who expect everything abroad to be just like it is at home. "Americans can be kind of arrogant," he says. Instead, he went out of his way to be friendly with the doctors, nurses, and hospital staff.

Wayne did a little homework before flying overseas and learned that Asian cultures appreciate gifts. To make a good impression, he brought some homemade truffles that were individually wrapped in boxes and offered them to the doctors and nurses. The gifts cost him a total of about $10, but the rewards from the gesture were priceless.

"The doctors and nurses were so grateful," he says. Thanks to those small gifts, Wayne thinks he received care that went above and beyond the usual: "They checked in on me so much in the hospital to see how I was doing, I actually had to tell them I needed a little time alone!"

For Wayne, the medical voyage has completely changed his life. About two months after surgery, he was able to take a trip to San Francisco and walk around the city for two hours. He's also back at work full-time, and he expects to be entirely off pain medications soon.

# Be Cool With Cultural Differences

As Dorothy said in *The Wizard of Oz,* "I've got a feeling we're not in Kansas anymore." You're likely to feel a bit like Dorothy when you land in your destination country. Often, the customs and traditions overseas may be very different from what you're used to at home.

For example, a few of the many cultural differences you might encounter include the following:

- ◆ When in Malaysia, avoid showing the bottoms of your feet to anyone.

- ◆ In Thailand, it's considered taboo to raise your voice to a Thai person.

- ◆ If you're a woman, dress to cover your legs and shoulders when in India.

To get the most out of your health-care trip, you need to be aware of such cultural differences. Even more important, you need to respect them. If you aren't willing to abide by these practices, you risk offending people in your host country.

# Can You Deal With Your Feelings?

I've studied the psychology of hundreds of medical tourists over the past few years and can guarantee that you will face some unpleasant feelings at some point during the planning of your health-care adventure. Having these feelings is completely normal and doesn't mean that you aren't fit for medical tourism. In fact, each year, thousands of medical tourists overcome these temporary psychological concerns and end up having successful experiences.

Common psychological issues you may encounter include the following:

- ◆ Fear

- ◆ Worry

- ◆ Anxiety

- ◆ Distrust

Here's a look at why you might have these feelings and what you can do to keep them in check.

## Fear of the Unknown

As you go through the planning process, you're very likely to experience fear. This feeling is usually considered a fear of the unknown. If you don't know what to expect from the medical tourism process, if you aren't familiar with the culture of your destination country, or if you don't know what's involved in your procedure, it's no surprise that you'd feel fearful and apprehensive.

To eliminate your fear, you need to become an informed medical tourist. The more you understand about medical tourism, your destination country, and your procedure, the less fearful you will be.

## Worrying About the "What Ifs"

Worry is concern about what will happen in the future. Ninety percent of what we worry about never happens, and the other 10 percent we have no control over. It's a mind game that revolves around the question "what if?" "What if my flight gets cancelled?" "What if the doctor operates on the wrong leg?" "What if I die?"

These thoughts can be very troublesome. Just ask Jerry Rice, former wide receiver for the San Francisco 49ers football team. He has been quoted as saying, *"The absolute worst thing a receiver can do is worry about not catching the ball or about getting hit."* What you focus on can become your reality.

Because of this, you need to minimize or eliminate those dreaded "what if" thoughts if you want to have a successful trip. If you don't have a positive attitude about seeking health care abroad, medical tourism isn't for you.

## Getting Anxious

*Anxiety* can produce an uneasy rushing feeling that can make your heart start beating uncomfortably fast and can make you break out in a sweat. If anxiety can worm its way into your thinking, it can feed off itself to produce even more anxiety.

## def•i•ni•tion

**Anxiety** is a feeling of distress or uneasiness of mind usually felt over an impending, anticipated, or even imaginary event. In severe cases, it can cause physical symptoms, including trembling, sweating, and heart palpitations.

Often, you may think that if you accomplish something or get something that it will make these feelings go away. Think about it. Have you ever thought that if only you lost 10 pounds, or if only you earned more money, your life would be perfect? But what happens after you do drop those 10 pounds or make that extra cash? You probably find something new to be anxious about. Anxiety is a never-ending cycle, like a dog chasing its tail.

To overcome anxiety, you need to first recognize that you have these feelings. While it isn't easy to change your thinking patterns, it can be done. With anxiety at bay, you'll be able to get much more enjoyment out of your medical voyage.

## Distrust Issues

The concept of medical tourism is still very new in this country, and it's common for people to have a sense of distrust about it. You may think it sounds too good to be true. Or you may not be sure that international hospitals, clinics, or doctors operate in the same honorable and ethical manner to which we've become accustomed in the United States.

Rest assured that there are several ways to check on the quality and credentials of medical providers overseas. In fact, we'll cover several ways to investigate hospitals and doctors in upcoming chapters. If you understand the high standards that international medical providers must meet, you can minimize or eliminate feelings of distrust.

# Can You Handle Peer Pressure?

As you plan your medical retreat, you can be sure that at least one person in your life will be vehemently opposed to what you're doing. Most of our clients have three to four "disbelievers" who try to talk them out of medical tourism.

When these people try to dissuade you from taking a health-care trip, remember that they probably don't have enough knowledge or understanding of the industry to allow them to feel any other way. It makes sense that if someone knows nothing about medical tourism, it might seem like a very scary proposition.

Just try to concentrate on the fact that you have taken the time to educate yourself about medical tourism and that you are better equipped to make a decision about whether it is right for you.

## The Least You Need to Know

   ◆ Not everyone is cut out for medical tourism.

   ◆ Ask a doctor if you're fit for travel.

   ◆ Attitude counts.

   ◆ Being flexible enough to roll with the punches is key to a successful trip.

   ◆ Medical tourism can bring up a variety of emotions.

# Part

## 2

# Planning Your Health-Care Adventure

If you're thinking that medical travel might be right for you, brace yourself. Planning a health-care voyage requires a major time commitment and a willingness to educate yourself about your medical tourism options. In the next few chapters, we explain the planning process and help you understand what you can do to ensure a successful medical trip.

# Chapter 8

# Do Your Homework

## In This Chapter

- Why you need to research your condition and treatment options
- How long it takes to plan a medical trip
- How timing your trip can maximize savings
- How to find reliable medical tourism info through the Internet
- What to consider when choosing a destination country

If you're contemplating medical tourism as an option, get ready to do some serious homework. Research is the crucial first step in the planning process. You can expect to log some major time in front of your computer as you search for information about your treatment and medical tourism options. Fortunately, all that research is likely to pay off handsomely in the end.

Being an informed patient and traveler has its rewards. With knowledge on your side, you can make wiser choices regarding medical travel, which means you'll be more likely to have a satisfactory overseas experience.

# Know What You Want

The first rule of medical tourism is: you must have a thorough understanding of your medical needs and desires before even considering going abroad. Unless you know exactly what you're looking for, you simply can't make an informed decision about the best country, hospital, or doctor to visit.

## Deciphering Your Diagnosis

If you're considering medical tourism for a procedure that's medically necessary, you need a thorough understanding of your diagnosis and recommended treatment course. For example, if your doctor recommends a hysterectomy, you need to comprehend why. Is it because you have uterine fibroids? Endometriosis? Irregular menstrual bleeding? Cervical cancer? Your particular condition may dictate which type of hysterectomy is recommended, or it may play a role in determining which surgical techniques are used.

Such variables exist for many procedures. Your underlying condition is what influences your physician's recommendations. The more you know about your medical condition, the more information you can relay to a foreign doctor.

## Understanding Your Procedure

Whether you're considering a medically necessary procedure or a cosmetic treatment, you should make an effort to educate yourself about your proposed procedure. In addition to understanding why the surgery is necessary, you should know:

- How the procedure is performed.
- How to prepare for surgery.
- What to expect from the recovery process.
- What side effects, risks, and complications are associated with the procedure.
- What will happen to you if you choose not to have the surgery.

That's a lot to digest, and you can't always count on your American doctor to give you all the details during your appointment. Some doctors simply are better than others at fully describing and explaining what to expect from surgery. Sure, some doctors will spend ample time with you clarifying the various ins and outs of a procedure. For instance, plastic surgeons typically schedule rather lengthy consultations so that procedures may be described in detail.

On the other hand, you might get no more than a two- to five-minute overview that glosses over a lot of pertinent information. You might find that after you leave your physician's office, questions start running through your head. How long is the incision? Will I need to stay in the hospital? Will I have to take time off from work? When will I be able to take a shower? When will I be able to resume normal activities? These are all important questions, and you should know the answers.

## Informed Consent

As a patient, you have a right to be informed about all aspects of a surgical procedure before agreeing to have an operation. That's why there's something called *informed consent*. Informed consent indicates that you have been sufficiently informed about your procedure, and that you have consented to have the treatment.

Informed consent is a legal requirement in the United States, and is supported by major medical organizations. The American Medical Association (AMA) calls the informed consent communication process an ethical requirement in addition to a legal necessity. The American College of Surgeons (ACS), the world's largest organization of surgeons (with more than 70,000 members), also endorses the principle of informed consent. According to the ACS, "Patients should understand the indications for the operation, the risk involved, and the result that it is hoped to attain."

The notion of informed consent is not exclusive to the United States. In many international settings, physicians and hospitals are either required to obtain informed consent or voluntarily do so.

To ensure that you are making an informed decision, you can expect to be provided with *informed consent forms* prior to a surgical procedure or other medical treatments.

## def•i•ni•tion

**Informed consent** is the process of communication between a physician and a patient, focusing on patient education. This process must result in a patient indicating that he or she has an adequate understanding of a procedure or treatment and that he or she is authorizing the physician to perform the procedure.

U.S. physicians are required to have patients read and sign **informed consent forms** before performing surgery. Many international surgeons also use these forms, which spell out the nature of the procedure, what to expect before and after surgery, and the risks involved.

Informed consent forms generally include the following information about your specific procedure:

◆ Indications (why you need the surgery)

◆ The procedure's nature and purpose

◆ Risks and benefits of having the procedure

◆ Alternatives to surgery

◆ Risks and benefits of alternative treatments

◆ Risks and benefits if you choose not to have surgery

Informed consent forms initially were designed to help educate patients and to offer detailed information that may not have been provided in person by the physician. Over the years, however, these forms have evolved into a veritable legal document used to protect physicians from lawsuits.

"Some doctors have you read and sign the form, but don't really care if you understand it," says Dr. Art Shoenstadt, a former practicing physician and founder of eMedTV, a website he created to counter what he saw as a lack of adequate patient education. "I thought there had to be a better way to educate people about diseases and procedures, especially for surgical procedures where there's so much to consider."

Because informed consent forms are now viewed as legal documents, they're often filled with boilerplate rhetoric that isn't specific to your procedure. The language describing pre-op requirements, surgical techniques, side effects, and post-op instructions may be rather generic in nature.

Don't expect to find a comprehensive list of surgical risks in the paperwork. When listing risks, informed consent forms often use phrases such as "Risks may include, but are not limited to, the following." This is another method used to protect physicians from lawsuits. Unfortunately, it doesn't serve to fully educate *you*, the patient.

> **Code Blue!**
>
> Informed consent forms may be generalized forms that don't spell out all of the specifics of your procedure. Make sure you carefully read all informed consent forms and ask questions if anything isn't clear.

For your safety and peace of mind, it's best not to rely solely on these forms to educate yourself about your procedure. Don't hesitate to ask your American or international doctor about the information presented in these forms and do your own research online to flesh out your knowledge.

## Medical Procedures 101

To pump up your knowledge, give yourself a crash course in your medical condition and in the procedures that interest you. Fortunately, numerous sources are available to help you improve your knowledge of medical conditions, diseases, treatment options, and cosmetic procedures. The good thing is, you don't even have to leave home to find reliable information—it's right at your fingertips, on the Internet.

A host of reputable websites offer detailed medical information that's geared toward patients and written in easy-to-understand, everyday language. Websites that cover a wide range of medical conditions and treatments in an authoritative and unbiased manner include the following:

- MayoClinic (www.mayoclinic.com)
- MedlinePlus (www.medlineplus.gov)
- WebMD (www.webmd.com)
- eMedTV (www.emedtv.com)

For cosmetic surgery, try the following websites:

- American Society of Plastic Surgeons (www.plasticsurgery.org)
- American Society for Aesthetic Plastic Surgery (www.surgery.org)

Many of these websites offer detailed overviews of medical conditions, including symptoms, diagnoses, treatment options, and more. You also can find procedure guides that take you step-by-step through the entire surgical process—from pre-op do's and don'ts to post-op recovery instructions.

A newer addition to the Internet is the use of patient education videos. At eMedTV, you can find more than 3,000 videos that take you through every step of dozens of procedures, including hip replacement, knee replacement, hysterectomy, and heart bypass surgery.

Why is it so important to understand every detail about your surgery? According to Dr. Schoenstadt, "When you understand more about your procedure, you're more likely to have realistic expectations about the outcome than if you simply read a doctor's informed consent form."

**Doctor's Orders**

If you're using the Internet for research, make sure you get your information on medical conditions, diseases, and treatments from reputable medical websites.

For example, let's say you're thinking about having hip-replacement surgery. You may understand that it involves replacing the hip joint, but how much do you know about the rehabilitation process? If you haven't done your homework, you may be in for post-surgical shock. "With these types of orthopedic procedures, the surgery is the easy part," warns Dr. Schoenstadt. "It's the recovery that's the tough part."

If the recovery process takes you by surprise, and you aren't willing or able to make the effort to rehabilitate your new hip, it may never function as well as it could. Ultimately, you might consider your medical tourism experience a failure even though the surgeon, nurses, and hospital did a first-rate job.

Now let's assume that you spend some time researching hip-replacement procedures, and you fully grasp what to expect following surgery and after you return home from your destination country. In this case, you're consenting to have the surgery knowing that you'll have to do your part to fully recuperate. By following through with the recommended post-op rehabilitation, you'll get a better result and you'll be more satisfied with your overall experience.

## Seeking Out Second Opinions

Should you get a second opinion of your diagnosis or treatment plan before checking into medical tourism as an option? You may have heard that it's a good idea to get a second opinion whenever surgery is recommended. But getting a second opinion in the United States can be costly, even if you have health insurance. If you're serious about medical tourism as an option, you're better off letting your overseas doctor provide you with that second opinion.

**Check-Up**

Many international surgeons and hospitals will review your medical charts and test results free of charge. Others may charge a nominal fee.

An overseas surgeon typically will check your magnetic resonance images (MRIs), x-rays, and other medical records, make treatment recommendations, and give you a quote before you commit to having a procedure. This evaluation basically serves as a second opinion. Should your overseas surgeon recommend a different course of treatment than your U.S. physician, you may want to seek a third opinion either from a U.S. doctor or another foreign physician.

After you've got a firm grasp on your diagnosis and treatment options, only then should you begin the planning process.

# It's All About Timing

When planning a medical voyage, consider the timing. That includes both the time required to plan your trip as well as the time of year you choose to go.

## When to Start Planning Your Trip

Give yourself ample time to plan your health-care voyage. Ideally, you should allow about six months for the planning process if you're taking the do-it-yourself approach to medical travel. You'll need to research hospitals, doctors, and destination countries.

In addition to the medical aspect of your trip, you also must consider the more mundane travel necessities, including passports, visas, flights, and accommodations. If you don't have a valid passport, you'll need to apply for one. According to the U.S. Department of State website, the time length required to receive your passport varies according to the type of service you choose. Routine service will get your passport to you within four weeks. With expedited service, you should receive your passport within three weeks.

To get your passport even faster, you have a couple of options. You can make an appointment at a regional passport agency, or you can hire a passport expediting service. Some agencies promise that you can have a valid passport in hand in as little as 24 hours. Of course, you'll have to shell out additional dough for the quick turnaround. For more information about applying for a passport, visit the U.S. Department of State website (travel.state.gov/passport/passport_1738.html).

For some foreign destinations, you also need to obtain a *visa*. This can add several weeks to the process. For information on obtaining visas and other travel requirements, check the U.S. Department of State website (travel.state.gov/).

To get the lowest prices on airfares and accommodations, you need to make your reservations at least one month in advance. That means you must make a final decision on your destination, hospital, and physician prior to that. If you have a valid passport, and the country you've chosen doesn't require a visa, you may be able to coordinate your trip more quickly.

### def•i•ni•tion

A **visa** is a document that may be required when visiting some foreign countries. Visas generally indicate the time length a person is legally allowed to stay in a foreign country. Different types of visas (for example, tourist and business visas) are available depending on the purpose of your trip.

## Choosing the Best Time to Go Overseas

Take care when choosing the dates for your medical trip. The time of year you select can either add to your savings or end up costing you extra. Most countries have a high season and a low season for tourist travel. The high season is when the greatest numbers of tourists descend on the country. During the low season, fewer tourists come to visit. In general, you can count on higher prices for airfares and hotels during the high season. Flights and hotels also fill up faster during the peak travel season.

During the low season, however, you can usually find the best deals on airfares and accommodations. Because fewer tourists are visiting, you may have a better selection of hotels and other accommodations. Note that a destination's low season may correspond with a rainy season or a very hot time of the year.

In addition to sidestepping the high tourist season, you need to avoid traveling during major foreign holidays or festivals. If you try to book a trip during a holiday, you'll be slapped with higher hotel prices and airfares. Not only that, you'll have to deal with an onslaught of tourists, which can make it more difficult to find a hotel room, get around town, make dinner reservations, and more. Holidays you may want to avoid include:

- Carnaval in Rio de Janeiro, Brazil, which is a four-day celebration that attracts thousands of visitors each year.

- Chinese New Year, which is celebrated in many Southeast Asian countries and draws a flood of tourists.

 **Code Blue!** _____

Don't book your trip during a major holiday in your destination country or you could wind up paying a lot more than you need to for flights and hotels.

The specific dates for these events change each year, so be sure to check them before making any reservations.

# Take Advantage of the 'Net

Medical tourism is a hot topic. In fact, a simple Google search for "medical tourism" or "medical travel" pulls up well over a million listings, including newspaper and magazine articles, websites, blogs, and Internet posts. With so much data available at your fingertips, you might think that coordinating a medical trip will be a snap.

The bad news is that there's almost too much information to wade through. Many sources offer conflicting accounts that can leave you scratching your noggin. Fortunately, we're here to help you decipher the sometimes confusing information you might come across.

## Surf the Web

To get the most out of an Internet search for medical tourism, you've got to pay attention to the information source. Many websites that promote medical tourism offer biased accounts to entice you to visit their particular country, to use their hospital, or to hire their agency.

When you do a Google search, you need to recognize that some of the websites that come up in the listings are actually paid advertisements. For instance, the listings on the right-hand side of a Google page as well as the listings highlighted in a different color at the top of the page are typically paid ads.

Start your search by checking out the listings that come up "naturally"—those that aren't paid ads. These usually are listed below the highlighted area at the top of a Google search page. Most likely, you'll find listings for several medical tourism agencies, websites promoting certain destination countries, websites promoting specific hospitals, and more. Visit several websites to gain a better understanding of the medical tourism process.

**Code Blue!**

> Marketing rhetoric and posh photos on the Internet can be very deceiving. In my travels to five continents around the world, I have personally experienced this type of misperception. How do you know which websites are telling the truth and which are "enhancing" reality? The truth is, you don't know until you have either experienced it firsthand or know of a trusting source that has had the experience.

## E-Mail for More Info

As you research medical travel, e-mail hospitals and other organizations for additional information about their services. Remember that when you're dealing with foreign medical providers, you may not get a quick response. Some international facilities are overwhelmed with requests and simply don't have the processes in place to handle all the inquiries. Our best advice is to be patient. Also, when e-mailing requests for more information, be sure to include specific details about your medical condition, your diagnosis, and the procedure or procedures you're considering.

# Narrow Your Destination Options

The destination country you choose is significant to the total value of your medical tourism experience. You should take into consideration numerous factors relating to the destination country; doing so could mean the difference between a truly wonderful experience and an unbearably frustrating trek. Here are some of the most important factors to consider about your destination country.

## Infrastructure Concerns

Many countries that offer substantial savings on health-care costs are considered to be emerging economies. That means that their infrastructure may be lacking many of the basics we take for granted in North America. Road conditions, communications systems, trash disposal, and general cleanliness may leave something to be desired.

In some countries, you could find that your modern hospital is located right next to a major slum. If so, the sights, sounds, and smells could prove to be very disturbing to you and could impede your recuperation. Even though the hospital is top-quality and the doctors are first-rate, the surroundings may taint your view of the entire medical tourism experience.

On the other hand, a number of destinations boast an infrastructure that rivals the status quo in North America. Do your homework to determine whether a country's infrastructure may be a problem for you.

## Navigating Around Town

Think about how easy or difficult it will be for you to get around town while you recuperate. Would you rather be in a crowded, hustle-and-bustle metropolis where you'll likely be jostled every time you leave your hotel? Or would you prefer a quaint, laid-back locale where you'll be able to take a leisurely stroll through town? Also consider the traffic. Will you sit in stop-and-go traffic to get to your doctor appointments, or will you cruise quickly to your destinations?

## Can You Stand the Climate?

Most medical tourism destinations are in tropical climates, so prepare yourself for some warm, humid weather. In some countries, temperatures can soar above 100 degrees during the summer months, and you may be breaking a sweat every time you step outside. Make sure the hospitals and hotels you choose have air conditioning to keep you cool and comfortable while you recover.

Countries with a tropical climate usually have a rainy season. If traveling solely for pleasure, you might want to avoid the rainy period. But rainy days aren't a big deal for medical travelers. Monsoon season is a different story. If your destination gets hit with annual monsoons, it's best to avoid traveling during that time of year.

## Consider the Culture

Every nation around the world has a unique and interesting culture. Styles of dress, eating habits, and social customs may be very different from what we're used to in the United States. It's a good idea to do a little investigating to find out about the cultural do's and don'ts in your destination country.

Be aware that some cultures are known for being friendly and hospitable, while others have a reputation for being more distant and uninviting. If you'd like a healthy dose of handholding while you're abroad, you may want to limit your search to countries where the doctors, nurses, and hotel staff will likely treat you like family.

## Language Barriers

The ability to effectively communicate while you're abroad is key. In several destinations, English is the second language, but there are still many countries where English isn't commonly spoken. This can be a real problem in the medical setting.

Imagine that you're in pain or that you need help getting to the restroom, but you're unable to communicate this to the nurse because of a language barrier. This can add a lot of stress to your recuperation and can wreak havoc on your peace of mind. If simple things such as ordering food in a restaurant or telling a taxi driver where to go are equally difficult to communicate, it can diminish your overall experience.

## Distance From Home

Convenience may play a role in your decision regarding where to go for your procedure. Destinations that are closer to the United States may be more appealing to you. For instance, you can hop from Miami to Costa Rica in less than three hours, whereas travel time to Southeast Asia or South America may hit 24 hours or more.

**Code Blue!**

Remember that countries in closer proximity to the United States tend to charge higher prices for their services. You'll have to decide which is more important to you: the convenience factor or the budget factor.

## Sightseeing and Travel Opportunities

The vacation aspect of your trip should fall to the bottom of your priorities list. It's much more prudent to focus on the medical portion of your trip rather than the sightseeing or travel opportunities. Just know that wherever you go, you'll find a host of interesting things to see and do. If your mind is set on an African safari or a jungle trek, remember that you may not feel up to it following surgery.

## The Least You Need to Know

- You must have a handle on why you need or want your procedure.

- The planning process takes time.

- Traveling during the low tourist season can be cheaper.

- Some medical tourism websites may offer biased information.

- Choosing a destination country involves several factors.

# Chapter 9

# Rx for Choosing Physicians

## In This Chapter

- How to decipher a foreign doctor's curriculum vitae (CV)
- Why you may want a doctor with international training
- What you can do to facilitate the selection process
- Why you must choose a physician who can effectively communicate
- Why referrals from former patients are the best things to go on

Whether you're looking for a plastic surgeon, an orthopedic specialist, or a dentist, choosing your overseas doctor is one of the most important decisions you'll make regarding medical tourism. The good news is that information about international medical providers is relatively easy to obtain. International hospitals understand that Americans want to know as much as possible about a doctor's qualifications, so they make this information readily available.

As a rule, you're likely to receive far more details about the qualifications of your overseas physician than you would about a U.S. doctor. In this chapter, we explain what qualifications to look for and what you can do to help zero in on the best doctor for your needs.

# Credentials and Experience: What to Look For

Of course, you want a doctor with first-rate credentials and experience. Fortunately, foreign physicians routinely send a copy of their CV to potential international patients, so you'll have the chance to evaluate his or her qualifications. As explained previously, a CV usually contains information about a doctor's education, training, certification, experience, and more. Here's an example of a CV that Dr. Suresh Kumarasamy, has graciously allowed us to print here.

---

Dr. Suresh Kumarasamy, M.B.B.S; M.ObGyn; M.R.C.O.G; A.M.
Date Of Birth: October 3, 1958
Birthplace: Penang, Malaysia
Sex: Male
Marital Status: Married

Gleneagles Medical Centre
1, Jalan Pangkor
Penang 10050, Malaysia
suresh@gmc.po.my

Telephone: 011-60-4-220-2102 (Clinic)
011-60-4-227-6111 (24-hr hosp. emergency)
Fax: 011-60-4-226-2994

Present Position: Consultant Obstetrician & Gynaecologist/Gynaecological Oncologist, Gleneagles Medical Centre, Penang, Malaysia.

Adjunct Senior Lecturer, Penang Medical College (A Medical College of the Nat'l Univ. of Ireland).

Medical Education: Bachelor of Medicine & Bachelor of Surgery (equivalent to M.D.), University of Mysore, India (1984); Member of the Royal College of Obstetricians & Gynaecologists, London (1992); Masters in Obstetrics & Gynaecology, University of Malaya (1992); Visiting Fellowship in Gyn. Oncology, Northern Gynaecological Cancer Centre, Gateshead, U.K. (1995–96); Fellowship of the Int'l Union Against Cancer, Dept. of Cancer Medicine, University of Sydney, Australia (1998).

---

Residency & Postgraduate Experience (1984–1998): St. James University Hospital, Leeds, U.K.; Stirling Royal Infirmary, Scotland, U.K.; Queen Elizabeth Hospital, Gateshead, U.K.; Royal Prince Alfred Hospital, Sydney, Aus.; Univ. of Malaya Medical Centre, Malaysia; Hospital of the Science Univ. of Malaysia; Queen Elizabeth Hospital, Malaysia; Kasturba Hospital, Manipal, India.

Awards: Traveling Oncology Scholarship, North of England Oncology Club, 1995; Overseas Fund Award, Royal College of Obstetricians & Gynaecologists, London 1997; Excellent Service Award, Ministry of Health, Malaysia, 1997; Organon Award, 9th Malaysian Congress of Obstetrics & Gynaecology, 1999.

Editorial Boards: Medical Journal Of Malaysia, 1996–2001; MIMS Obstetrics & Gynaecology.

Committees: Chairman, Sub-Committee on Gynecological Oncology, Obstetrical & Gynecological Society of Malaysia (1996–1999, 2001–2007); Malaysian Cervical Cancer Prevention Advisory Board; Clinical Practice Guidelines Committee for Cervical Cancer, Ministry of Health, Malaysia; Council Member, Malaysian Medical Association (1997–1999); Vice-Chairman Joint Penang Ethical Committee (2002–2006); Expert opinion on SERMs in the management of post-menopausal osteoporosis, Eli Lilly & Company.

Medical Societies: Royal College Of Obstetricians & Gynaecologists, London; Obstetrical & Gynecological Society of Malaysia; Malaysian Medical Association, Chairman Penang Branch 1997–1999; Malaysian Menopause Society.

Medical Registration (Medical License): General Medical Council, U.K.; Malaysian Medical Council; Karnataka Medical Council, India.

Academic: Senior Lecturer at Penang Medical College; Examiner for the National University of Ireland (Penang Medical College). Lectures at int'l meetings including: Taiwan Pediatrics Soc. Annual Conference (2008); All India Congress Of Ob/Gyn (2008); 5th Int'l Conference On Ob/Gyn, Oman (2007); Assn. of Southeast Asian Nations Conference on Primary Health Care (2007); Overseas Scientific Meeting of the Ulster Ob/Gyn Society (2006); Int'l Society Of Gynecological Endoscopy Conference (London 2005, Kuala Lumpur 2004); 5th Singapore Congress of Ob/Gyn (2005); Karnataka Ob/Gyn Conference, India (2005); Int'l Federation of Ob/Gyn Societies Gynecological Oncology Conference (2003); Fed. Of Ob/Gyn Societies Of India Conf. (2003); Ministry Of Health, Brunei (2001); Royal Thai College of Ob/Gyn, Johns Hopkins Int'l (2000); Joint Mtg. Royal College of Surgeons, Ire. (2000);

*continues*

*continued*

Xvith Asian & Oceanic Congress of Ob/Gyn (1998). Over 100 lectures at national and regional medical meetings. Examiner, Board of Mid-Wives, Malaysia 1992–2001. Introduced microwave based ablative technology (MEA) in Malaysia for the treatment of menorrhagia. Trained gynecologists in the use of this treatment in other parts of Asia.

Clinical: *I perform routine and complex radical surgery for both cancer-related as well as benign gynecological conditions on a regular basis. On average I perform six major operations each week. I established a referral service for gynecological cancer and complex non-cancer surgery in 1996. I receive referrals from other parts of Malaysia as well as neighboring countries for complicated surgery. I also manage patients requiring additional surgery after initial treatment elsewhere.*

Other Medical Interests: *One of my key interests is in promoting safe practices in obstetrics and gynecology particularly during gynecological surgery. I have co-authored a book "Reducing Litigation Risk in Obstetrics & Gynaecology" with professor Dermott McDonald of Ireland. This guide for obstetricians & gynecologists provides advice on safe practice and emphasizes techniques and procedures to minimize the risk of complications during gynecological surgery. I assist the Malaysian courts as well as medico-legal defense societies in providing expert medical opinions on medico-legal matters.*

*I have a keen interest in introducing new innovations that improve the lives of women with gynecological problems. I am regularly asked to consult for multinational corporations on gynecological issues. I was clinical consultant—Asia, Australia and New Zealand—for Microsulis Medical Limited, a U.K. based medical device company from 2001 to 2005. I also regularly lecture and train fellow gynecologists on new techniques and treatments both in Malaysia as well as abroad.*

Obviously, there's a lot of information provided in this CV. But how do you decipher what it all means?

## Decoding the Abbreviations

In the United States, a doctor's name usually is followed by the initials M.D. Unfortunately, not every country uses M.D. to indicate a person who has met the education and training requirements necessary to practice medicine. On a foreign doctor's CV, the doctor's name often is followed by a series of cryptic abbreviations. For example, Dr. Kumarasamy's name is followed by the initials M.B.B.S., M.ObGyn., M.R.C.O.G., and A.M.

Confused? You're not alone. Don't worry, though; we're going to help you decode these confusing abbreviations. Let's start with M.B.B.S. This stands for a dual Bachelor of Medicine and Bachelor of Surgery, which is considered the equivalent of the M.D. and is awarded by medical schools in the United Kingdom. Foreign designations that you may come across during your research and that are considered the equivalent of an M.D. include the following:

- M.B.B.S.
- M.B.B.Chir.
- M.B.B.Ch.
- M.B.Ch.B.
- B.M.B.S.
- D.N.B.
- Titulo de Medico Cirujano

If a doctor's name is followed by any of the above designations, it indicates that he or she is qualified to practice medicine.

Let's go back to our sample CV. M.ObGyn. stands for master of obstetrics and gynecology. Physicians who have advanced degrees in a medical or surgical specialty earn the designation "master of [specialty name]." This designation may be master of surgery, or M.S. The M.S. degree also may be abbreviated in any of the following ways:

- M.S.
- Ch.M.
- M.Ch.
- M.Chir.
- D.M.

For dentists in the United States, the abbreviations D.D.S. or D.M.D. are used. Abbreviations that international dentists may use include the following:

- D.D.S.
- D.M.D.
- B.D.S.
- M.D.S.

On the sample CV, A.M. and M.R.C.O.G. also are listed. A.M. means that the physician is registered (licensed) as a specialist with the Academy of Medicine in Malaysia. M.R.C.O.G. stands for member of the Royal College of Obstetrics and Gynaecology. The Royal College of Obstetrics and Gynaecology is an international society of obstetricians and gynecologists who have met stringent educational and training requirements and who have passed comprehensive membership examinations.

North American and international physicians include abbreviations after their names to indicate memberships in national and international medical organizations, associations, and societies. Here are just a few of the many, many abbreviations for medical societies that you might find on a foreign doctor's CV:

- F.R.C.S. (Fellow of the Royal College of Surgeons)
- F.R.A.C.S. (Fellow of the Royal Australasian College of Surgeons)
- F.R.C.P. (Fellow of the Royal College of Physicians)
- F.E.S.C. (Fellow of the European Society of Cardiology)

There are dozens more abbreviations that physicians may tack on to the end of their names. If you receive a CV from a foreign physician and you aren't sure what the abbreviations stand for, don't hesitate to ask for clarification.

# Education

Throughout the world, people are required to complete several years of specialized education before becoming a doctor. In the United States, an undergraduate degree is followed by four years at an accredited medical school. Upon graduation from medical school, the M.D. degree is attained.

In many other countries, the educational requirements are similar but vary slightly. For instance, in India, the equivalent of a U.S. undergraduate degree is completed during the eleventh and twelfth grades of high school. Medical school starts immediately after that and lasts about four and a half years.

To become a dentist in the United States, a candidate must graduate from an undergraduate program and then successfully complete four years of dental school. Worldwide educational requirements for dentists are similar to those in the United States, but differ slightly depending on the country.

When reviewing a doctor's CV, you may want to see if he or she has any experience with education or training abroad, such as in the United States, United Kingdom, or

Australia. Many overseas physicians boast international training, which may make you feel more confident in their abilities. The lack of international training, however, in no way indicates an inferior education.

## Internships

Doctors in the United States also must complete an *internship* before being able to practice general medicine unsupervised. Additional training called a *residency* is required if a doctor wants to specialize in a certain type of medicine, such as dermatology, plastic surgery, or obstetrics and gynecology. After completing the residency, some physicians may choose to continue their education with a specialized training program called a *fellowship*.

## def•i•ni•tion

An **internship** typically lasts one year and involves medical training in a hospital setting. A **residency** is a hospital-based training program that lasts approximately two to seven years. A **fellowship** offers advanced, specialized training in a specific branch of medicine to doctors who have already completed their residency. Fellowships are voluntary.

In other countries, training requirements may differ slightly. Again using India as an example, graduation from medical school is followed by a mandatory one-year internship. After completing the internship, doctors are considered qualified to practice medicine. Indian physicians who want to specialize in a specific area, such as neurology or cardiac surgery, must complete additional training.

## Continuing Education

Many physicians worldwide choose to continue their education throughout their careers. Continuing education keeps surgeons and other doctors up-to-date on the latest surgical techniques and medical innovations. Look for physicians who not only attend continuing education classes and lectures, but also who are speakers at professional conferences and seminars.

## Medical License Required

In every country that promotes medical tourism, doctors must be licensed to practice medicine. In most countries, a medical license gives a doctor the right to diagnose and treat patients, but it isn't specific to any particular specialty. In general, each destination has some form of medical council or association that grants licenses to physicians. Some of these councils have websites where you can find information on licensed physicians.

For example, the Malaysian Medical Council (mmc.gov.my/v1/) offers a medical register through which you can search for a licensed physician by name. You simply enter the name of the doctor you're researching, and you can see their degree (such as M.D.), undergraduate school, and a year-by-year list of facilities where they've practiced. Similarly, the Singapore Medical Council (www.smc.gov.sg/html/SMC_Home.html) offers an online medical register.

## Board Certification

You've probably heard the term "board-certified," but do you know what it means? In the United States, when a doctor is board-certified, it means that he or she has met rigorous educational and training requirements in a specific medical specialty, such as cardiology, obstetrics and gynecology, or plastic surgery. Board certification, which can be granted in 1 of 24 specialties sanctioned by the American Board of Medical Specialties, is a completely voluntary process.

> **Doctor's Orders**
>
> Although board certification may be voluntary, it demonstrates a physician's commitment to excellence and continuing education. Because of this, you may feel more secure in the hands of a board-certified physician or surgeon.

Board certification can be obtained in many other countries as well. For instance, in the United Kingdom, the General Medical Council grants board certification to physicians who meet stringent requirements. In Canada, it's the Royal College of Physicians and Surgeons. In Australia, it's the Australian Specialist Medical Colleges, such as the Royal Australasian College of Surgeons.

Some overseas doctors who have international training are board-certified by a United States, United Kingdom, Canadian, or Australian organization. Others may be board-certified by a medical council in their own country.

## Associations and Affiliations

Top-flight foreign physicians often boast membership in prestigious national and international medical associations, and many have affiliations with U.S. medical organizations. For example, a select group of foreign plastic surgeons are either members of the American Society of Plastic Surgeons (ASPS) or are international corresponding members of the ASPS.

To become a member of the ASPS, a plastic surgeon must be highly trained in cosmetic and reconstructive plastic surgery. He or she also must be board-certified by the American Board of Plastic Surgery (ABPS) or the Royal College of Physicians and Surgeons of Canada (RCPSC).

International corresponding membership is reserved for plastic surgeons practicing outside the United States or Canada. To be considered for this honor, a surgeon must have achieved distinction in the field of plastic surgery and must be a member in good standing with his or her national plastic surgery association. However, corresponding members aren't necessarily board-certified by the ABPS or the RCPSC.

The ASPS website offers online physician-finder tools that allow you to search for the following:

◆ ASPS member surgeons practicing abroad (www1.plasticsurgery.org/ebusiness4/patientconsumers/findintsurgeon.aspx)

◆ International corresponding member surgeons (www1.plasticsurgery.org/ebusiness4/patientconsumers/findcorrsurgeon.aspx)

Using the online physician finder is easy. You simply choose a destination country from a pull-down menu, and a list of plastic surgeons comes up. You'll find names, addresses, phone numbers, and e-mail addresses for the plastic surgeons listed.

International plastic surgeons also may be members of the American Society for Aesthetic Plastic Surgery (ASAPS), which requires either board certification by the ABPS or a similar organization in the respective country. The ASAPS website offers a physician-finder tool where you can search for international members by country: www.surgery.org/public/find_a_surgeon.

Look for affiliations with international societies. For example, many board-certified plastic surgeons are members of the International Society of Aesthetic Plastic Surgery (ISAPS). Founded in 1970, this organization has 1,300 members from more than 70 countries. The ISAPS website lets you search for board-certified plastic surgeons by country: www.isaps.org/index.php.

**Check-Up**

The countries with the most plastic surgeons listed on the International Society of Aesthetic Plastic Surgery are the United States and Brazil.

Let's return to our sample CV, in which the surgeon has listed membership in the following organizations: Royal College Of Obstetricians and Gynaecologists (London), Obstetrical and Gynecological Society of Malaysia, Malaysian Medical Association (Chairman Penang Branch), and Malaysian Menopause Society.

Membership in such organizations often reflects a certain level of competence. You may want to search the Internet for more information on any associations listed in your doctor's CV to find out exactly what is required to become a member. You may discover that a surgeon or physician must meet high standards to earn membership.

## Experience with the Procedure You Want

It's very important to choose a physician who is very experienced in performing the specific procedure you want. For example, an orthopedic surgeon may be highly skilled in hand surgery, but may not perform many hip replacement procedures. Or a plastic surgeon may do hundreds of liposuction procedures each year but only a few rhinoplasty operations.

Sometimes, a doctor will list the number of procedures he or she has completed (for example, "more than 500 hip replacements"). If not, be sure to ask how much experience he or she has with your procedure.

# Getting the Most Out of Preliminary Consultations

Typically, you'll have some form of communication with a foreign doctor you're considering, before making your trip abroad. E-mail often is the preferred method of communication when dealing with international medical providers. In part, e-mail is more convenient because the time differences between the United States and many medical tourism destinations can make a phone call tough to schedule. For example, when it's 8 A.M. in Los Angeles, it's 10 P.M. in Bangkok, Thailand. To reach a surgeon during working hours, you might have to call in the middle of the night.

## Prepare a List of Questions

Whether your communication takes place via phone or e-mail, prepare a list of questions to ask the surgeon. Questions you may want to ask the overseas doctor include the following:

- What procedure or procedures do you recommend for me?

- How will the procedure be performed?

- How long will I stay in the hospital?

- What are the possible risks and complications?

- How often have you performed this procedure?

- What is your success rate for the procedure?

- What's involved in the recovery process?

- What is the total cost for the procedure?

If a doctor doesn't provide satisfactory answers to your queries, find a different doctor.

## Sending Medical Reports and "Before" Photos

For a physician to assess a medical condition, recommend appropriate treatment, and give you a quote, he or she first will need to see all of your medical reports. Any magnetic resonance images (MRIs), x-rays, computed tomography (CT) scans, lab reports, or other medical documents pertaining to your condition will need to be sent to the doctor via e-mail.

For cosmetic procedures, you'll probably be asked to e-mail "before" photos of the areas you want treated. For instance, if you're interested in a face lift, you may need to send front and side views of your face. For a tummy tuck, front and side views of your abdomen may be necessary.

Whether you're going abroad for a medically necessary procedure or for a cosmetic nip/tuck, your surgeon will make recommendations based on the documents or images you send. You need to remember, however, that those recommendations may change after your surgeon has evaluated you in person.

**Check-Up**

Note that "before" photos don't have to be professional in quality. Images taken with just about any digital camera will suffice.

Say you're in the market for eyelid surgery to get rid of those droopy lids. When your surgeon sees you up close, he or she may decide that a forehead lift or brow lift might be more appropriate or might be required in addition to the eyelid surgery to produce the desired results. Be aware that such changes may alter the cost of your procedure.

**Check-Up** _____

I had one client who was told by a United States orthopedic surgeon that she needed a bilateral knee replacement. When the foreign surgeon examined her in person, however, he determined that she actually only needed one knee replaced. He explained that the patient had been compensating for the damaged knee by putting more stress on the other one, causing it to hurt. The patient ended up saving even more money because of this. After she had recovered from the procedure and was able to walk normally, her other knee stopped hurting.

# Communication Is Key

Being able to effectively communicate with your doctor is extremely important. Your health is at stake here, so it's vital that you and your doctor comprehend each other. You also need to know that you can reach your surgeon when necessary and that he or she will respond to your needs.

# English, Please!

You may be heading to a foreign country, but that doesn't mean you have to take a crash course in a foreign language. To ensure that you can communicate well, insist that your doctor speak English. Many doctors in international settings speak English, but some don't. In addition, some physicians have very strong accents that are difficult to understand.

# Get Your Doctor's Cell Phone Number

Some overseas surgeons will gladly give you their cell phone number so you can easily contact them in case you experience complications after your surgery, or if you have questions or concerns. This shows a real commitment to providing you with the best care possible. Always ask your surgeon for his or her mobile phone number.

# Responsiveness Counts

Remember that if you're taking the do-it-yourself approach to medical tourism, it often can take several weeks to receive responses to your phone or e-mail queries to foreign doctors. Of course the best surgeons are usually the busiest, so it may take longer to hear back from them. However, if you haven't received a response after more than a month, you may want to move on to another physician.

# Talk to Former Patients

One of the best ways to find a surgeon abroad is through patient referrals. Talking to other Americans who already have had surgery with the doctor can give you a better feel for the experience. Former patients can tell you whether they're pleased with their results and whether they're satisfied with the care they received.

Be sure to ask any doctor you're considering for referrals to former patients from the United States. The doctor should be able to put you in contact with several former patients. If not, try another doctor.

Questions you may want to ask former patients include the following:

> **Code Blue!**
>
> Insist on speaking to a doctor's former patients before making your final decision. Any doctor who can't or won't put you in contact with several American patients they've treated isn't worth your time.

- ◆ Were you well-prepared regarding the expectations of your procedure?

- ◆ Was the doctor able to effectively communicate?

- ◆ How often did you see the doctor after your procedure?

- ◆ Were there any hidden costs?

- ◆ Are you happy with your results?

- ◆ Would you recommend this doctor?

After you've talked to a few former patients, you should feel more confident about making your decision.

## The Least You Need to Know

- ◆ Choose a doctor who has the proper credentials and who is experienced with your procedure.

- ◆ You may feel more comfortable with a surgeon who has American or international training.

◆ Surgeons with international training aren't necessarily more skilled or experienced.

◆ Prepare a list of questions for your doctor.

◆ Choose a doctor who speaks English.

◆ Talk to former patients before choosing your surgeon.

# Hospital Hints

## In This Chapter

- ◆ How to find international hospitals or dental clinics
- ◆ Why hospital accreditation is so important
- ◆ Why you might want to look for hospitals that have connections to U.S. medical centers
- ◆ Why you need to go to a hospital that caters specifically to Americans
- ◆ Why you should go to a hospital rather than an outpatient clinic

Throughout the world, there are hundreds of high-quality hospitals, which is a good thing for anyone considering medical tourism. However, the sheer number of top-notch international medical facilities can be overwhelming. How do you wade through them and select the best one for your particular needs?

Here, I help you sort through the many options and give you the inside scoop on what to look for when choosing an international hospital. Remember, I've spent years researching and visiting the world's best medical facilities so you don't have to.

# Finding a Foreign Hospital

If you were looking for a good hospital in the United States, you'd probably ask your family and friends for referrals or ask your own physician for recommendations. The same principle applies when searching for a hospital beyond American borders. If you know someone who had surgery in a foreign country and had a successful experience, ask him or her for a referral. Similarly, your doctor may have other patients who have gone abroad for medical care and might be able to share some insights with you.

**Doctor's Orders** _____

The best way to find an international hospital is through a referral from someone who has already been to that hospital: a friend, an acquaintance, a doctor, or a company that specializes in medical tourism.

If you don't know anyone who's taken the plunge with medical tourism, you might feel like you're looking for a needle in a haystack. If you do a quick Internet search for medical tourism, however, you'll find dozens of articles and websites that include references to various international hospitals.

**Code Blue!** _____

If you visit medical tourism websites that have forums where visitors can post messages about their overseas care, be wary of postings that seem overly exultant. It just might be that the hospital being lauded created the posting itself.

Among the hundreds of medical tourism websites out there, you might find some blogs or forums where people post messages about their own experiences with overseas medical care. These websites might provide you with more personal insight into some international hospitals that treat American patients.

However, we must caution that you can never be sure who is actually writing that glowing review of "such-and-such hospital" in "this exotic locale." Be aware that it isn't unheard of for some international hospitals to promote themselves with manufactured postings on such forums.

As you visit various websites dedicated to medical tourism, you'll probably notice many of the same foreign hospitals mentioned over and over. Start making a list of these medical facilities, and then do some investigating to find out more about them.

Check to see whether the hospitals on your list have a website, and make sure the website is in English. If it isn't, consider that a red flag. If a hospital isn't willing to create an English version of its website, it can't be very serious about catering to U.S. patients.

Spend some time tooling around each hospital website. Most of them should include a section in which they list their medical specialties. If the specialty you need (such as cardiology or orthopedics) isn't listed, cross that facility off your list. After you've got your short list of possible hospitals, it's time to do some serious digging.

# Accreditation Counts

Any hospital you're considering should be accredited, which means that it has met stringent patient safety and quality of care standards set by a third-party accrediting agency. Looking for accredited hospitals sounds like an easy task, but it can get very confusing considering that overseas hospitals may be accredited by a wide variety of agencies, including national or international organizations. Each accrediting agency formulates its own set of standards. In this section, I introduce you to some of the most common overseas hospital accrediting agencies.

> **Doctor's Orders**
> Remember that hospital accreditation in the United States and overseas is a completely voluntary process.

## Joint Commission International (JCI)–The Gold Standard of Hospital Accreditation

A growing number of hospitals that promote health-care services for international patients are accredited by the Joint Commission International (JCI). JCI is the international arm of the Joint Commission on Accreditation of Healthcare Organizations (JCAHO), the organization that accredits more than 90 percent of U.S. hospitals.

Note that JCI standards for international hospitals are similar to—but not exactly the same as—the JCAHO safety and quality standards required of American hospitals. That's because JCI takes differing international laws and customs into consideration when creating international benchmarks. This means that the requirements vary slightly from country to country. Nevertheless, the JCI seal of approval can give you peace of mind that a foreign hospital is on par with the safety and quality standards to which we are accustomed in the United States.

> **Check-Up**
> International hospitals that want to earn JCI accreditation must meet more than 300 individual standards.

JCI began offering accreditation to international hospitals in 1999. Since that time, it has awarded accreditation to about 150 international health-care facilities in Asia, Latin America, Europe, and the Middle East. For a list of international hospitals that have earned JCI accreditation, visit www.jointcommissioninternational.org/23218/iortiz/.

Although JCI accreditation is a plus, don't limit yourself to the hospitals on this list. There are many world-class foreign hospitals that don't have JCI accreditation. In some cases, they may be accredited by another international or local agency, or they may be in the process of attaining JCI accreditation, which typically takes at least one year to complete.

## Understanding International Organization of Standards (ISO) Certification

Another type of international certification you may come across in your research is *International Organization of Standards (ISO)*. Based in Geneva, Switzerland, this international organization sets worldwide standards for management practices, quality control, and reporting practices for all sorts of businesses, not just health-care facilities. Although ISO accreditation is not specifically geared toward hospitals, it can provide some assurance that certain quality, safety, and management standards are being met.

## Is National Accreditation Good Enough?

International hospitals often are accredited by agencies within their own countries. Foreign accrediting organizations may set standards similar to those of U.S.-based accrediting agencies, such as JCI. You should be aware, however, that the standards may vary from country to country. Just a few of the many national accrediting organizations include the following:

## def•i•ni•tion

The **International Organization of Standards (ISO)** is a Swiss-based organization that sets quality standards for businesses in a variety of industries, including the health-care industry.

- ◆ Institute of Hospital Quality Improvement and Accreditation (Thailand)
- ◆ Singapore Accreditation Council
- ◆ Malaysian Society for Quality in Health (MSQH)

You can look up more information on these organizations on the Internet.

## The Inside Scoop on International Society of Quality Healthcare (ISQua)

You also may want to consider hospitals that are accredited by agencies that are members of the International Society of Quality Healthcare (ISQua). ISQua is an international umbrella organization for accrediting agencies requiring similarly high standards of hospitals. A number of international and local accrediting agencies are among ISQua's members, including:

- JCI
- The Australian Council on Healthcare Standards
- Canadian Council on Health Services Accreditation
- Australian General Practice Accreditation Limited
- Irish Health Services Accreditation Board (HIQA)
- Council for Health Service Accreditation of Southern Africa
- Taiwan Joint Commission on Healthcare Accreditation
- Quality Improvement Council, Australia
- CHKS Healthcare Accreditation Quality Unit, United Kingdom

As members of ISQua, these accrediting agencies have shown that they meet the highest international benchmarks for standards, training, and processes.

# Affiliations with U.S. Hospitals

In your search for an overseas medical facility, look for institutions that boast affiliations with renowned U.S. medical centers. Among the many U.S. hospitals that have affiliations with foreign hospitals are:

- Harvard Medical International
- The Johns Hopkins Hospital
- Cleveland Clinic
- Mayo Clinic
- Baylor University Medical Center
- New York–Presbyterian Hospital
- Weill Cornell Medical College

With these international partnerships, physicians from the overseas hospital may travel to the U.S. facility for additional training, and vice versa. Such partnerships also encourage information sharing between the two institutions.

Many international hospitals are actively seeking affiliations with American hospitals as yet another way to differentiate themselves from the growing number of health-care facilities catering to American medical tourists. In general, you can be sure that foreign hospitals with U.S. affiliations are interested in working with Americans and American patients.

Go online to find lists of overseas hospitals that have affiliations with the following American medical institutions:

◆ Harvard Medical International: www.hmi.hms.harvard.edu/main/home/index.php

◆ The Johns Hopkins Hospital: www.jhintl.net/glo/projects/

Foreign hospital administrators understand that strong connections to U.S. institutions can be very attractive to American patients. Therefore, if an overseas hospital has an affiliation with a U.S. facility, it is likely that this information will be included on its website.

# International Patient Centers

To handle the growing number of medical tourists, more and more foreign hospitals are creating international patient centers. These departments are designed to facilitate the medical tourism process and may include services, such as …

◆ Translation.

◆ Appointment scheduling.

◆ Booking accommodations.

◆ Ground transportation to and from the hospital.

If you're taking the solo approach to medical tourism, you may want to choose a hospital that offers these additional services. Be aware, however, that many of these centers are new and may not be adequately staffed. Or in some cases, they may be staffed by marketing personnel as opposed to individuals with a medical background.

> **Code Blue!**
>
> Be sure to call or e-mail international patient centers to inquire about a hospital's services. The response level you receive may be indicative of the care you would receive on-site. For example, do they respond quickly and make you feel special? Or do they treat you like a number?

# Location, Location, Location

Your hospital's location also can play a role in your decision. For example, is it situated in a nice part of town or is it located near a poverty-stricken slum? Will you feel safe walking around outside the hospital? How far is it from the hotel where you will be recuperating? Remember, you'll have to return to the hospital for follow-up appointments, so you want it to be conveniently located near your hotel.

# Experience Working With American Patients

As Americans, we have certain needs and expectations as patients. Hospitals that have experience dealing with American patients understand these needs and know how to deliver a satisfactory experience. Be sure that your overseas hospital routinely treats Americans.

# Experience With Procedures and Success Rates

It's a good idea to find out how much experience a hospital has with the type of procedure you want. Usually, this amounts to asking how many times your procedure has been performed in the facility. Beware: there's no magic number.

For example, if you're on the hunt for a hysterectomy, you may find that one hospital's gynecological surgeons have performed more than 500 hysterectomies while another hospital's surgeons have performed 1,000. This doesn't mean that the hospital that has performed 1,000 of them is better than the hospital that's done 500. You simply want to ensure that the procedure you want is being performed on a regular basis. That said, if a hospital's surgeons have performed less than 50 hysterectomies, you might want to consider a different facility.

Another element you want to investigate is a hospital's success rate with the procedure you want to have. Success rates aren't typically included on a hospital's website, so you need to inquire with hospital personnel.

# Is Bigger Better for Medical Tourists?

A few international hospitals have emerged as major players in the field of medical tourism. In fact, some treat hundreds of thousands of foreign patients each year. You might think that indicates that these are the best hospitals for medical tourists. But that isn't the case for everybody.

In reality, some of these hospitals may be so busy with the onslaught of international patients that you may not get the personalized treatment you'd like. Sure, your surgeon may be highly skilled, and you may save a good chunk of change, but you may feel like a number.

In addition, some of the most popular foreign hospitals have a "come see us and we'll figure it out" attitude toward your medical needs. Rather than going through thorough pre-consultations and treatment recommendations before you commit to taking a trip, they expect you to hop on a plane first and then get your diagnosis and surgery plans on-site. Understandably, you may be hesitant to take such a leap of faith.

In some cases, you may find that overseas hospitals that don't make the medical tourism headlines may actually provide you with a more pleasant overall experience. In these facilities, you may be more likely to receive the VIP treatment in addition to high-quality health care.

Of course, it's up to you to decide what's most important to you. Do you want the assurance that comes with an institution that has processed hundreds of thousands of foreign patients? Or would you prefer a more personalized experience in a high-quality hospital with decidedly less hustle and bustle?

# Hospitals vs. Clinics

If you're heading abroad for a medically necessary procedure, you'll definitely want to limit your search to hospitals. If you're in the market for liposuction or any other cosmetic procedure, you may be tempted to go to one of the thousands of plastic surgery clinics around the world. Many of these outpatient facilities offer high-quality care and boast excellent success rates for their procedures.

**Check-Up**

Many of the world's finest plastic surgeons operate out of clinics or day hospitals rather than full-fledged hospitals.

Even so, I need to point out a couple of problems with clinics as a medical tourism option. Most plastic surgery outpatient clinics aren't accredited by the same organizations that offer hospital accreditation. Some may not be accredited at all. JCI has launched an *Ambulatory Care* Accreditation Program for international clinics. As of this writing, however, no plastic surgery clinics are listed as JCI accredited on the JCI website (www.jointcommissioninternational.org/23218/iortiz/). Because of this, it can be very difficult to determine whether a clinic meets the quality and safety standards you want.

I also must warn you that these outpatient clinics may not be equipped to handle major complications that can occur during or after surgery. Major hospitals, on the other hand, are fully equipped and staffed to deal with all sorts of emergencies and complications.

For these reasons, I strongly urge you to have surgery in an accredited hospital rather than in a plastic surgery clinic.

## def•i•ni•tion

**Ambulatory care** refers to any type of medical care, including surgery, which is provided on an outpatient basis.

# Dental Clinics

If you're thinking about heading abroad for a smile makeover or some routine dental work, you need to find a dental clinic that offers first-rate care. Rest assured there are thousands of top-notch dental clinics circling the globe. To find a foreign dental clinic that caters to medical tourists, particularly Americans, you can use many of the same strategies described for finding a hospital.

Start by asking friends or your own dentist for referrals. Your own dentist may be hesitant to offer any recommendations to foreign dental clinics and may try to dissuade you from venturing abroad for dental care. In part, this may be due to the fact that your dentist would rather have you spend your money with him or her. He or she also may be genuinely concerned about your health and well-being and may be unaware of the high-quality dental offerings in many other destinations.

The Internet can be a great resource for locating international dental clinics that cater to medical tourists. By searching for the terms "medical tourism" or "dental medical tourism," you'll likely find several websites promoting dental clinics in a variety of countries. If you have an idea of which country you'd like to visit, do an Internet search for dental clinics in that country (for example, "Argentina dental clinics").

Make a list of the clinics you find and do a little sleuthing. Are the dentists board certified? Do they speak English? Do they specialize in the type of dental work you want? Call or e-mail for more info to see how responsive they are.

## The Least You Need to Know

◆ You can follow a variety of strategies to search for hospitals or dental clinics.

◆ Many international hospitals boast U.S. affiliations.

◆ It's best to choose an overseas medical facility that routinely works with American patients.

◆ Hospitals usually are a safer choice than clinics for medical tourists.

◆ A hospital that's conveniently located near hotels and that's in a safe neighborhood is ideal.

# Should You Hire a Medical Travel Agency?

## In This Chapter

- ◆ Discover the different types of agencies
- ◆ Find out what agencies can do for you
- ◆ Learn about pricing and fee structures
- ◆ Reasons why U.S.-based agencies may be best
- ◆ What to look for in an agency

Trying to research and plan your own medical care abroad quickly can become a headache. With so many hospitals, doctors, and other variables to research, it's easy to get bogged down in the details. Luckily, you don't have to go it alone when planning a health-care journey. As the popularity of medical tourism soars, a new breed of professionals has emerged to help you navigate the medical tourism process.

Whether you need to find an international hospital, schedule appointments, or secure lodging, these medical tourism specialists can help. With experience on their side, they can usher you through the process to make it as smooth and stress free as possible.

# What Is a Medical Travel Agency?

An organization managed by a medical tourism specialist (or specialists) who coordinates overseas health-care trips may be referred to as a medical travel agency. A professional health-care trip planner also may go by a laundry list of other monikers, including …

- ◆ Medical travel agency
- ◆ Medical tourism service agency
- ◆ Medical concierge services provider
- ◆ Health-care facilitator
- ◆ Overseas health-care facilitator

Whatever name they use, an agency can help you coordinate the details of your health-care travel.

# Types of Medical Travel Agencies

To meet a growing demand, approximately 200 medical travel agencies have popped up in recent years. Most of these agencies are small, independent operations that fall into one of two categories: referral services or full-service agencies.

## Referral Services

The vast majority of medical travel agencies—about 95 percent—are considered referral services. These companies typically offer a limited menu of services, such as scheduling appointments and booking air travel and lodging.

Often, these health-care facilitators work with a rather limited number of international medical providers. For example, they may work with a couple of hospitals and a few surgeons in a particular destination country. Sometimes, they may provide services for a single hospital or even a single surgeon within a destination.

> **Code Blue!**
>
> Be wary when dealing with referral services that work solely with one hospital or one surgeon. Although the medical provider may be highly qualified for some types of procedures, they may not be right for the specific treatment you're seeking.

# Full-Service Agencies

Full-service agencies offer A-to-Z assistance with every aspect of a health-care adventure. With these operations, you can expect a welcome amount of handholding throughout the entire process. In addition to assisting you with the planning, these companies often have an English-speaking representative in your destination country to take care of all your needs while you're abroad.

## CASE STUDY

| | |
|---|---|
| Name: | Eileen |
| Age at time of surgery: | 56 |
| Residence: | Florida |
| Procedure: | Hip replacement |
| Destination country: | Malaysia |
| Cost in United States: | $32,000–$45,000 |
| Total cost abroad (travel included): | $11,000 |

Eileen had been limping for a long time, due to a sore hip, when she had some x-rays taken. A U.S. doctor told her she needed a hip replacement. Unfortunately, Eileen didn't have health insurance and couldn't afford surgery, so she continued suffering. A few years later, Eileen could no longer walk and was in severe pain every day. That's when she saw a TV show that included a feature on medical tourism.

The idea of having surgery at a fraction of the cost sent Eileen straight to her computer. She looked up medical tourism and came across a full-service medical travel agency. She scoured the website for medical tourism details and filled out a form asking for more information. About two minutes later, Eileen was pleasantly surprised to get a call back from the agency. "And this was on a Sunday afternoon," she says. The representative spoke with her for well over 30 minutes, answering all of her questions. "He was so nice and made me feel very comfortable about the whole idea," she remembers.

From that point on, the agency led her through the process, sending her bios of doctors and information about hospitals and hotels. After Eileen made her choices, the real planning began: choosing a surgery date, sending x-rays to the surgeon, booking a flight, and more. The agency filled her in on what to expect while abroad, giving her packing tips and insights into the foreign culture. They arranged for a driver to pick her up at the airport and take her to the hospital.

Eileen's surgery and her overall experience were very successful, and she says she wouldn't hesitate to do it again. She's especially grateful that she had a full-service agency by her side to guide her through the experience. "There's no way I could have done it on my own," she says. "I wouldn't have known where to begin. They did everything for me."

Full-service providers advise you on everything to ensure a safe and enjoyable trip that meets your medical needs and fits within your budget. Just like a regular travel agency, they can help you with the routine travel arrangements; but what is especially valuable is that they usually work with multiple hospitals and surgeons in numerous countries, so you have more options than with a referral service.

In many cases, these pros have personally visited international facilities to ensure that they are indeed world-class centers. They likely have contracted with the hospitals to provide the very top surgeons for their clients. Thanks to the in-person meetings, they likely have developed strong relationships with destination hospitals, physicians, and hotels.

> **Check-Up**
>
> Having a full-service agency on your side can be a big advantage while overseas. Hospitals don't want to lose their business because the facilitator may send hundreds of patients their way. This gives the agency a lot of clout, which helps them get quicker responses and immediate action when a problem occurs. If you aren't an agency customer, you're just one patient; unfortunately, that means you aren't as important to the hospital.

Having a solid relationship with foreign hospitals can come in very handy. For instance, full-service agencies can usually help you get speedier responses to your questions to international hospitals and doctors. Plus, if you have any problems while you're overseas, an agency can typically reach the higher-ups at the hospital to resolve the issues. If you're on your own and you run into a problem, you won't know who to go to within the hospital, and you probably won't get the same quick action.

## Referral Services vs. Full-Service Agencies

How do you know which medical travel agency is best for you? It depends. The agency you choose depends on your budget, your level of travel experience, and your personality. If you're a savvy traveler, you may be fine with nothing more than a referral to a hospital, surgeon, or dentist. On the other hand, you may feel more comfortable with a full-service agency that can offer assistance every step of the way.

# What Medical Travel Agencies Do

Health-care facilitators offer a vast array of services to meet your needs. In this section, we detail some of the many ways agencies can simplify the medical tourism process for you. Remember, referral services typically offer a limited set of services, whereas full-service agencies are more likely to offer many or all of the following services.

## Matchmaker, Matchmaker, Find Me a Doctor and More

One of the primary tasks for any agency is helping you choose a destination, hospital, and doctor. It's important to remember that health-care planners are not licensed physicians and cannot offer advice about your treatment. Nor should they tell you which hospital or doctor to choose. Although agencies typically won't make the choice for you, they should provide you with a list of top-notch facilities and physicians that meet your requirements. The final decision should be entirely up to you.

**Doctor's Orders**

When working with referral services that represent a sole physician or hospital, you won't have as many options regarding your care. You'll need to do some independent investigating to make sure the hospital or physician fits your needs. Check the hospital's website to see whether your procedure is listed among its specialties. Ask for the doctor's curriculum vitae (CV) to determine whether they have the proper training and experience with your procedure.

To help you choose a doctor, your agency also may arrange an international phone consultation for you. At the very least, the agency should provide you with the doctor's e-mail address so you can ask questions about your treatment and about his or her credentials and experience.

The best agencies perform extensive research on a destination country's surgeons and hospitals to seek out the most qualified providers. Some even perform on-site inspections and interview medical staff before agreeing to include a facility on their roster. In this case, only pre-screened facilities and physicians that offer the particular treatment you want will be presented to you.

Medical travel agencies have good reason to make sure the facilities and physicians in their network are top-notch. In fact, their success depends on it. Remember, agencies are in the business of satisfying their clients—that means you—so it's in their best interest to promote only the best of the best.

## Booking Air Travel, Lodging, and More

Medical travel agencies can save you the hassle of making travel arrangements. Plus, many agencies have negotiated discounts with airlines, hotels, and other tour agencies and can pass the savings on to you. Agencies may help you with the following routine travel arrangements:

- Flights
- Hotel reservations
- Recovery center accommodations
- Obtaining visas
- Applying for or renewing passports
- Immunization recommendations
- Ground transportation in your destination country
- International cell phones and calling cards
- Concierge services

When booking hotels or recovery centers, agencies will keep your budget in mind. In many cases, you may find that you're able to afford five-star accommodations that are more luxurious than anything you could afford in the United States.

Some agencies may charge a nominal fee to assist you with things like obtaining a visa or applying for a passport. In this case, you're paying for the convenience. Rather than scouring the Internet for the proper forms or waiting in line at the appropriate government agencies, you can have health-care planners handle the process for you.

**Check-Up**

Having pre-arranged transportation from the airport can give you peace of mind. It eliminates the hassle of hailing a taxi or finding public transportation. Plus, you won't need to worry about the possibility of getting overcharged or getting lost.

Facilitators often stay on top of any public health concerns in their destination countries and will inform you about any immunizations that are required. In general, medical tourism hospitals are located in cities where public health concerns aren't an issue.

A medical travel agency may offer door-to-door service with pre-arranged ground transportation in your destination country. With this service, someone will meet you at the airport to whisk you off to your hotel or to the hospital for your in-person consultation. This ensures that you will get exactly where you need to go on time.

To help you stay in touch with friends and family back home, an agency also may provide you with an international cell phone or a calling card. More important, this gives you an opportunity to call the agency in case you run into any unexpected snafus.

To make your stay more enjoyable, some agencies also provide concierge services. These services may include things such as laundry service, tickets for entertainment events, or other VIP services. These little touches can make a big difference when you aren't feeling 100 percent.

## Arranging Medical Appointments

After you've selected a doctor and chosen a date for your procedure, you can count on your medical travel agency to schedule and confirm all your consultations, appointments, and medical tests abroad. Depending on the type of treatment you're having, you may have one or more consultations in addition to some routine lab tests before your procedure and at least one follow-up appointment after treatment.

An agency can ensure that you have ample time for all your pre- and post-operative appointments. Because agencies have long-standing relationships with medical staff, they can help out with rescheduling if your appointment times change due to unforeseen emergencies. Knowing that your appointments are pre-scheduled and confirmed can give you peace of mind so you can relax.

**Doctor's Orders**

Make sure your agency is available to reschedule consultations and lab tests if necessary.

## Managing Your Medical Documents

Keeping track of all your medical reports, diagnoses, test results, x-rays, and magnetic resonance images (MRIs) can be time-consuming. Trying to send these documents to hospitals or doctors overseas can be especially challenging. Many foreign facilities require that documents be in digital form, and you may not have access to digital files.

Letting a medical travel agency manage your medical documents can be a big relief. Most full-service agencies can transfer your records into digital files and will ensure that your records get into the proper hands abroad.

Similarly, some health-care planners will make sure that all your documentation from your treatment abroad is placed in your file for recordkeeping or is sent to your doctor at home. By keeping all of your files in one place, you can be sure that your physicians will have the necessary information to provide you with the best treatment possible.

## A Helping Hand From Arrival to Departure

To help make your overseas experience as smooth as possible, some agencies provide a bilingual representative in the destination country. From the moment you step off the plane, this English-speaking personal assistant will be by your side, providing translation services and other assistance as necessary.

Depending on the agency and the level of service you've chosen, this assistant may escort you to all of your appointments and tests before and after your procedure. He or she also may accompany you to your surgery and back to your hotel or recovery resort after you've been discharged. A personal assistant can be a real lifesaver overseas, catering to all your needs and ensuring that you have a satisfactory experience.

## Assisting With Vacation Plans

If you hope to include some sightseeing during your medical voyage, an agency can make arrangements for you. In many cases, agencies partner with local tour agencies in the destination country so your vacation desires can be met.

Keep in mind that, as you recuperate from surgery, you need to take it easy and possibly refrain from taking part in any vigorous sightseeing expeditions. Your agency may be able to help you choose activities in your destination country that don't require a lot of physical exertion.

# Agency Fees—Getting Something for Nothing?

With everything a medical travel agency offers, you may be thinking that it must be really expensive to hire one. Wrong! Your costs actually may be no more than if you planned the whole trip yourself. In fact, you could end up paying less than you would on your own—thanks to agency-negotiated discounts with hospitals, hotels, and tour operators.

Agencies use a variety of fee structures to charge their customers. In this section, I take a closer look at the various pricing models commonly used. Be sure that all fees and charges are spelled out in writing.

## Membership Fees

Some agencies require that you pay a one-time nonrefundable membership fee. By becoming a member, you'll be given access to the agency's planning services. In most

cases, the membership fee is applied toward your health-care journey if you book a trip through that agency. However, if you don't hire the agency to plan your trip, you will lose that money. Membership fees typically won't break the bank; they run about $50–$300.

> **Code Blue!**
>
> Insist on a detailed list of all charges before you go abroad, so you understand what is included and what isn't.

## Package Deals

One of the most common pricing structures among agencies is the package deal. Agencies usually offer a variety of package deals that include a set number of services. These deals may range from bare-bones, budget-style service to luxury VIP treatment.

Basic packages may include little more than the cost of surgery, a few days in the hospital, and associated medical costs. Luxury packages may feature five-star accommodations, airfare, a personal assistant, cell phone service, concierge services, sightseeing options, and more. With package deals, the cost is mainly dependent on the type of procedure you're having and the level of service you want.

> **Code Blue!**
>
> Beware of package deals. You may find out that you have to pay for extras after you arrive at your destination. Ask about any additional costs you might incur.

One problem with package deals is that they don't take into account the fact that every patient is different and has different needs. For example, you may require a longer hospital stay than what's included in the package. Or you may find out that additional pre-op tests or prescription medicines are necessary. Or if you have diabetes or a heart condition, the surgeon may need to take extra precautions during your procedure to ensure your safety. All of these things can add up to extra costs for you.

## Commissions and Flat Fees

Many referral services charge a flat fee or commission for their services. A commission usually is a percentage of the price of a surgery or a hotel stay. For instance, if you book a surgery with one of their doctors, you'll pay a fee. If the surgery will take place in a hospital referred by the agency, that's an additional fee. If you choose to stay in a hotel they suggested, you'll pay yet another fee. If you don't end up scheduling a procedure with any of the providers the agency recommended, you pay nothing.

If you feel comfortable doing much of the other legwork, this kind of arrangement may be ideal for you. These agencies often don't offer any handholding after you're in your destination country, so be prepared to fend for yourself if you run into any problems.

## Deposits

Agencies typically require that you make a deposit prior to your departure. Deposits range from 10 to 50 percent of the overall cost of your surgery or package if you're going with a package deal.

Some agencies require you to pay 100 percent of the costs up front. In general, it's best to avoid paying the total cost before you take your trip. You want to ensure that you're satisfied with the hospital and the physician before making your final payment. Note that most reputable agencies don't require full payment before services are rendered.

In general, deposits can be made using a credit card, a personal check, a money order, or loan financing. Be sure to ask whether there are any international transaction fees if you use a credit card because these fees can be substantial.

Always ask whether the deposit is refundable if you decide to cancel your trip. Also, ask if you can get your money back after you've arrived in your destination country if the hospital doesn't meet your expectations or if you aren't happy with the surgeon.

# U.S. Agencies vs. International Outfits

Medical travel agencies are popping up all over the world, not just in the United States. Some facilitators have set up shop in medical tourism destinations, such as India or Brazil. Usually, these international operations specialize in facilitating medical tourism in the country where they're located. Because they are on location, they may have a keen understanding of that country's medical system and a very good relationship with the local hospitals and surgeons. In some cases, these foreign-based facilitators may be Americans who have moved abroad for some reason, or they may be natives of that country.

Something you should be aware of, however, is that some foreign-based agencies actually may be sponsored by a foreign hospital. That is, the hospital hires the facilitator to try to increase its medical tourism business. In this case, you aren't getting an unbiased, independent agency. You're getting someone who wants to bring as many patients as possible to that hospital, regardless of whether it's the most appropriate facility for your needs. The real trouble with this scenario is that these facilitators may masquerade as independent agencies.

Because of this, you may want to confine your search to U.S.-based agencies. There are several other benefits of going with a facilitator in the United States. For example, you'll be dealing with English-speaking people so you can minimize the risk of miscommunication. Additionally, U.S.-based facilitators have a better understanding of the needs and expectations of American patients. Time-zone differences within the United States also make it easier to stay in contact with your agency, whereas coordinating communication with agencies that are 10 or more hours ahead of the United States can be very difficult.

> **Code Blue!**
>
> Make sure your agency is an independent operation as opposed to an offshoot of a foreign hospital. Otherwise, you may be railroaded into going to a hospital that may not be ideal for you.

For a number of reasons, some international facilitators try to give the impression that they're located in the United States. Their websites may be built to create the appearance that the organization is an American firm.

How can you tell if an agency is really U.S.-based rather than foreign-based? Here are some tips to help you figure out where an agency is located based on its website:

- Check the "Contact Us" page for the address and phone number.
- If there's no phone number or address listed, that may be a sign that it is not U.S.-based.
- Call and talk to someone, and note how well they speak English.
- Look for awkward sentence structure and misspellings, which may indicate non-native English speakers.

In your initial communications with an agency, you should ask where they are located.

# What to Look for in a Medical Travel Agency

Whether you decide to go with a referral service or a full-service agency, avoid new agencies that don't have a proven track record. Many operators start a business hoping to cash in on the medical tourism trend without doing enough homework. In the end, these agencies tend to come and go quickly. The last thing you want is for your agency to close up shop before you take your trip.

Make sure the agency can refer you to former patients. You certainly don't want to be an agency's first customer or "guinea pig" when you're dealing with your health and well-being. When talking to former patients, ask how the agency performed and if you had any problems with them.

Don't go with a facilitator unless they have voyaged overseas to inspect the hospitals they're representing. If they haven't, they can't really vouch for the hospital's condition. If any problems arise while you're abroad, they may not have a strong enough relationship with the hospital to help get your problem resolved.

When you contact a medical travel agency, ask the following questions:

- Have you been to the countries?
- Have you visited the hospitals?
- Have you met with hospital administrators, executive staff, and chief surgeons?
- Have you explained the needs of American medical tourists to the administrators and doctors?
- Do you have a proven process?
- Do you have good relationships with the hospitals?
- If there's a problem while I'm overseas, can you take care of it?
- How many patients have you facilitated?
- Can you give me referrals to former patients?
- Do you offer some form of guarantee?

Based on an agency's responses, you should get a better idea of its experience and ability to provide you with the level of service you desire.

Considering that you're dealing with your health and well-being, don't rely solely on what an agency tells you. Do some investigating on your own. Do an Internet search for the company to see whether it's mentioned in any articles on medical tourism. Check with the Better Business Bureau to see whether there are any complaints lodged against the firm, and if so, whether the complaints were resolved.

# Are Agencies Accredited?

As of this writing, there is no accreditation program for medical travel agencies. Likewise, there are no licensing requirements for health-care facilitators. That means there is no third-party organization evaluating the quality of service provided by agencies, and there are no educational or training requirements for planners. Literally anyone can hang out a shingle and call himself or herself a health-care facilitator.

There is talk within the industry of creating some form of accreditation process, but it may be years away. Because of this, you need to be even more vigilant when checking out a company's experience and qualifications.

## The Least You Need to Know

- ◆ Referral services typically offer limited services.
- ◆ Full-service agencies provide a wide range of services.
- ◆ Using an agency actually may lower your overall costs.
- ◆ Choose an agency that has a proven track record.
- ◆ Ask about guarantees and refund policies.
- ◆ Thoroughly research an agency.

# Part 3

## Dollars and Sense

Sure medical travel can save you a bundle, but you may still need to shell out a significant amount of money for an overseas health-care trip. In this part, we spell out the various costs associated with medical travel to simplify your budget plan. We'll also examine other money matters, such as financing options, insurance coverage abroad, and tax breaks. You'll also discover insider tips to help you ensure that you get what you pay for.

# Treatment Costs

## In This Chapter

- ◆ What is and isn't covered in the surgeon's fee
- ◆ What your hospital bill includes
- ◆ What fees you need to pay
- ◆ How to use a budget worksheet to help you estimate costs

Whether you have a medical procedure performed in the United States or abroad, a number of costs are involved. To get an accurate estimate of your overseas treatment costs, you need to be aware of all the possible fees and charges associated with your procedure. In this chapter, we introduce you to the many possible treatment costs you may need to pay.

## Physician Fees

Physician fees often make up the bulk of overseas treatment costs. The surgeon's fee usually includes the following:

- ◆ The pre-consultation
- ◆ The procedure

♦ Hospital visits

♦ All follow-up appointments

Other costs (such as anesthesia) may or may not be included in the surgeon's fee. Cosmetic surgeons often use local anesthetics with sedation for cosmetic procedures and administer the drugs themselves; in this case, it's likely that anesthesia fees will be included in the surgeon's fee. However, for more involved procedures using general anesthesia, a separate anesthetist and thus a separate fee are usually required.

**Doctor's Orders**

If you're going with a lump-sum package deal that includes your procedure, travel, and accommodations, make sure you get an itemized list of exactly what is included. You don't want any surprises after you land overseas.

If you have complications during or following surgery, you may be subject to additional surgeon fees. Be sure to ask your surgeon about his or her policy regarding complications. This way, you'll have an idea of what you'll have to pay in case of complications.

Here's the good news regarding complications. Some overseas surgeons choose not to charge extra fees when unforeseen problems occur. They want to please American medical tourists and want to encourage referrals to other U.S. medical travelers. Because of this, they may be willing to forego the extra fees they would normally charge to ensure your satisfaction.

**Check-Up**

I had a patient whose surgery was scheduled to take four hours, but due to complications, it ended up taking eight hours. Normally, a surgeon would tack on extra fees for the additional time required to complete the surgery. But the overseas surgeon was more interested in making the patient happy, so he didn't charge any additional fees.

Similarly, if you're having a cosmetic procedure, inquire about your surgeon's revision policy. For instance, what fees will you be responsible for if you aren't happy with your results and feel like you need a follow-up procedure?

As you plan your medical trip, you should ask potential doctors to give you written, detailed estimates for your treatment. Be aware that the quotes you receive may be all-inclusive or may include only a portion of the required fees. Be very careful when evaluating and comparing the quotes you receive to ensure that you're comparing apples to apples.

**Check-Up** _____

I've noticed that some surgeons give you a quote that's on the high side just to be safe. Then you actually end up paying less than the original quote. This promotes goodwill and makes patients more likely to recommend the doctor to others.

# Hospital Fees

The facility where you have your procedure may bill you for a wide variety of things. Common foreign hospital charges include fees associated with your procedure as well as your recovery, if you stay in the hospital after your operation. The hospital should provide you with a comprehensive quote for all of these things. As always, ask whether there will be any additional fees that aren't included in the quote.

**Code Blue!** _____

Although I understand that lower prices are the main motivator for seeking medical travel, never choose a hospital or physician solely because they offer the cheapest price. Your health depends on your choice of the most qualified medical providers offering the best value, not the lowest price.

## Procedure Fees

Whether your surgery takes place in a hospital or an outpatient clinic, you're likely to be charged for the following:

- Operating room
- Operating room nurses
- Medical supplies
- Medical equipment usage
- Medications
- Prosthetics or medical devices, if necessary

Fees for the operating room (OR) and OR nurses are usually charged by the hour. The quote you receive usually will be based on the number of hours your surgeon anticipates your procedure will take. If your procedure ends up taking more than the allotted time, you may be charged additional fees.

While you're having surgery, a variety of medical supplies, monitoring equipment, and medications are used. You'll be charged for the use of all of these items. These fees should be included in the hospital's price estimate.

Prosthetics or medical devices include things like breast implants, artificial knee or hip joints, and artificial discs. Typically, the hospital (rather than the surgeon) charges for these devices. Even if you're having a breast-augmentation procedure in a plastic surgery clinic, you usually have to pay a separate fee for the breast implants in addition to the surgeon's fee.

## Recovery Fees

If your procedure requires a hospital stay, you'll be charged for a host of things during your recuperation, including ...

◆ Daily room rate

◆ Nursing services

◆ Medical supplies

◆ Use of monitoring equipment

◆ Medications

◆ Food

◆ Physical therapy sessions, if necessary

◆ Physical therapy supplies, if necessary

**Check-Up**

A few times, hospitals have mistakenly underestimated prices for my clients. I've made them stick to those numbers, which amounted to additional savings for my clients. If you're venturing abroad on your own without an agency, you may not get that kind of treatment.

The price quote you receive generally specifies the number of days you'll spend in the hospital. Usually, this is based on the average number of days patients stay for the procedure you're having. For instance, if you're having hip replacement, a seven to 10 day stay is common. For minor procedures, a couple of days may be the norm. If you end up staying longer than planned, you may be faced with extra fees. On the other hand, a shorter stay than anticipated may mean a price break for you.

During your recuperation in the hospital, a variety of medical supplies will be used, and a number of medications may be administered to control pain and prevent infection. In addition, your vital signs likely will be monitored using sophisticated equipment. These costs also should be included in the price estimate.

For procedures such as knee or hip replacement, post-op physical therapy will be required. Make sure that the costs for the therapy sessions and any supplies used are included in your quote.

# Sample Hospital Bill

To help you get a better idea of what's included on a hospital bill, here's an example from a real medical travel procedure. This patient had hip replacement surgery and spent six days recuperating in the hospital. Note that this sample only shows the total cost for each category. The actual bill itemizes each expenditure within each category. For instance, under the "Medications" heading on the actual bill, every solution used in the intravenous (IV) site, every pill, and every injection is listed separately with its individual cost.

## Sample Hospital Bill

| Description | Cost (rounded to nearest dollar) |
| --- | --- |
| Hospital accommodation (room, nursing care, food for six days) | $968 |
| Blood infusion | $112 |
| Consignment supplies | $2,425 |
| Lab tests | $56 |
| Medical gases | $176 |
| Medical supplies | $545 |
| Medications | $1,249 |
| Miscellaneous | $9 |
| Operating room | $420 |
| OR medical supplies | $253 |
| Procedure fee | $11 |
| Medical equipment rental | $473 |

*continues*

## Sample Hospital Bill  (contineud)

| Description | Cost (rounded to nearest dollar) |
| --- | --- |
| X-rays | $92 |
| Consultants (surgeon, anesthesiologist, physical therapist) | $3,528 |
| Total | $10,317 |

# Anesthesiologist Fees

For surgical procedures, some form of anesthesia usually is required to control pain and to induce relaxation and drowsiness. Either the surgeon or a licensed anesthetist will administer the anesthetics. A separate fee usually is charged when a licensed anesthetist handles the anesthesia. This fee generally includes a pre-consultation with the anesthetist, administration of the anesthetic agents, monitoring during the procedure, and post-operative monitoring.

**Code Blue!**

Make sure a licensed anesthetist or your own surgeon will be administering the anesthesia, and ask which type of anesthesia will be used. Local anesthetics combined with sedation are commonly used for many cosmetic surgery procedures; general anesthesia is often used for major surgical procedures.

**Check-Up**

Even if you've had x-rays or other tests done in the United States, you may need to have them done again or have additional tests performed while you're abroad. These may be additional costs or may be included in your hospital estimate.

# Lab, X-Ray, and Imaging Fees

Prior to or following your procedure, you may need to have any number of lab tests, x-rays, magnetic-resonance imaging (MRIs), computed tomography (CT) scans, or other tests performed. The quote you receive from the hospital should include the cost of tests normally performed for the procedure you're having. If these tests are performed while you're in the hospital, they generally will be included as part of the hospital quote.

## Additional Consultation Fees

It is common practice, in the United States and abroad, for surgeons to consult with other physicians regarding your care. There are many reasons why a surgeon might enlist the aide of another doctor. It may be to perform diagnostic tests or to deal with certain aspects of your care. Consulting physicians typically charge a fee for their services. These charges are usually included in the hospital fee.

# Other Fees

In addition to these charges, you may be responsible for a number of other fees relating to your medical care. Take note that these fees may not be included in the quotes you receive from overseas surgeons or hospitals. If not, you'll have to add these costs to your total out-of-pocket expenses.

## Paying for Prescriptions

While you're in the hospital, any medications used will be included in the hospital fee. However, you'll need to pay out-of-pocket for any prescriptions you'll need after being discharged from the hospital. The good news is that medication costs abroad can be as little as one-tenth the amount you would pay in the United States. Always ask your surgeon whether there are any medications you might need that aren't available in your host country. If so, you may want to fill those prescriptions in the United States before you head overseas.

## Pre-Travel Evaluation and Post-Op Follow-Up at Home

In some cases, your overseas physician will ask you to visit an American doctor to ensure that you are healthy enough to travel. This visit may include a number of routine tests, including blood work, an electrocardiogram (ECG), a chest x-ray, and more. If you don't have health insurance, you'll have to pay for the visit and the tests yourself.

You also may want to check whether this American physician will be available for appointments should you need any follow-up care after you return home. For example, you may need to have some stitches or a drain removed after you come home. Seeing an American physician for such things will be an additional cost.

# Digitizing Medical Documents

Foreign doctors only can provide you with an accurate quote after reviewing your medical documents, including any x-rays, MRIs, or CT scans. To e-mail these items to a physician, you'll need to have them converted to a digital format. Several firms provide this service at a reasonable cost—usually no more than $10 per copy.

# Medical and Incidental Supplies

Aside from the prescriptions and medical materials you might get from the hospital, you may need additional supplies. For example, if you're having liposuction, you may need to wear a compression garment for several days or weeks following your procedure. Or, if you're having breast augmentation, you'll be instructed to wear a sports or support bra for several weeks. It's best to purchase these garments before your departure and take them with you rather than waiting to buy them in your host country.

### Doctor's Orders

If you're required to wear a compression garment following a cosmetic procedure (such as liposuction), buying two such garments rather than one can really pay off. Doctors recommend wearing the garment at all times for a week or more after your procedure. These garments can become sweaty and sticky, especially in hot and humid climates, and will require washing. Some doctors say that you can wash the garment and dry it in 20 minutes using a hair dryer. But some of my clients have found that the garments still are wet more than 30 minutes later, and they're very uncomfortable if you try to put them on when they aren't completely dry. With a second garment on hand, you can wear one while you wash the other.

Simple things like salves, ice packs, and heating pads may improve your comfort as you recover. These items won't be included in your hospital bill, so plan on bringing some money to cover these costs.

# Gifts for Nurses and Doctors

When traveling abroad for medical care, you may want to consider taking small gifts for the hospital and nursing staff, especially if you'll be visiting a country in Asia. There's a long tradition of gift giving in this area of the world, and a small gesture is much appreciated and can translate into even better care for you. Gifts don't need to be expensive—just a token of appreciation will do.

# Treatment Costs Budget Worksheet

To help you come up with a good estimate of what you'll have to pay for your treatment abroad and of how much you'll save by going overseas, we've included this handy chart. Simply fill in the estimates for your treatment costs abroad and then compare them to the costs quoted for having the same procedure at home.

## Budget Worksheet: Treatment Costs

| | Cost Abroad | Cost At Home |
|---|---|---|
| Pre-travel fees | _____ | _____ |
| Physician | _____ | _____ |
| Lab, x-ray, imaging | _____ | _____ |
| Digitizing documents | _____ | _____ |
| Medical supplies (compression garments, support bras, etc.) | _____ | _____ |
| Procedure fees | _____ | _____ |
| Anesthesiologist | _____ | _____ |
| Additional consultation | _____ | _____ |
| Surgery facility | _____ | _____ |
| Medical devices | _____ | _____ |
| Recovery fees | _____ | _____ |
| Hospital room/ recovery center | _____ | _____ |
| Physical therapy | _____ | _____ |
| Prescriptions | _____ | _____ |
| Incidental supplies | _____ | _____ |
| Rental equipment (wheelchair/crutches) | _____ | _____ |
| Gifts | _____ | _____ |
| At-home follow-up fees | _____ | _____ |
| Physical therapy | _____ | _____ |
| Other | _____ | _____ |
| Treatment costs total | _____ | _____ |

## The Least You Need to Know

- ◆ Surgeon fees should cover the consultation, procedure, and all follow-up visits.

- ◆ Hospital charges usually are in addition to the physician's fees.

- ◆ Get all fee estimates in writing.

- ◆ Ask if any charges aren't included in the quote.

- ◆ Budget for follow-up care at home if necessary.

# Chapter 13

# The Price of Travel

## In This Chapter

- ◆ Choosing your level of luxury
- ◆ Getting the most for your money with an agency's help
- ◆ Finding the best airfares
- ◆ Balancing quality and cost for hotels and recovery retreats
- ◆ Adding optional expenses
- ◆ Covering needed at-home costs

When you're considering medical travel, you've got to budget for travel in addition to medical treatment. Airfare, hotel charges, and other fees will add to the total cost of your health-care journey. Here, I detail the many possible costs associated with traveling abroad for medical care.

Of course, it's impossible to say exactly how much you should expect to pay for travel expenses. Your actual costs will depend on the chosen destination country, travel preferences, sightseeing desires, and more. Keep this in mind as you budget for your trip.

# Budget Trip or Five-Star Service?

When you take a health-care voyage, you can opt for a penny-pinching budget excursion or a luxurious five-star extravaganza. If you're severely strapped for cash, you may want to scrimp on the travel portion of your trip. As a rule, it's better to economize on your travel rather than on your medical care.

Going all-out for the VIP treatment can add to the overall cost of your trip, but it may be worth the higher price tag. In fact, I usually recommend splurging a bit while you're recuperating. A little pampering and TLC can go a long way when you're recovering from surgery and may help you heal faster. When you're relaxed and at ease, your body tends to heal more quickly than if you're uncomfortable and anxious.

Even if you're on a tight budget, you may still be able to afford a little luxury overseas. In many medical tourism destinations, taking the deluxe route is very affordable by U.S. standards.

# Planes, Trains, and Automobiles

In general, using a medical travel agency should not increase the overall cost of your trip. In fact, it is more likely to reduce your travel costs because agencies boast relationships with airlines, hotels, and tour operators. Even so, an agency may charge a membership fee, a commission, or some other form of fee for coordinating your trip. Be sure to factor this into your budget.

Airfare to and from your destination usually will be a high-ticket item. For instance, round-trip economy flights from the United States to Southeast Asia can cost up to $1,500. Round-trip airfare to South America starts around $1,000, and round-trip tickets to Central America may come in under $1,000. Remember that you may get a price break if you buy your tickets through a medical travel agency.

> **Doctor's Orders**
>
> When flying to far-off destinations, such as Southeast Asia or South America, consider breaking up your flight into legs. You may find this preferable to a nonstop 15- or 18-hour flight.

Generally, I recommend trimming costs by flying in economy class rather than splurging on first-class tickets, which can cost thousands of dollars. Even though you may be in the air for 8, 12, 18, or more hours, the additional cost for first-class fare usually isn't worth it. Most of my clients prefer to spend that money on nicer hotels and better food in their destination country.

When you're traveling internationally for medical care, you may need to make changes to your airline reservations. Because of this, you must purchase plane tickets that can be changed. When you book through a medical travel agency, changes usually can be made for a nominal fee. Always ask the agency about fees incurred when you make adjustments to your reservations.

### Check-Up

I've had clients who have had to postpone their trips due to health problems. For example, a client developed a gum infection prior to her trip and had to reschedule. Her surgeon said it wasn't safe for her to undergo surgery until the infection was under control. Because she had booked her trip through an agency, she was able to make changes without financial consequences.

On the other hand, if you book your tickets on an Internet travel site, you may not be able to make any changes to your ticket, or you may have to fork over a hefty sum in penalties to make changes. In the worst-case scenario, if your ticket isn't changeable and it's nonrefundable, you could end up being forced to purchase new tickets. Ouch!

### Doctor's Orders

You may want to arrange for a wheelchair at the airport for your return flight. Your doctor in your destination country will need to write a note for you, which you must give to airport authorities. If you've had some form of orthopedic surgery, this can be a lifesaver. Arrangements also can be made for airport personnel to pick you up at your gate and shuttle you to your next gate. Medical travel agencies routinely coordinate such services.

In addition to your airfare, you'll need to budget for ground transportation in the United States and in your destination country. At home, you'll need transportation to get to and from the airport. In your final destination where you'll be treated, you may need a taxi to get to and from various medical appointments. To be safe, agree on a price before getting into a foreign taxi.

### Code Blue!

Arrange for a driver to pick you up at the airport for a pre-set fee. This prevents you from having to find a cab and having to negotiate the fare to your destination.

# Hotels and Recovery Centers

Along with your airfare, accommodations typically are your biggest travel expense. Fortunately, hotels and recovery centers in medical tourism destinations are relatively inexpensive compared to hotels in the United States. In many locations, you can find luxury accommodations for $100 to $200 per night.

## Hotels

Because hotel prices are so reasonable in medical tourism destinations, you may be able to swing a stay in a five-star hotel that you could never afford back home. You should note, however, that hotel prices in India are higher than most countries due to a shortage of upscale accommodations.

When looking for a hotel, price isn't the only factor to consider. Amenities you may want to put on your wish list include the following:

◆ Room service

◆ Buffet breakfast included in price

◆ American cuisine

◆ Pleasant and safe surroundings

◆ Restaurants within walking distance

◆ Handicap accessibility (particularly important if you're having orthopedic surgery)

◆ Proximity to the hospital

◆ Connection or relationship with the hospital

Choosing a hotel that offers these amenities can improve your overall experience. For instance, when you're first discharged from the hospital, you may not want to leave your room or the hotel, so room service and hotel dining services come in handy.

When you're ready to venture outdoors, it's a plus to have restaurants and shopping within a short walking distance. This way, if you start to feel fatigued, you can easily head back to your hotel. If dining and shopping spots require a lengthy cab or bus ride, it may take you a long time to make it back to your hotel. This can be cause for concern if you are returning because you started feeling tired, achy, or weak.

If you're scheduled for orthopedic surgery, selecting a hotel that's handicap accessible is key. Initially, when you're discharged from the hospital, you'll likely be required to use a wheelchair. If your lodging isn't wheelchair-friendly, it can be very frustrating and difficult for you to get around. Also, look for hotels that offer railings in the bathrooms and potty chairs on the toilets, which make it easier to get up and down.

Always find out how close a hotel is to the hospital. Because you'll have to go back and forth for follow-up appointments, it's best to book a room in a nearby hotel. In addition, some hotels routinely deal with neighboring hospitals and their patients. With this kind of connection, the hospital and the hotel may coordinate changes to your reservation dates if your hospital stay becomes longer or shorter than anticipated.

Keep all of these things in mind when evaluating hotel prices for your health-care adventure. Sometimes, the lowest price isn't necessarily the best bargain, and the highest priced luxury hotel may not be best suited for your needs.

A medical travel agency often can help you get the best deals on hotels. Thanks to relationships with the hotels, an agency may be able to negotiate a lower price, or may secure a number of upgrades at no extra cost to you.

Another reason you may want to have an agency book your accommodations is that it gives you some assurance as to the overall quality of the facility. Agencies are in the business of making their clients happy so it's in their best interest to place you in a suitable hotel.

> **Check-Up**
>
> Some of the hotels I deal with have long-standing relationships with nearby hospitals. Because of this, the hotels often won't charge you for days you miss when your hospital stay is extended. And they'll go the extra mile to make room for you if you get discharged from the hospital earlier than expected.

> **Code Blue!**
>
> Don't always believe the hotel photos you see on the Internet. They aren't always realistic. To avoid being disappointed, get an unbiased opinion from someone who's actually stayed in the hotel.

If you book a hotel on your own, solely based on what you see on the Internet, you may be in for an unpleasant surprise. I've found that some hotels don't live up to what is depicted on their websites.

## Recovery Centers

In some destinations, recovery centers are another affordable lodging option for your recuperation. Rates usually are similar to what you would pay for an upscale hotel. What differentiates them is that these centers specifically cater to medical tourism patients, so they may have a better understanding of your needs.

Recovery facilities often offer professional post-operative caretakers or nurses to see to your needs. This can be a great benefit and can give you peace of mind, knowing that professional care is available should you need it. Thanks to the aftercare provided, these facilities may be ideal if you're having surgery in an outpatient clinic rather than in a hospital. If you're spending several days to a week or more in the hospital, you usually won't require nursing care after you've been discharged.

Also called treatment centers, these accommodations often include three meals a day and beverages in the price. If you like the idea of having all your meals in the facility, this can be a real money-saver. If you're a little more adventurous, however, and would prefer to try some of the local restaurant fare, you may end up paying twice for your meals.

Most recovery centers are located in older homes or apartment-type buildings that lend a homier feel. To make you feel even more at home, many offer rooms equipped with refrigerators, coffee makers, microwave ovens, and even small kitchens.

Other amenities that may be offered in recovery facilities are massage services, facials, and other spa-type treatments. These are in addition to typical hotel room amenities, such as room service, air conditioning, television, and Internet access.

**Check-Up** _____

Recuperating with other medical tourists in a recovery center can offer a number of benefits. But just like any group setting, some people in a recovery center may not be as supportive as others. For instance, I've visited some recovery centers where patients have said things like, "My surgery turned out better than yours. You should have gone to my doctor."

In a recovery center, you often will meet other recuperating guests in common areas, such as courtyards and dining rooms. If you're a very social person, you may enjoy the camaraderie of swapping surgery stories with other medical tourists. If you aren't feeling up to mingling, however, you might prefer a little more privacy. It's up to you to decide how much socializing or quiet time you need.

Recovery centers offer a number of benefits, but there are some disadvantages, too. For instance, many facilities weren't built with patients in mind. The walls in these older buildings may be thin, and it's possible that you might hear other patients moaning throughout the day or night. This can be disturbing and may interrupt your rest.

Spending a week or more in close contact with other recuperating patients can be a bit too much togetherness for some people. Consider the fact that following surgery, you—and the other guests—probably won't be at your best and you may feel cranky, grumpy, or downright ornery. This can lead to personal disagreements, which can add stress to your recuperation.

# Passports, Visas, and International Entry/Exit Fees

No matter which country you decide to visit, you'll need a valid passport. The current fee for a new passport is $100. Renewing an existing passport costs $75. On top of these fees, you'll need to cover the price of passport photos and mailing costs. It's best to apply for your passport at least a few months prior to your departure. If you need to rush your passport's delivery, you'll have to tack on another $60 fee for expedited service and the cost of overnight shipping for both your application and your passport delivery.

**Check-Up**

Many countries require that your passport be valid for a certain time period following your entry or exit date. This may be 30 days from your entry date or six months from your departure date. Be sure your passport is valid for the required amount of time.

Some destinations also require that you obtain a visa before entering the country. For example, you'll need a visa if you intend to visit Brazil or India. The fee for a visa ranges from about $75 to $150. Apply for your visa at least one month prior to your departure date.

**Check-Up**

Medical travel agencies or other passport/visa service agencies can assist you with obtaining a passport or visa for a nominal fee. If you need your passport or visa in a hurry, these agencies have the know-how to make it happen. In some cases, next-day service may be available. Agency fees for rush jobs may run you about $100 to $200.

Depending on where you travel for your medical care, you also may have to pay entry and exit fees. Averaging about $30, these fees typically must be paid in cash. U.S. dollars often are the preferred currency, so make sure you have some U.S. money with you.

# You Think You're on Vacation?

When it comes to the "tourism" portion of a medical travel adventure, you can spend a bundle or next to nothing. Extravagant tour expeditions, like a safari or a jungle trek, can eat away at your budget. But, many sightseeing opportunities don't cost a thing.

## Sightseeing

As previously mentioned, it's best to wait until after your surgery to see how you're feeling before booking vacation activities. You should always get clearance from your surgeon before venturing out for any physical tourist activities. The last thing you need is to rip open your stitches while rock climbing or trekking through the jungle. Plus, if you book in advance and then aren't feeling up to going, you may be subject to stiff cancellation fees.

## The Cost of Bringing a Companion

Don't forget about the added travel costs if a spouse, family member, or friend will be joining you on your medical adventure. You'll have to add an extra plane ticket to the tab, as well as meals and incidentals. There also may be additional lodging costs.

> **Doctor's Orders** _____
>
> It may not be advisable to have your traveling companion share your hospital room. For one thing, the day bed or pull-out bed may not be the most comfortable. And more critically, he or she may be exposed to infection, which is a possibility in every hospital whether it's in the United States or abroad.

In some foreign hospitals, if you have a private suite with a day bed, your companion can stay in the room with you at no extra cost. Some hospitals offer daily meal plans for visitors staying with you. Even so, your companion may prefer not to be at the hospital 24/7. When this is the case, your companion will need a hotel room while you're in the hospital. Of course, after you're discharged from the hospital, you and your companion can share a hotel room.

## Fast Food, Fine Dining, and More

Regardless of the destination you choose, you can find a variety of dining options to fit any budget. Nearly every medical tourism locale offers a range of eateries from cheap fast food joints to fine-dining establishments, and everything in between. Your hotel staff should be able to provide you with recommendations in your price range. If you're staying in a recovery center, your meals already may be included in the price.

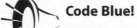

**Code Blue!**

Stay away from street vendors. You might not be used to some of the foods or spices they use. Plus, street vendors may use tap water for cooking, which can cause stomach problems.

## Shopping Options

As a rule, you can find great values while shopping in medical tourism destinations. The amount you spend on local wares depends on your budget. If your pocketbook is thin, you can limit yourself to a few inexpensive souvenir items. If you want to take advantage of low prices on clothing or other goods, you may want to include this in your budget.

**Doctor's Orders**

To get the best deals while shopping in some foreign countries, try bargaining. In certain destinations, negotiating prices is perfectly acceptable and even expected. Just be prepared to follow through if you make an offer. In many countries, it's considered a no-no to renege on an offer.

# It's the Little Things That Get You

Sure, you've budgeted for your procedure, your hotel and your travel, but that's not all you need to include. A host of other expenditures can add to the overall cost of your trip.

## Converters and Adapters

If you're planning on packing any electric appliances, such as hair dryers, electric shavers, or cell phone chargers, you may need to invest in an alternating current (AC) power converter and/or an AC plug adaptor. Many foreign hotels offer these items, but availability depends on demand. Therefore, you can't assume that your hotel will have these devices available for you upon your arrival. Plug adapters fall into the $10 to $15 range, while converters may cost about $30 to $40.

## Credit Card Exchange Fees

When you use your credit card abroad to pay for hotels, dining, shopping, or other expenditures, be prepared to pay transfer or exchange fees. These fees are charged when purchases made in a foreign currency are converted into U.S. dollars on your bill. You may want to contact your credit card company ahead of time to find out how much these fees will be.

## The Cost of Keeping in Touch

Staying in touch with loved ones back home can cost an arm and a leg if you don't plan ahead. For example, if you use your hotel phone to call friends and family back home, you may be charged in excess of $2 per minute, depending on the country. At these rates, you easily can add hundreds of dollars to your hotel tab.

Similarly, if you take your cell phone with you, you may be charged hefty roaming fees for every call you make or receive while you're abroad. These fees can add up fast, and could put a serious dent in your budget if you spend a lot of time on the phone. Plus, if your cell phone isn't equipped to work overseas, you may need to purchase a subscriber identity module (SIM) card to make the phone operable.

Luckily, there are cheaper ways to communicate when traveling abroad. For instance, you may be able to rent or purchase a cell phone in your host country and take advantage of low local calling rates. Purchase prices for these phones range from about $50 to $100, but you might get lucky and find one for less. Ask the hotel staff where you can get good deals on cell phones. With these phones, charges for international calls to the United States are just fractions of a dollar per minute. Even better, these phones often come with unlimited free incoming calls, no matter where the calls originate.

**Check-Up**

Sometimes, purchasing a cell phone abroad may actually cost less than renting one. Compare costs before buying or renting a cell phone.

Cell phones are yet another item that some medical travel agencies offer to clients free of charge. You pay nothing for the phone; you only pay for the minutes. Always check with your agency to see if they provide international cell phones.

International calling cards are another inexpensive alternative for phoning home. These pre-paid cards don't require a contract and don't have an expiration date. Often, they also can be used to make international calls from the United States, so if you don't use up all your minutes while you're overseas, you can use them after you return home.

If you're taking a laptop computer with you, you can take advantage of other inexpensive communication options, such as e-mail. Many hotels offer access to the Internet, or you can log on for a nominal fee in one of the many cybercafés that have popped up in many medical tourism destinations.

With a laptop in tow, you also can take advantage of Skype. This free software program allows you to make free calls via your computer to anyone else on Skype, anywhere in the world. Skype also allows you to call landlines and cell phones at very cheap rates.

## Adding Up Financing Fees

If you take out a loan to finance your medical excursion, you'll need to remember that you'll have to pay interest on the loan amount. Depending on the type of financing you choose, the interest rate can vary widely from less than 10 percent to more than 20 percent. Factor the total amount you'll pay into your budget.

## Travel Insurance

You may want to consider purchasing travel insurance to minimize any financial loss in the unlikely event that you must postpone or cancel your travel plans. Travel insurance firms typically offer coverage for trip cancellations, trip interruptions, travel delays, baggage delays, and lost or stolen luggage. Insurance providers also can assist you with cash transfers, replacing lost or stolen travel documents or credit cards, tracing lost luggage, and more. Prices for coverage depend on the airfare and your age, and range from about 3 to 10 percent of the cost of your plane ticket.

**Check-Up**

If you book your trip through a medical travel agency, you probably won't need travel insurance. Agencies usually can work to get you a refund if you need to cancel or postpone your trip for legitimate reasons.

## At-Home Costs

While you're overseas having surgery, you may incur additional costs at home. For instance, if you're a pet owner, you may need to board your pets or hire a pet sitter or dog walker. If you don't like the idea of leaving your home empty, you might want to hire a house sitter. In addition, you've got to remember that the bills keep coming in at home even though you aren't there. Before leaving for your trip, it's a good idea to pre-pay bills, such as utilities, credit cards, satellite or cable television, Internet, phone, and cell phone.

> **Doctor's Orders** _____
>
> When you return home, you may be fatigued from jet lag and the surgery experience. Give yourself a few days to ease back into the swing of things. If you've boarded your pets, you might want to think about keeping them there for a few days after your return. Similarly, you may want to spring for someone to take care of your lawn or to do the housework after you return.

## Lost Wages

Don't forget to factor in any lost wages you'll incur if you have to miss work to take your health-care voyage. If you can use vacation time or personal days for your trip, you may not be missing out on any income. But, if you won't get paid for the time off, you'll need to count that as part of your costs.

# Travel Costs Budget Worksheet

Use the following chart to tally your travel costs. Obviously, most of these travel costs wouldn't be incurred if you were having your procedure at home. However, some expenses may apply. Add these costs to your treatment costs to come up with an estimate of the total cost of medical travel versus the total cost of having surgery at home.

## Budget Worksheet—Travel Costs

|  | Cost Abroad | Cost At Home |
|---|---|---|
| **Pre-travel fees** | | |
| Medical travel agency | _____ | _____ |
| Airfare | _____ | _____ |
| Transportation (to airport) | _____ | _____ |
| Passport | _____ | _____ |
| Visa | _____ | _____ |
| Travel insurance | _____ | _____ |
| AC power converter | _____ | _____ |
| AC plug adapter | _____ | _____ |
| Other | _____ | _____ |
| **In-destination fees** | | |
| Entry/exit fees | _____ | _____ |
| Ground transportation | _____ | _____ |
| Lodging | _____ | _____ |
| Meals | _____ | _____ |
| Sightseeing | _____ | _____ |
| Shopping | _____ | _____ |
| Credit card fees | _____ | _____ |
| Communication fees | _____ | _____ |
| Other | _____ | _____ |
| **Companion fees** | | |
| Airfare | _____ | _____ |
| Lodging | _____ | _____ |
| Meals | _____ | _____ |
| Other | _____ | _____ |
| **At-home costs** | | |
| Transportation (from airport) | _____ | _____ |
| House sitter | _____ | _____ |
| Pet sitter/boarding | _____ | _____ |
| Lawn care | _____ | _____ |

*continues*

## Budget Worksheet—Travel Costs    (continued)

| | Cost Abroad | Cost At Home |
|---|---|---|
| Housekeeper | _____ | _____ |
| Other | _____ | _____ |
| **Other costs** | | |
| Lost wages | _____ | _____ |
| Financing fees | _____ | _____ |
| **Travel costs total** | _____ | _____ |
| **Treatment costs total** | _____ | _____ |
| (from other table) | | |
| **Total Costs** | _____ | _____ |

# The Least You Need to Know

◆ Determine your overall budget.

◆ Consider hiring an agency to handle travel plans.

◆ Fly economy class and use the money you save in the destination country.

◆ Decide if you'd prefer staying in a hotel or a recovery center.

◆ Give your budget some wiggle room for extras like shopping and sightseeing.

◆ Pre-pay your bills at home before your departure.

# Chapter 14

# What About Insurance?

## In This Chapter

- Why your insurance provider may someday offer global health care
- How self-insured companies are taking steps to cover medical tourism
- What incentives insurers may offer to medical travelers
- How insurance companies currently are covering foreign medical treatment
- Why medical malpractice insurance is key for patients and insurers

As of this writing, very few health insurance providers are willing to pay for you to go abroad for medical care. That is, however, expected to change in the coming years. Just like you, insurance providers are looking for ways to cut rapidly rising health-care costs. Medical tourism may be the answer.

Insurance companies and self-funded employers have been making strides toward a future in which medical tourism may be offered as an option. In fact, some providers already are developing medical tourism pilot programs. In the future, the list of network doctors and hospitals you get from your insurance company may include medical providers in India, Singapore, Thailand, Malaysia, Dubai, and a host of other countries. Who knows?

# Does Insurance Cover Medical Tourism?

For now, in most cases, the answer is no. Most insurance providers don't currently give their members the option to seek affordable medical care in a foreign country. However, according to a 2008 survey from the International Foundation of Employee Benefit Plans, 11 percent of the organizations surveyed claimed to offer some form of coverage for medical tourism. This number doesn't necessarily mean that these organizations cover medical tourism in its truest sense. Rather, it's more likely that they cover emergency medical services required while traveling in a foreign country.

What's keeping insurance carriers from offering global health care to medical tourists? Some of the main sticking points that may be keeping major insurers from taking the medical tourism plunge include the following:

- Liability issues

- Continuity of care issues

- Public perception issues

- Regulatory issues

- Administrative issues

According to attorney Dale Van Demark of Epstein Becker & Green (a national law firm that specializes in the health-care industry), potential liability issues present a major concern for all industry participants, including insurance providers. For instance, if an insured goes abroad for surgery and has a bad outcome, he or she could attempt to sue the insurer.

**Check-Up**

As of this writing, there are no known court cases involving an American medical tourist who experienced a bad outcome and attempted to sue an insurance company, an employer, or a medical tourism facilitator in the United States, according to Dale Van Demark (an attorney at Epstein Becker & Green).

Insurers also may want to ensure that continuity of care is available following an overseas health experience. They understand that problems could arise if members don't have access to care at home, if complications occur, or if follow-up treatments are necessary.

Similarly, insurers might be concerned that the public may not view their efforts to offer medical tourism in a positive light. If the public thinks that insured members are receiving subpar care abroad—even if it's an erroneous notion—or that insured members are being forced to seek care in far-flung locations, it could damage a provider's reputation.

Van Demark indicates that a number of regulatory issues also pose potential problems if insurers adopt some form of a medical tourism plan. As an example, insurers must comply with U.S. privacy standards in accordance with the *Health Insurance Portability and Accountability Act (HIPAA)*. HIPAA was enacted to assure that patient health information is properly protected. As Van Demark explains, HIPAA doesn't regulate international hospitals, foreign physicians, or even U.S.-based medical tourism facilitators. To comply with HIPAA, the foreign providers and intermediaries must enter a business associates' agreement that ensures the appropriate treatment of a patient's health information.

## def•i•ni•tion

Enacted in 1996, the **Health Insurance Portability and Accountability Act (HIPAA)** established a set of national standards designed to protect individuals' health information. U.S.-based insurance companies, medical providers, and other entities must meet these standards. However, international medical facilities and foreign surgeons are not required to meet HIPAA standards.

Van Demark also points out that state regulators must approve all insurance products. Insurance requirements, such as mandatory coverage, may hinder the ability to offer a medical tourism insurance product. Only California has enacted legislation to specifically allow for a so-called "cross border" plan. According to Van Demark, how most state regulators will view a medical tourism product remains an open question.

In addition to these potential concerns are administrative obstacles. Insurers need to create systems to administer the medical tourism process and must develop relationships with overseas hospitals and physicians. These are no small tasks and could take years to implement after making the decision to pursue medical tourism.

# Do Self-Funded Employers Cover Medical Tourism?

Many self-funded corporations currently are investigating medical tourism as a possibility. For the most part, however, they have yet to begin sending employees abroad for medical treatment. As previously explained, self-funded employers are companies that pay out-of-pocket for the health-care services their employees actually receive, rather than paying monthly premiums. Typically, this means that the employer establishes a fund out of which it pays the medical expenses for its workers and their dependents. In some cases, employers may pay medical expenses out of cash flow.

Setting up a self-funded plan is a common way for medium-size and large employers to realize significant savings on their health-care costs. In fact, some 40 million private and public workers currently are covered by such plans. But there is some risk involved when opting for self-funding rather than a group health-care plan. Think about it. If several employees fall seriously ill and require ongoing or expensive care, it could end up costing the employer even more than a traditional health-care plan. In fact, it could wipe out the employer's medical fund or even bankrupt the company.

To avoid this kind of potential financial devastation, self-funded employers may purchase what's called *stop loss insurance*. With this type of insurance, the employer pays only medical claims up to a pre-determined dollar amount, at which time the stop-loss insurer steps in and foots the bill for any additional claims.

## def•i•ni•tion

**Stop-loss insurance** can prevent self-insured companies from suffering financial losses due to medical expenses. The insurance kicks in after a self-funded employer has paid out a pre-set amount. This deductible either can apply to expenses paid for a single employee or for the entire workforce.

Because self-funded employers are paying out-of-pocket for their employees' medical claims, they are always looking for ways to cut costs. Medical tourism is increasingly becoming one of the options being explored. In fact, "Companies are coming to us asking what medical tourism is, if it's right for them, how much they can save, and how to implement it," says Bruce Barwick, CEO of Trigram America, the leader in education, training, and resources for companies and insurance carriers interested in medical tourism.

Trigram America provides a three-step process for self-insured companies that want to offer medical tourism as an option for their employees. These steps are as follows:

1. Educate the employer about medical tourism.

2. Perform an assessment of the company to determine whether offering global health care will be beneficial.

3. Implement a medical tourism program.

According to Barwick, many U.S. firms currently are in phase one or phase two of the process, but very few have reached the implementation phase.

What's holding them back? Employers share many of the same concerns held by other insurance providers. They want to ensure that foreign hospitals are safe and accredited and that doctors are properly credentialed. Continuity of care after a patient returns home is another area of concern. Employers need to make sure that their employees can receive appropriate follow-up care in the United States.

### Check-Up

"Many self-funded employers have employees working overseas," explains Bruce Barwick, CEO of Trigram America. "They already send these workers to hospitals and medical providers in the countries where they're working. So they're already dealing with worldwide medical providers. For these companies, it's a much more natural progression to allow their U.S.-based employees to visit those same hospitals and doctors. At that point, it's really just about the travel."

Like insurance companies, employers also face liability issues. If medical malpractice occurs, or an employee isn't satisfied with the outcome of his or her procedure, could the employer be considered liable? Employers definitely want to put programs in place to protect themselves from possible lawsuits before they start sending employees to foreign countries.

In addition, Barwick explains that self-funded corporations need to consider how their stakeholders might react if they go ahead with a medical tourism program. For example, how will local hospitals respond when the company's employees start going overseas for treatment instead of using their services? If a firm's workers are unionized, will the union object to the idea of the company sending union members overseas for surgery?

### Check-Up

According to several media reports, a paper products company in North Carolina was planning to send an employee to India for rotator cuff and gall bladder surgery in 2006. But the self-insured firm caught flak from the United Steelworkers union, which sent protest letters to prevent the company from sending its union members overseas for medical treatment. Faced with the opposition, the company opted not to go through with its medical tourism plans.

Barwick is convinced that after a few pioneers take the initiative and begin offering medical tourism as an option to their employees, other companies quickly will follow. He anticipates that by the end of 2009, some self-funded firms will be testing the waters with global health-care offerings. Within a few years, the floodgates will open, and medical tourism will begin to be a more common option for employees of self-insured businesses.

# How Insurance Coverage Might Work in the Future

When insurance companies or privately funded corporations do begin offering high-quality, low-cost medical care abroad, it likely will be presented as a voluntary option or alternative to U.S.-based care. It is extremely unlikely that insurers or companies will mandate that members or employees hit the road for medical care. The choice will be entirely up to you.

However, to entice insured members or employees to take advantage of medical tourism, providers may offer some form of incentive to seek treatment overseas. Here's an example of a popular incentive model a provider might offer.

You may be eligible for the following incentives from your employer or insurer:

- ◆ Your deductible is waived.

- ◆ Your co-pay is waived.

- ◆ Your companion's travel expenses are paid by the insurer.

- ◆ You're allowed an extended stay in the destination for recuperation.

- ◆ You're offered a cash incentive to have your procedure abroad.

Sounds pretty good, doesn't it? Instead of forking over approximately $5,000 to $6,000 in co-pays, you actually might be paid $5,000 to $6,000. And, you get an extended vacation with a companion on top of that. From the insurer/employer standpoint, they'll be racking up the savings, too. For example, a bilateral hip replacement would cost about $45,000 to $65,000 in the United States, but only about $20,000 abroad, including all the travel costs. That means the insurer is saving 50 percent or more even after paying you a cash incentive. That sounds like a win–win situation.

Other scenarios are possible, too. For instance, self-funded employers may choose to roll the savings back into the company's health-care plan to expand their offerings. For example, the savings could be used to expand vision or dental care programs. Basically, it will be up to each individual insurance provider or company to determine what to do with the money that's saved when an insured member or employee goes abroad for medical care.

# Health Insurance Medical Tourism Programs

Although the vast majority of health insurance providers have yet to add medical tourism to their menu of options, a few providers currently cover some form of medical tourism. Here's a look at some of the providers who have given medical tourism the green light.

## BlueCross BlueShield of South Carolina

As one of the first U.S.-based health insurance providers to offer medical tourism as an option to its members, BlueCross BlueShield of South Carolina (BCBSSC) is a veritable pioneer within the insurance industry. BCBSSC launched its initiative in 2007 with a partnership with Bumrungrad Hospital in Bangkok, Thailand. The program has since expanded to include affiliations with Joint Commission International accredited hospitals in Costa Rica, Singapore, Turkey, and Ireland. Contracts with additional international hospitals are underway.

This breakthrough program was the brainchild of David Boucher, a BCBSSC executive who is now the CEO of a BCBSSC subsidiary specifically launched to facilitate medical tourism for its members. Boucher first read about the growing medical tourism phenomenon in a magazine article and thought it might be a good fit for BCBSSC and its 1.5 million members. The former hospital CEO began seriously researching the medical tourism landscape and zeroed in on Bumrungrad Hospital in Thailand as a possible partner.

**Check-Up**

Insurers and patients share many of the same concerns about medical tourism. They want to be certain that overseas medical facilities are safe and that English is spoken or that an on-site interpreter is available.

Boucher scheduled an overseas trip and spent four and a half days at the hospital, performing an informal evaluation from a consumer standpoint. He spent a full day with the medical director touring the facility, including the operating room and the recovery room. He even checked out the dietary offerings. "I was thoroughly impressed with what I saw," says Boucher.

Based on the positive evaluation, Boucher decided to approach executives at BCBSSC with his idea. They decided to move ahead with the plan to offer medical tourism as a value-added service to its members. The plan doesn't require its members to go abroad nor does it use financial incentives to encourage members to travel overseas. According to the BCBSSC website, members who opt for health care abroad receive the following:

- ◆ Significant cost savings

- ◆ Surgical services

- ◆ Travel arrangements

- ◆ VIP transfers to and from airports and hospitals

- ◆ Appointment scheduling

- ◆ Assistance obtaining passports and visas

- ◆ Superior hospitality services

- ◆ Private or deluxe hospital room accommodations

- ◆ On-site interpreters

To date, only a smattering of BCBSSC members have taken advantage of the opportunity. That number is expected to grow as more members learn about medical tourism as an option.

The press has been helping spread the word about the BCBSSC medical tourism model. The insurance provider already has garnered a healthy dose of attention in the media, which could spark other insurers to test drive a global health-care plan of their own.

## BlueShield of California's Access Baja Plans

The Access Baja plans offered by BlueShield of California allow its members to receive medical care in Baja California. The plans are available to members who live or work in the Mexican municipalities of Tijuana or Mexicali or in the United States within 50 miles of certain U.S.-Mexico border crossings. Because medical care costs so much less in Mexico than in the United States, these plans offer significant savings to its members in terms of premiums and co-pays.

Although these Access Baja plans cover medical care in a foreign country, they don't really fit the true sense of medical tourism. In general, these plans are geared to Mexican nationals who may cross the border every day to go to work for a U.S.-based company. They aren't targeting the general American population in search of more affordable health care.

## Salud con Health Net

Similar to the Access Baja plans, Salud con Health Net allows its Latino members to seek health-care services across the border in Mexico. Members who live either in California or in Mexico are eligible for the plans, which generally offer lower co-pays for medical care provided in Mexico. Members aren't required to seek care in Mexico; they also can visit network physicians within California.

# Medical Malpractice Liability Insurance

As mentioned earlier in this chapter, the risk of medical malpractice occurring in a foreign country is a major concern for health insurance providers, self-funded employers, and patients alike. For instance, if while abroad something goes wrong in the operating room, what recourse do you have as a patient?

In the United States, if a negligent error occurs, you can call a lawyer and sue the hospital and/or the doctor. But overseas, you're dealing with a different country, a different culture, different customs, and different laws. In some foreign courts, you may not be allowed to sue for medical malpractice. Or you may find that malpractice settlements in your medical tourism destination are far less than what you might receive in U.S. courts. For many people, the fear of having little or no recourse in the event of a negligent error is enough to prevent them from booking a health-care trip.

Similarly, insurance carriers and self-insured employers need to think about their liability if one of their insured members or employees is the victim of medical malpractice while overseas. Here's a scenario employers need to consider: Let's say an employer gives an employee a cash incentive to have medical treatment in a foreign destination, and something goes wrong. If the employee has no recourse to sue in the foreign country, that employee may choose to sue the employer instead. This risk is one of the main reasons self-funded companies are not yet offering medical tourism as an option for its employees.

Soon, you'll begin to see a new type of insurance offered to mitigate these risks: medical malpractice insurance. Introduced in 2008 by Aos Assurance Company Limited, medical malpractice insurance is specifically designed with medical tourism in mind. Policies are available to individuals who are heading overseas on their own or through a medical tourism agency. Self-funded employers and insurance carriers also can take advantage of policies that will protect them from the liability issues they might face if an insured or an employee encounters medical malpractice overseas.

> **Code Blue!**
>
> Although nobody likes to think about the possibility of something going wrong when you're about to have surgery, it can happen. Medical malpractice can occur in the best hospitals in the United States or in the most modern medical facilities abroad. It is a real risk, and it can happen anywhere. If you're contemplating a health-care voyage abroad, purchasing medical malpractice insurance may give you more peace of mind.

For individuals, "the policies work in a similar way as travel insurance or even car insurance," says Aos Assurance's director and founder Paul Laverty. Laverty offers the following example of how it works: "If you go to India for knee replacement, and your knee isn't working properly after you get home, you might see a doctor here in the U.S. to find out why. Let's say the doctor discovers that the surgeon in India left gauze inside or made an error. You would call us, and we would open a file—much like what happens if you get into an accident in your car, and you call your car insurance. We'll perform due diligence and get information from the doctors involved. Then we adjudicate the claim and make a settlement offer."

According to Laverty, because there are no lawyers involved, the entire claims process is relatively quick compared to the amount of time it takes to resolve medical malpractice cases in the United States. "In the U.S., it can take years to settle a case—even longer if a case goes to court," explains Laverty.

Aos Assurance's group policies are geared toward insurance providers and self-funded employers and are designed to mitigate the liability risk associated with sending insured members or employees overseas for medical treatment. For instance, if an insured member experiences a negligent error and decides to sue his or her insurance carrier or employer, the policy provides coverage for both the insured member and the provider. With these policies available, insurers and employers may be more inclined to add medical tourism to their offerings.

# Continuity of Care Insurance

Another innovative insurance product that's poised to hit the market is continuity of care insurance. With this type of insurance, you can purchase a short-term policy that will cover you in case you experience complications after you return home. The policies will work similar to the way a preferred provider organization (PPO) plan works. If you experience complications after you've come home, you can choose to visit a local doctor from a vast network of U.S. physicians. With the emergence of this type of insurance product, it may allay any fears you have about possibly needing follow-up care in the United States.

## The Least You Need to Know

- ◆ Many insurers and employers are investigating medical tourism as an option.

- ◆ Certain concerns need to be addressed before insurers or employers will cover medical tourism.

- ◆ Smaller insurance providers will be more likely to cover medical tourism than large carriers.

- ◆ Many self-funded companies are expected to add global health-care benefits in the next few years.

- ◆ The availability of medical malpractice insurance may encourage employers and insurers to offer medical tourism.

- ◆ Continuity of care insurance may ensure that you'll have access to necessary treatments back at home.

# Chapter 15

# Financing Options: The Many Ways to Pay

## In This Chapter

◆ How to pay for medical tourism on the cheap

◆ How friends and family can help share the costs

◆ How to creatively fund your health-care voyage

◆ What financing methods cost the most

◆ Why medical and dental loans may not work for overseas procedures

◆ How a chart can help you compare financing options

When it comes to paying for medical treatment overseas, you have numerous options. If you've got money socked away, you can always use that. But what if you aren't sitting on a bundle of cash? Don't worry. There are multiple traditional financing methods, along with a host of not-so-traditional ways to come up with the cash for your trip. In this chapter, I explore a variety of these methods so you can determine which is best for you.

# Use Your Savings

There's no question that the best and most economical way to pay for a health-care journey is with your own savings. When you foot the bill with cash you've got in the bank, under the mattress, or in a shoebox, you avoid any additional financing fees or interest costs. The vast majority of my clients use their savings to cover the costs of their medical treatments and travel expenses.

If you're still in the early phase of contemplating an elective procedure, such as cosmetic surgery, you may want to open a savings account to fund your medical tourism. Of course, saving enough money to cover all your costs may take some time. Just ask Didi (featured in Chapter 2), who for several years put about $20 a month in her face lift fund. It was only after Didi realized that she'd never reach the roughly $20,000 she needed to pay for a face lift in Beverly Hills that she decided to use the money in her account to go to Costa Rica.

---

**CASE STUDY**

| | |
|---|---|
| Name: | Mark and Willie |
| Age at time of surgery: | 57 and 55, respectively |
| Residence: | California |
| Procedure: | Mark received rhinoplasty and a neck lift; Willie received a face lift, neck lift, eyelid lift, arm lift, liposuction, and breast reduction |
| Destination country: | Malaysia |
| Cost in United States: | $80,000–$100,000 |
| Total cost abroad (travel included): | $20,000 |

Mark had his nose fixed in 1977, while he was in the military, but he was never satisfied with the result. He still felt like his nose was too big for his face. To make matters worse, he'd had trouble breathing for 30 years—that is, ever since he'd had the procedure. His wife, Willie, started thinking about facial cosmetic surgery to rejuvenate her looks. The couple saw a feature about medical tourism on a television show and started thinking about the possibility of going overseas for cosmetic surgery.

The couple had recently sold their home and put aside some money from the sale to pay for their medical tourism trip. "We didn't realize that you could make payments for something like this," admits Mark, "so we just paid in full with the money from the sale of the house."

---

After about six months of planning, the couple headed to Southeast Asia where Mark and Willie met with a plastic surgeon who had practiced in Chicago for 12 years and who spoke perfect English. During the consultation, Willie brought up other procedures that interested her in addition to the facial procedures she had already scheduled. By the end of her consultation, Willie had decided to have a breast reduction, arm lift, and liposuction.

Willie had already been considering having her breasts reshaped prior to going abroad, but she chose to wait until she'd met the surgeon in person to bring it up. Why? The couple had been asked to e-mail photos of the various areas they wanted treated, and she and Mark understandably felt uncomfortable sending photos of her bare breasts across the Internet.

Fortunately, the surgeon was able to accommodate Willie's desire for additional procedures. The next day, Mark had his surgery, and the day after that, Willie went under the knife. The surgeries were very successful, but Willie experienced a post-op glitch. Her pain medication was available only through the hospital in the form of an injection. There was no pill form on hand for her to take after being discharged, so she ended up experiencing more pain than anticipated.

Today, the couple is very happy with the results. Mark says Willie looks 15 years younger. And that nose of his? Not only does Mark love its new shape, but he's also thrilled that it allows him to breathe better than ever.

# Got a Health Savings Account?

If you have a *Health Savings Account (HSA)*, you may be able to use pre-tax dollars to pay for qualified medical expenses, including some of the costs associated with medical tourism. In general, you can have an HSA if you don't have any health insurance, or if you have a high-deductible health insurance plan. Typically, to take advantage of an HSA, you can't be enrolled in Medicare, and you can't be claimed as a dependent on someone else's tax return.

How does an HSA work? Each year, a maximum amount of money can be contributed to the account. In 2007, that number was $2,850 for an individual, and $5,650 for a family. The numbers are somewhat higher if you're over 55 years of age. Contributions can be made to the account in numerous ways. Of course, you (the account holder) can put money into the account. But, additional contributions also can be made by your employer or by others on your behalf. You also may be able to transfer a certain

**def•i•ni•tion**

Available since 2003, the **Health Savings Account (HSA)** is a special pretax account that an individual uses to pay for medical expenses.

amount of funds from an individual retirement account (IRA) to your HSA without incurring penalties.

# Don't Be Afraid to Ask Friends and Family

If you want or need a procedure but can't cover the costs, reach out to your friends and family for help. You might be surprised to discover that the people who care about you just might be willing to dig into their pockets for you. Your efforts to raise money can be as simple as making a few phone calls to your closest pals. If you're really gung-ho, you can create a mass e-mail campaign that's sent to all of your contacts. Or you can even hold a fundraiser.

---

### CASE STUDY

| | |
|---|---|
| Name: | Judy |
| Age at time of surgery: | 63 |
| Residence: | Nevada |
| Procedure: | Hip replacement |
| Destination country: | Malaysia |
| Cost in United States: | about $45,000 |
| Total cost abroad (travel included): | about $17,000 |

A former Las Vegas showgirl and a ballroom-dancing instructor, Judy's livelihood has always centered on dancing. But due to increasingly severe hip pain, the Nevada resident hadn't been able to dance for more than a year. In fact, simply walking and standing had become painful. Without health insurance, she couldn't afford to pay for the hip replacement she needed. Judy decided to take the more affordable medical tourism route thanks to a recommendation from one of her students.

Judy's students did more than just recommend going abroad for surgery. One couple told her that they wanted to donate money to her trip and that they wanted to take up a collection with her other students. "I was so embarrassed at the thought of asking my students for money," says Judy. "I've always been so independent. I told the couple I could never ask for donations." But Judy didn't have to ask. The couple said they were going to do the asking for her. And they did. Many of Judy's students were happy to contribute to her medical tourism fund, and thanks to their generosity, nearly the entire amount of her trip was covered.

Judy says she could have scraped together enough money to pay for her trip through savings, but it would have been a real hardship. She's extremely grateful to her students and can't wait to have her surgery. "The U.S. doctor said I'd be able to dance again, and I would be so happy to have another chance to dance," she says.

Remember that if people are donating money to help you pay for your health-care journey, there may be some tax implications. The money you receive may need to be reported on your tax returns, and you may need to pay taxes on it. Talk to your accountant or a tax specialist to find out what your tax obligation might be and keep this in mind when coming up with your fundraising goals.

> **Doctor's Orders** _____
>
> If you're considering seeking contributions to cover your medical tourism costs, consider having a friend or family member take the lead. It's often easier for a loved one to ask others for donations toward your procedure.

Even if your friends and family can't afford to give you cash gifts to help fund your trip, they may be able to help in other ways. For instance, they may be willing to offer you a no-interest or low-interest loan that you can pay back over time. If you're thinking about asking for a loan from a friend or family member, make sure to keep it professional. Draft a promissory note—you can find customizable samples of them online—that details a payment plan, and stick to it. Remember that relationships can be ruined if loans aren't repaid, so tread carefully when seeking money from the people you love.

# Leverage Your Assets: Home-Equity Loans and More

If you own your own home, you may be able to take advantage of the equity you have to finance your overseas health-care journey. Your options may include a home-equity loan or a reverse mortgage.

Before taking money out on your home, consult with your accountant or with a financial specialist. An expert can help you determine whether this is the best way for you to finance your trip.

## Home-Equity Loans

A *home equity loan* may allow you to secure a significant amount of credit at a relatively low interest rate. Other names for a home equity loan include the following:

♦ Home equity line of credit

♦ Second mortgage

## def•i•ni•tion

With a **home equity loan,** your home serves as collateral for the loan. The loan basically is a type of revolving credit, which requires you to pay interest on any unpaid balances.

- ◆ Debt consolidation loan
- ◆ Home improvement loan

Rates for home equity loans may be variable or fixed and are commonly less than the rates associated with other financing options. What makes home equity loans even more attractive is that the interest you pay on the loan may be tax deductible.

To obtain a home equity loan, you'll need to fill out an application from a lender. The lender will review your income, debts, and financial obligations to determine whether you should be approved for a loan and, if so, what the credit limit will be. Credit limits often are determined using a formula that takes the current value of your home and subtracts the amount you owe on the existing mortgage. Depending on the state in which you live, you may be able to borrow from about 75 percent to more than 100 percent of the equity you have in your home.

You should be aware that a home equity loan isn't free. Costs may include an application fee, a property appraisal fee, and other charges. Be sure to factor these costs into the overall price you're paying for the loan.

## Reverse Mortgages

If you're a homeowner who's 62 years of age or older, you may be able to take advantage of a loan called a *reverse mortgage*, which allows you to cash in on the equity you have in your home. Whether you live in a condominium, townhouse, or single-family dwelling, you may be eligible for a reverse mortgage. With this loan, you can receive your money in a variety of ways:

## def•i•ni•tion

A **reverse mortgage** is a loan that allows homeowners who are 62 or older to convert the equity in their home into cash.

- ◆ A lump sum
- ◆ A line of credit
- ◆ Fixed monthly payments
- ◆ A combination of the above

If you plan to use the money solely to fund a medical voyage, you may want to opt for a lump sum or a line of credit rather than monthly payments. The benefits of opting for a reverse mortgage include the following:

- You don't need to have an income to qualify.

- The money you receive is tax free.

- You're only charged interest on the proceeds you receive.

- You don't have to sell your home.

- You maintain the title to your home.

- You don't have to make monthly payments on the income.

These benefits may make a reverse mortgage attractive if you need financing to pay for your health-care trip. Be aware, however, that reverse mortgages come with their own costs. For example, the majority of reverse mortgages include a variable interest rate, although some are offered with a fixed rate. You also may need to pay a monthly service fee to manage your reverse mortgage. And remember, the loan plus interest, must be repaid if you sell your home or move out.

**Code Blue!**

By law, you must consult with an independent financial counselor before applying for a reverse mortgage. This rule is built in to the reverse mortgage program to ensure that you fully understand the program and your alternatives.

# Borrowing From 401(k) Accounts

If you have a 401(k) account, you might consider borrowing from the retirement fund to help pay for your medical tourism expenses. Most 401(k) plans allow you to borrow up to 50 percent of your vested balance (up to $50,000). Take note that some plans place restrictions on what you can do with the money you borrow from your 401(k). Fortunately, paying medical expenses is an accepted use.

There are pros and cons to borrowing from your 401(k). Among the benefits, you don't need to fill out any kind of application, and interest rates are generally relatively low. On the downside, a 401(k) loan could leave you with a significantly smaller nest egg. The capital you take out of the account is no longer appreciating or earning any interest. When you repay the loan, you must do so using after-tax dollars rather than the pre-tax dollars that initially went into the account. In addition, 401(k) loans aren't tax deductible so you won't get a tax break on the interest you pay.

Most 401(k) loans must be repaid within five years. If, however, you leave your employer prior to repayment, you may have to immediately repay the loan in full. If you aren't able to do so, you could be faced with additional penalties or taxes.

# Borrowing From Other Investment Accounts

If you have investment accounts, such as CDs, government-backed bonds, corporate bonds, stocks, or mutual funds, you may be able to use those funds as collateral for a bank loan to help you pay for your health-care voyage. Sometimes, banks will allow you to borrow a percentage—from approximately 50 percent to 100 percent—of the amount of money in the investment, according to Adam Schwartz, a financial guru and president of consulting firm ALS Consulting, Incorporated. The amount you can borrow typically depends on the type of account you have.

The following chart shows approximations of the maximum percentage and maximum amount you might be able to borrow with the full value of your investment account as collateral. Keep in mind that percentages vary among institutions, and there are no guarantees that you will, in fact, be able to obtain such a loan.

## Approximate Maximum Loan Amounts on Investment Accounts

| Type of Account | Amount in Account | Percentage Available For Loan | Amount of Loan |
|---|---|---|---|
| CD | $25,000 | 100% | $25,000 |
| Government-backed bonds | $25,000 | 90% | $22,500 |
| Corporate bonds | $25,000 | 80% | $20,000 |
| Stocks/mutual funds | $25,000 | 50% | $12,500 |

These loans are considered secured loans, which typically come with relatively low interest rates. The interest rates you'll have to pay will depend on the type of investment account you have, the amount of money in the account, the size of the loan, and the time length given to repay the loan in full. Secured loans such as these can be a good financing option in tough economic times, when banks are less open to lending without collateral.

# Taking a Loan Against Your Life Insurance Policy

With certain types of life insurance policies, you may be able to take out a loan against the policy to finance your medical excursion. Qualifying policies include the following:

- Whole life insurance

- Universal life insurance

- Variable universal life insurance

Such policies are known as *cash value insurance policies*, and they may allow you to access some of the money you have paid into the policy. Schwartz explains how it works. "Let's say the premium payments on a $250,000 term life insurance policy were about $25 per month for a total of $300 per year. But with a cash value policy for the same $250,000 death benefit, you were to pay considerably more, say $150 a month for a total of $1800 a year," says Schwartz. "Over a 10-year period, you would have paid $18,000. And you may be able to take out a loan for a percentage of that amount— maybe as much as $10,000."

**def•i•ni•tion** _____

> With **cash value insurance poli-cies,** you typically pay initial pre-miums that are higher than other types of life insurance policies. The additional money you pay into the policy builds a cash value that you may be able to access via a loan.

In general, loans on a cash value life insurance policy come with a low interest rate. You'll need to pay the interest on the loan along with the insurance premiums. However, payback of the amount loaned may actually be optional. If you choose not to repay the loan, your beneficiaries would simply receive the death benefit minus the loan amount in the case of your death. For example, if your death benefit was $100,000, and you took out a $5,000 loan from the policy, your beneficiaries would get $95,000. This arrangement may be appropriate if you want to avoid taking on additional debt to finance your medical trip. Terms of the loan depend upon the insurance company.

# Unsecured Personal Loans

Unsecured personal loans aren't backed by any kind of collateral. These typically can be used for almost any purpose, including medical expenses. This sounds great, but note that the rates on these loans usually depend on your credit rating. The better your credit rating, the lower the rate you'll pay. If you have a poor credit history, you may be stuck paying 20 percent interest or even more.

# Charge It! Using Your Credit Cards

Using your credit cards to finance your medical tourism expenses is yet another option. With this method, you don't need to fill out an application or wait to be approved—the funds are immediately available. On the flip side, you need to have an ample credit line to cover your costs, and high annual percentage rates could prove costly if it takes you a long time to repay. Think about how much you'll be able to pay each month to determine how long it will take you to pay off the debt and how much that time will cost you in interest.

# A Last Resort—Medical and Dental Loans

As a result of the skyrocketing health-care costs in the United States, and the popularity of pricey cosmetic procedures, a new breed of patient financing has emerged. Medical and dental loans for a wide variety of elective procedures are now offered through a number of lenders. Interest rates on medical loans vary widely. You could pay less than 10 percent if your credit rating is in tip-top shape. But if you have bad credit, you could be forking over 20 to 25 percent in interest charges.

Note that patient financing lenders may pay directly to the medical providers rather than sending you the cash payout. This may pose a problem for you as a medical tourist because some of the lenders only do business with doctors in the United States and will not forward payments to physicians or hospitals abroad. In some cases, if an overseas surgeon or hospital is affiliated with a U.S. facility, you may be able to circumvent this issue by having the funds delivered to the U.S. entity. Always find out whether the lender will authorize an overseas payment before signing on the dotted the line.

# Sell Your Stuff

If you need a little extra cash to help pay for your trip to Singapore, Costa Rica, or Brazil, but you'd prefer to avoid going into debt, consider hosting a garage sale or selling some of your stuff on eBay. Those golf clubs that haven't been touched in years, those tools you got for Christmas but never used, or those clothes that just didn't fit quite right could fetch some cash for you.

Who knows? You could pull in a few hundred bucks or even a few thousand dollars depending on what's lurking in your closets. The money you earn from sales could help you meet the cost of your procedure or could simply provide some extra spending dough in your destination country.

# Work It Off

To avoid hefty interest rates and financing fees, you can always ask for additional hours at work or take on a part-time gig to augment your medical tourism fund. Considering that it often takes three to six months to plan a health-care voyage, you may want to use that time to pump up your income. By funneling your extra income into an interest-bearing savings account, you may be able to sock away a tidy sum by the time you leave for your trip.

# Find Your Best Financing Options

Obviously, you have a lot of options when it comes to financing medical tourism. To help you sort through the advantages and disadvantages of the various alternatives, use this handy chart.

## Financing Options

| Method | Need to Apply | Interest Rates | Additional Fees | Collateral Required | Tax Implications |
|---|---|---|---|---|---|
| Savings | No | No | No | No | No |
| Health Savings Account (HSA) | No | No | No | No | No |
| Friends/ family donations | No | No | No | No | Maybe |
| Friends/ Family loans | No | Maybe— Low | No | No | Maybe |

*continues*

## Financing Options    (continued)

| Method | Need to Apply | Interest Rates | Additional Fees | Collateral Required | Tax Implications |
|---|---|---|---|---|---|
| Home equity loans | Yes | Yes—Low | Yes | Yes | Yes |
| Reverse mortgage | Yes | Yes | Yes | Yes | Yes |
| 401(k) | No | Yes—Low | No | No | Maybe |
| Personal Loans | Yes | Yes—Low to High | Yes | No | Maybe |
| Credit Cards | No | Yes—Low to High | No | No | No |
| Medical/ dental loans | Yes | Yes—High | Yes | No | Maybe |

## The Least You Need to Know

◆ Most medical tourists use savings to pay for their trip.

◆ Seeking donations from friends and family can really pay off.

◆ If possible, choose financing options that offer low interest rates.

◆ Using your credit cards can be a pricey proposition.

◆ For medical tourism, medical and dental loans may not be the answer.

# Chapter 16

# Tax Talk

## In This Chapter

- ◆ How to deduct medical tourism expenses from your taxes
- ◆ What procedures don't qualify for tax deductions
- ◆ When your companion traveler's expenses may be deductible
- ◆ Where to get the tax forms you'll need
- ◆ Why you need to keep a record of all your medical tourism expenses
- ◆ Why consulting with a tax professional is a must

Medical tourism can do more than just slash your health-care costs. It might also earn you a tax break from Uncle Sam. Specifically, you may be able to deduct some of what you pay for your overseas health-care excursion from your income tax return. These deductions can lower the amount of taxes you need to pay, which ultimately saves you even more money.

Take note, however, that tallying your medical expenses for deductions can be tricky business, according to Mark G. Argianas, CPA. "The IRS rules regarding what does and doesn't qualify as a medical expense aren't always clear-cut," he explains. In general, the Internal Revenue Service (IRS) describes allowable medical expenses as "the costs of diagnosis, cure, mitigation, treatment, or prevention of disease, and the costs for treatments affecting any part or function of the body."

In this chapter, I will give you the information you need to determine which medical tourism expenses may be deductible and which expenses can't be written off. However, you shouldn't view the information presented here as a blueprint for filling out your tax return. In fact, every medical tourist's situation is different, and what may be tax deductible for one person may not be for another. Therefore, we strongly urge you to consult with a tax professional about your medical expenses.

# Who Can Deduct Medical Expenses?

You can deduct or itemize only medical expenses on your income tax return if you meet certain criteria. According to IRS's *Publication 502*, which details the ins and outs of medical and dental expenses, you can deduct only expenses that exceed 7.5 percent of your adjusted gross income. If your medical and dental expenses don't add up to more than 7.5 percent of your adjusted gross income, you can't deduct them.

## def•i•ni•tion

**Publication 502** is an IRS document that includes 30-plus pages of detailed information about medical and dental expenses. It explains which expenses are deductible and which expenses can't be written off. This document also provides guidelines for calculating your deductions and for reporting them on your income tax return. You can download Publication 502 from the IRS website, www.irs.gov/formspubs/index.html.

If you're flying overseas for a surgical procedure and you're paying out-of-pocket for your treatment, it's very possible that you'll pass the 7.5 percent threshold. If, however, you're heading abroad for minor treatments or minimal dental work, you may not hit that mark. Following are two examples to help you understand how the 7.5 percent rule works.

## Example A

Let's say your adjusted gross income is $50,000. That means that only the medical expenses that exceed 7.5 percent of $50,000—or $3,750—would be deductible. Now, let's assume your expenses for a hip replacement in Singapore total $20,000. That means $16,250—the costs above $3,750—may be deductible.

## Example B

Let's use $70,000 as your adjusted gross income. To qualify for itemized deductions, your medical expenses would have to be more than 7.5 percent of $70,000, or $5,250. Now, let's say you traveled to Costa Rica for some dental work—two crowns and a root canal—and paid a total of $3,500, including your travel expenses. In this case, you would not be able to deduct these expenses from your tax return.

# Tax-Deductible Procedures

You should take note that not all medical procedures qualify for tax deductions. Only expenses related to certain medical procedures are tax deductible. This holds true whether you're traveling overseas for surgery or going to the local hospital for treatment.

## Medically Necessary Procedures

In general, any procedure that is deemed medically necessary qualifies for a tax deduction. This includes the costs of any doctor's appointments necessary to diagnose a condition and the costs of any surgical procedures or other remedies recommended to treat the condition. Surgical procedures that fit this description include all sorts of cardiac, orthopedic, spinal, and gynecological procedures, among others. In addition, some infertility treatments, such as in vitro fertilization (IVF), meet the requirements for a tax deduction.

## Dental Procedures

Dental procedures that are medically necessary—such as root canals, tooth extractions, crowns, bridges, and implants—typically qualify for a tax write-off. Deductible expenses include the amount you pay for the actual procedure as well as any x-rays and temporary or permanent devices.

## Vision Treatments

Procedures that treat eye conditions and diseases usually are tax deductible. You also can write off the costs of any eye examinations required to diagnose a condition. Procedures that qualify include LASIK, cataract surgery, and other eye surgeries. The costs of eyeglasses and contact lenses also are deductible.

# Procedures That Aren't Tax Deductible

As a rule, you can't claim a tax deduction on any procedure that isn't considered a medical necessity. This includes any elective cosmetic surgery or cosmetic dentistry. Because the procedures don't qualify for a deduction, neither do any physician fees, examinations, x-rays, hospital fees, and other costs associated with these procedures.

## Cosmetic Surgery Procedures

In general, expenses associated with elective cosmetic surgery can't be deducted on your income tax return. According to the IRS, cosmetic surgery includes any procedure that is primarily aimed at enhancing your appearance rather than improving bodily functions or treating illness or disease. Procedures that fall into this category include face lifts, liposuction, breast augmentation, hair transplants, and more.

However, when cosmetic surgery is necessary to correct a deformity due to a congenital abnormality, an injury, or a disease, the expenses are tax deductible. An example of this includes breast reconstruction following mastectomy. If a woman has a mastectomy as a cancer treatment and then has the breast reconstructed, the costs are tax deductible.

Similarly, if a cosmetic procedure improves functions of the body in addition to enhancing your appearance, some portion of the costs associated with the procedure may be deductible. For example, if a rhinoplasty procedure enhances the appearance of your nose but also addresses breathing problems, you may be able to deduct some of your expenses.

Likewise, expenses arising from a tummy tuck that removes excess skin and fat from the abdomen usually aren't considered tax-deductible. If, however, the folds of skin and fat cause medical problems, such as skin rashes or infections, then the removal of the bulges may be partly deductible.

To take advantage of medical expense deductions, you'll need documentation indicating that the procedure was a medical necessity. For example, if you're hoping to write off some of the costs of a rhinoplasty procedure, you should have documentation showing that you've visited a doctor about your breathing problems. To claim deductions for a portion of your tummy tuck, you'll need verification that you've had skin rashes, infections, or other problems associated with excess abdominal flesh.

**Check-Up**

An excessive amount of skin and fat that hangs in folds from the abdomen may be called a panniculus. A panniculus can cause a variety of skin irritations and infections within the folds of skin. Therefore, the removal of the panniculus may be considered medically necessary. However, the simple removal of the panniculus—called a panniculectomy—doesn't typically provide the same aesthetic benefits as a tummy tuck, which not only removes excess skin and fat but also tightens underlying abdominal muscles and tightens the remaining skin. Consequently, many patients opt for a panniculectomy and a tummy tuck in the same operation. The fees for the panniculectomy portion of the procedure may be tax deductible, but the charges for the tummy tuck would not be deductible.

## Cosmetic Dentistry

Giving your pearly whites a cosmetic makeover generally doesn't qualify for a tax write-off. Treatments, such as teeth whitening, veneers, and bonding can't be included in your list of medical expenses. Hence, none of the office visits, x-rays, or devices used can be deducted either.

# Chart of Treatments You Can and Can't Deduct

Use this chart to help you determine whether the costs associated with your procedure can or can't be deducted from your income tax return.

## Deductible and Nondeductible Procedures

| Procedure | Deductible | Notes |
|---|---|---|
| Face lift | No | |
| Eyelid lift | Maybe | If drooping eyelids affect your vision, you may qualify. |
| Rhinoplasty | Maybe | If breathing problems are corrected, a portion of the procedure may qualify. |
| Brow lift | No | |
| Otoplasty | No | |
| Liposuction | No | |

*continues*

## Deductible and Nondeductible Procedures    (continued)

| Procedure | Deductible | Notes |
| --- | --- | --- |
| Tummy tuck | Maybe | If you have a history of skin rashes, irritations, or infections, a portion of the procedure may qualify. |
| Breast augmentation | No | |
| Breast lift | No | |
| Breast reduction | Maybe | If performed to correct problems like shoulder and neck pain, irritations from bra straps, or rashes beneath the breasts, this procedure may qualify. |
| Breast reconstruction | Yes | |
| Thigh lift | No | |
| Buttock lift | No | |
| Lower body lift | Maybe | If skin irritations or infections have been documented, a portion of the procedure may qualify. |
| Arm lift | No | |
| Hip/knee replacement | Yes | |
| Hip resurfacing | Yes | |
| Spinal fusion | Yes | |
| Spinal disc replacement | Yes | |
| Angiogram | Yes | |
| CT angiography scan | Yes | |
| Bypass surgery CAB | Yes | |
| Heart valve replacement | Yes | |
| Coronary angioplasty | Yes | |
| Hysterectomy | Yes | |
| LASIK | Yes | |

| Procedure | Deductible | Notes |
|---|---|---|
| Cataract surgery | Yes | |
| Eyeglasses/contact lenses | Yes | |
| IVF | Yes | |
| Acupuncture | Yes | |
| Chiropractic treatment | Yes | |
| Crowns | Yes | |
| Bridges | Yes | |
| Implants | Yes | |
| Veneers | No | |
| Root canal | Yes | |
| Extractions | Yes | |
| Bone grafts | Yes | |
| Teeth whitening | No | |

# Other Deductible Medical Expenses

In addition to procedure fees, a host of other expenses associated with medically necessary treatments may be deducted from your tax return. Depending on the foreign hospital where your procedure takes place, these expenses may or may not be included in your hospital bill. Typically, you'll need to itemize these expenses on your tax return so you should ask the hospital for a breakdown of fees and charges.

## Medical Supplies

Medical supplies required for your recuperation and recovery are considered tax deductible. If you have to pay out-of-pocket for any of the following items, you typically can write them off:

- Wheelchair
- Walker
- Cane
- Bandages

Wheelchairs and walkers are commonly required following orthopedic procedures, such as hip and knee replacement or hip resurfacing. In most destination countries, you can rent wheelchairs and walkers rather than purchase them outright. Whether you rent or purchase, these fees are deductible.

Rental arrangements for wheelchairs and walkers make sense for most medical tourists because by the time you're ready to leave your destination country, you'll probably no longer need the equipment to help you get around. Renting allows you to pay only for the time period you actually use the equipment and prevents you from having to travel back home with bulky devices. You may, however, still require the assistance of a cane.

**Check-Up**

If necessary when returning home, you can arrange to have a wheelchair available for you at the departing airport and at your home airport. Wheelchairs typically are provided free of charge by the airports so there is no additional expense for this service.

Bandages are a very common post-surgical supply for which you may need to pay. If you need a bandages supply for your recovery after you've been discharged from the hospital, you usually can purchase them in a drug store or pharmacy.

## Prescriptions Medications

The costs of medications prescribed by your overseas physician or your local doctor are tax deductible. Be aware that only expenses for prescription medications fall into this category. If you buy over-the-counter drugs or medications, such as pain relievers, you can't write off these costs.

## Imaging Costs and Lab Fees

If a medically necessary procedure requires any x-rays, magnetic resonance imaging (MRIs), computed tomography (CT) scans, or other imaging tests, the costs of these tests can be deducted. Whether the tests are performed before (as a means of diagnosis), after, or both before and after your procedure, they are typically deductible.

Similarly, any fees associated with necessary lab tests count as medical expenses, according to the IRS. Common lab tests include blood work, urinalyses, and electrocardiograms (ECGs), among others. Often, a series of pre-operative lab tests are required to ensure that you are healthy enough to undergo surgery.

## Nursing Services

If you use any nursing services after you've been discharged from the hospital or released from an outpatient clinic, you can write off the cost of these services. If you've had surgery in an outpatient clinic, it's likely that you may require some post-operative nursing care. If, however, you stay in the hospital following your procedure, you usually won't require additional nursing services after being discharged.

# Can You Deduct Your Travel Expenses?

With medical tourism, travel costs can be substantial. The good news is that, in some cases, some of your travel expenses may be deductible. If your procedure is considered medically necessary, then a portion of your related travel expenses can reduce your tax obligation. If you're going abroad for cosmetic surgery, cosmetic dentistry, or some other procedure that isn't considered medically necessary, then any associated travel costs won't be deductible.

## Airfare

According to the IRS, you can deduct the costs of traveling to another city for necessary medical services. Although the IRS code doesn't specifically mention transportation to another country, it is generally accepted that airfare can be deducted if you're traveling abroad primarily for a medically necessary procedure.

In general, only the price of a coach ticket is deductible. If you purchase a first-class or business-class ticket, you will be able to deduct only what you would have paid for a ticket in coach.

## Lodging—Hospitals, Hotels, and Recovery Centers

Some of the lodging costs during your medical retreat may be deductible. To deduct lodging expenses, the lodging must meet all of the following four requirements:

+ The lodging must be primarily for medical care and essential to your medical care.

+ A doctor in a licensed hospital (or in a medical care facility that is the equivalent of a licensed hospital) must provide the medical care.

+ The lodging must not be considered extravagant or lavish.

+ The travel away from home must not include any significant element of vacation, recreation, or personal pleasure.

For medical tourists, hospital stays qualify for deduction. Similarly, recovery centers that have professional caregivers on staff are likely to meet all of these conditions. However, a five-star hotel may not meet the last two requirements.

For lodging that meets the necessary criteria, you can deduct a maximum of $50 per night from your tax return. For example, if you spend 10 nights in a recovery retreat at $150 per night, your total bill will come to $1,500. Even though you spent $1,500, you can deduct only $500 ($50 per night × 10 nights).

## Ground Transportation

You can take deductions for costs related to transportation within your destination country, provided the transportation is necessary for medical care. For example, you can write off the costs of shuttling to and from the hospital or your overseas doctor's office via bus, taxi, or train. Similarly, if you rent a car in your host country, you may be able to deduct rental charges and the cost of filling up the tank. Other transportation charges that may be deducted include parking fees and tolls.

## Meals

The meals you eat while you're a patient in the hospital are considered medical expenses that you can deduct. In some cases, the cost of food served in a recovery center also may meet IRS requirements for a deduction. However, when you dine in a hotel or a restaurant in your destination country, you usually can't write off these costs.

## Can You Deduct Companion Expenses?

If you travel abroad with a companion, some of your companion's expenses may qualify for a write-off. In general, if your companion is going to act as your caregiver and will be administering medications, changing bandages, or offering other assistance while you recuperate, deductions may be allowed. Deductible expenses for your caregiver typically include his or her airfare and lodging.

To deduct companion expenses, be sure to get a written note from your doctor explaining both the necessity of your procedure and the necessity of having a companion travel with you. You don't need to submit this documentation with your tax return, but you must have it in the event of an audit.

## Travel Expenses You Can't Deduct

Even if you've gone overseas for a medically necessary procedure, you can't write off any expenses associated with vacation or recreation activities in your destination country. For example, sightseeing excursions and tours aren't deductible. Neither are jungle treks, safaris, boat outings, or other activities. Similarly, shopping for anything other than medical supplies doesn't qualify for a tax deduction.

Because you can't write off these activities, you also can't deduct the transportation costs of getting to and from such vacation-related activities. Likewise, any dining expenses incurred during tourist excursions are excluded.

# Use the Right Tax Forms

If you're going to itemize your medical tourism expenses on your income tax return, you'll need to do it on the proper IRS form. Medical expenses must be itemized on Schedule A—Itemized Deductions, Form 1040. Note that you can't itemize medical expenses on Form 1040A or Form 1040EZ.

**Doctor's Orders** _____

Download Schedule A and B—Itemized Deductions and Interest and Ordinary Dividends—and instructions for filling out Schedule A and B from the IRS website (www.irs.gov/formspubs/lists/0,,id=97817,00.html).

# When Can You Deduct Medical Expenses?

You can include only deductions for medical expenses paid in the year of the tax return. For example, if you're completing your 2008 income tax return, you can include only deductions for charges paid in 2008. Even if your procedure took place in Brazil in 2007, you can deduct only the costs associated with that procedure in the year you actually paid for them. If you use your credit card to pay for medical treatment, deduct the expenses the year the charge is made as opposed to when you pay it off.

Considering that you may have to make a deposit a few months before you travel abroad, and will likely have to book flights at least a month in advance, you may end up having expenses for your health-care voyage in more than a single year. For example, if you're going abroad for surgery in February 2010, you may need to book your flight and pay a deposit in December 2009. In this case, your medical expenses would be spread over 2009 and 2010.

> **Doctor's Orders** _____
>
> If you're hoping that your medical expenses will be high enough to allow you to take tax deductions, you may want to make sure that all of your expenses will occur within the same calendar year. If the costs are spread out over more than a single calendar year, they may not be high enough in each of those years to warrant a tax deduction.

If you neglected to deduct medical expenses on a previous tax return, you may be able to amend that tax return. To do so, you'll need to file Form 1040X Amended U.S. Individual Income Tax Return for the year when the charges were incurred. As a rule, you must submit an amended tax return within:

◆ Three years from the original file date.

◆ Two years from the date the tax was paid.

The later time limit option marks the date by which you must file an amended tax return.

> **Code Blue!** _____
>
> If you forgot to deduct your medical expenses on a past tax return, don't simply deduct those expenses on your current tax return. This is not allowed. The only way to take advantage of the tax deductions is to file an amendment to the previous tax return.

# Keep Your Receipts

According to Argianas, "the most important thing you need to do is keep all your receipts, cancelled checks, and credit card bills." Hanging on to all of your invoices, bills, and other receipts provides you with a record of all your medical expenses. You don't need to submit your receipts with your tax return, but they come in handy when calculating your deductions. And of course, if you're ever audited, you'll need to provide this documentation.

To help you keep track of your expenses, we've created a simple chart that you can take with you overseas. Use it to record all of the out-of-pocket costs associated with your medically necessary procedure. Check the sample first to see how to fill in the chart.

## Sample Record of Medical tourism Expenses

|    | Date | Provider | Address | Service Provided | Amount Paid |
|----|------|----------|---------|------------------|-------------|
| 1. | 2/1 | Cathay Pacific | N/A | Flight | $1,350 |
| 2. | 3/6–3/15 | Gleneagles Medical Centre | Penang, Malaysia | Hysterectomy | $4,400 |
| 3. | 3/15–3/29 | G Hotel | Penang, Malaysia | Accommodations | $700 |
| 4. | 3/5–3/29 | Benz Limo Services | Penang, Malaysia | Ground Transportation | $55 |

## My Record of Medical Tourism Expenses

|    | Date | Provider | Address | Service Provided | Amount Paid |
|----|------|----------|---------|------------------|-------------|
| 1. | _____ | _____ | _____ | _____ | _____ |
| 2. | _____ | _____ | _____ | _____ | _____ |
| 3. | _____ | _____ | _____ | _____ | _____ |
| 4. | _____ | _____ | _____ | _____ | _____ |

# Consult a Financial Advisor

As you can see, figuring out what is and isn't tax-deductible for medical tourism can be tricky. "That's why it's best to consult a tax professional," says Argianas. "There are many gray areas, and you could get into trouble if you do it incorrectly." Plus, you need to realize that every situation is different. Expenses that may be deductible for one medical tourist may not be deductible for you depending on various circumstances, and vice versa.

## The Least You Need to Know

♦ Only expenses related to medically necessary procedures qualify for a tax deduction.

♦ Costs for cosmetic surgery and cosmetic dentistry aren't deductible.

♦ Only the cost of coach-class airline tickets can be written off.

♦ You must use Schedule A to itemize your medical expenses.

♦ Keep a written record of your medical tourism expenses.

♦ Always consult with a tax specialist before filing.

# Chapter 17

# More Money Matters

## In This Chapter

- ◆ The cheapest ways to exchange money abroad
- ◆ Which payment methods are best for international hospitals
- ◆ Why you need to check your hospital bill's bottom line
- ◆ Why it is difficult to sue a foreign medical provider
- ◆ How to tip in medical tourism destinations

No matter how you're going to finance your trip, you want to get the most for your money. You want to make sure that you don't run into any financial hiccups while you're overseas. In this chapter, I provide you guidance on when and where to exchange your dollars for foreign currency to avoid getting stuck with exorbitant fees. Plus, I outline the most acceptable ways to pay international medical providers so you don't end up scrambling at the last minute to come up with an alternate payment method.

This chapter also reveals the steps you need to take before your departure to ensure that you can get your money back, if necessary. You'll also find out why it's extremely difficult to try to sue an international doctor or hospital in the event that you aren't satisfied with your outcome. And that's not all. We offer a number of helpful hints on local tipping customs so you don't waste your money by overtipping. On the flip side, these hints may help you avoid insulting anyone by neglecting to give a gratuity when expected.

# Foreign Currency Tips

Before you hit the road for your medical excursion, take a crash course in your destination country's foreign currency. The more you know about the cash you'll be using and the exchange rates, the more confident you'll be about your overseas spending and the more you'll understand how much you're really paying for products and services abroad.

## Familiarize Yourself With Foreign Currency

Prior to your trip, hit the Internet and look up your destination's currency. Check out photos of the paper and coin currency you'll be using, if possible. Get to know the denominations that the currency comes in and by all means, know the name of the currency. By taking the time to familiarize yourself with the foreign cash, you'll be more confident that you're paying the proper amount for your purchases.

**Check-Up**

Banknotes.com (www.banknotes.com) features a world currency gallery that displays thousands of bank note images from around the world. No matter where you're headed for your procedure, you probably can find images of your destination country's currency on this website.

To help you with your search, here's a chart of currencies for popular medical tourism destinations.

## Foreign Currencies for Popular Medical Tourism Destinations

| Country | Currency |
| --- | --- |
| Argentina | Peso |
| Brazil | Real |
| China | Yuan |
| Costa Rica | Colón |
| India | Rupee |

| Country | Currency |
|---------|----------|
| Malaysia | Ringgit |
| Mexico | Peso |
| Philippines | Peso |
| Singapore | Dollar |
| South Korea | Won |
| Taiwan | Yuan |
| Thailand | Baht |
| United Arab Emirates (UAE)/ Dubai | Dirham |

# Exchanging Money

Although credit cards are widely accepted in most foreign countries, you'll need to have some of the local currency on hand to pay for taxicabs, cappuccinos, and tips (more on tipping later in this chapter). To get your hands on some of the local cash, you'll need to exchange U.S. dollars into the foreign currency.

Exchanging money is easy and can be accomplished in a number of places, including the following:

◆ Foreign ATMs

◆ Online currency exchange sites

◆ United States and international currency exchange outlets

◆ Foreign hotels

Fortunately, global ATM machines have become commonplace worldwide, making it easy for you to obtain foreign currency in almost any foreign country. Almost every airport has ATM machines in English where you can simply insert your ATM or debit card and withdraw cash just like in the United States.

# Exchange Rates and Currency Conversion Fees

Exchange rates for foreign currencies change daily, so you may want to begin monitoring the rates as soon as you decide to go abroad. This will give you a better idea of the actual costs you'll be paying for your medical treatment and your accommodations. To find out the current exchange rates for the currency you need, visit a foreign currency exchange website, such as XE.com (www.xe.com).

No matter what currency exchange method you choose, you'll need to pay an exchange fee or a currency conversion fee each time you exchange money. Conversion fees may be a percentage of the purchase amount, a flat fee, or a combination of both.

Typically, the least expensive way to exchange dollars for foreign currency is to use ATM machines in your destination country. Conversion fees for ATM purchases typically range from about one to three percent of the purchase or may be up to $5 per withdrawal for flat fees.

Depending on where you're traveling for your medical treatment, you may be able to eliminate any flat fees for ATM transactions. No-fee international withdrawals are possible if your ATM card is from a bank that's part of the Global ATM Alliance.

The Global ATM Alliance is a network of international banks that allow their customers to make ATM withdrawals with no fees at any of the banks within the network. For example, Bank of America is a member bank that lets you use your ATM card or check card at the following banks with no fees:

- Barclay's (United Kingdom)

- BNP Paribas (France)

- China Construction Bank (China)

- Deutsche Bank (Germany)

- Santander Serfin (Mexico)

- Scotiabank (Canada)

- Westpac (Australia and New Zealand)

As you can see, there aren't many banks from popular medical tourism destinations included in the alliance.

Online currency exchange websites, such as XE.com, also charge relatively low exchange fees. However, you should steer clear of currency exchange outlets and hotels, which tend to have the priciest fees. Currency exchange outlets may charge up to of 10 percent, and hotel fees can top 20 percent.

**Check-Up** _____

XE.com (www.xe.com), a foreign currency trading website, also offers a great online travel expenses calculator at www.xe.com/tec/table.shtml. You simply plug in your overseas expenses, your payment method, and the conversion fee percentages, and it calculates your total expenses. You can use the calculator to figure out the real cost of your medical expenses.

## How Much Money Should You Exchange?

As a general rule, you shouldn't carry a lot of cash with you in a foreign country. If it gets lost or stolen, you don't have any recourse to get it back. In addition, if you're going into the hospital soon after your arrival, you won't need much cash. In fact, it's better not to have a lot of cash with you in the hospital. Just like in the United States, personal belongings can sometimes disappear in hospitals.

I recommend that you exchange only about $100 at an ATM upon your arrival in your destination airport. If you would feel more comfortable having some of the foreign cash in hand before you leave home, you always can exchange a small amount of money at your bank or through an online currency exchange website. After you've been discharged from the hospital, you can withdraw more money from an ATM to cover your incidental expenses.

# Payment Methods Overseas

When you go abroad for medical care, you'll be expected to pay the bulk of your procedure fee when you register at the hospital or outpatient clinic. Be aware that many overseas medical facilities only accept certain types of payments, such as credit cards. Because of this, you should find out which payment methods your overseas medical providers accept before embarking on your trip.

## Credit Cards and Debit Cards

By far, credit cards and debit cards are the most commonly accepted payment methods among foreign medical facilities. International hospitals trust the credit card companies, which operate on a global basis. In addition, credit card payments are immediately processed, which medical providers appreciate.

> **Code Blue!**
>
> If you're going to use your credit card to cover the costs of your procedure and your travel, you'll need a high credit limit. To ensure that you won't exceed your credit limit, you may want to pre-pay your credit card bill before your departure. Contact your credit card company to find out if pre-payment is an option. In addition, inform your credit card provider that you'll be traveling abroad and using your card overseas. If you don't, your card may be declined when the international hospital tries to process the transaction. That's because your credit card company may suspect the transaction is fraudulent activity.

Using your credit card to pay for overseas medical treatment makes sense for you, too. When you pay with your credit card, you can dispute charges if necessary, and you have some protection in case of fraud or errors. Plus, in the rare event that your credit card is lost or stolen, you can call your provider to prevent any unauthorized purchases.

## Cold, Hard Cash

Cash including local currency or U.S. dollars, may be accepted by some medical providers. In fact, some medical providers may offer some form of discount for cash payments. However, carrying thousands of dollars in cash to a foreign country isn't wise, and I can't recommend making cash payments for pricey procedures. If you pay for services in cash, you generally have no recourse to get your money back if you aren't satisfied with the outcome.

## Traveler's Checks

Paying with traveler's checks is another option. However, many international medical providers refuse to accept traveler's checks because of lengthy processing requirements. If a hospital or medical facility does accept traveler's checks, it may only accept a specific type of check. Be sure to check with your foreign medical providers to determine which traveler's checks, if any, are accepted.

# Get It All in Writing

It's always a good idea to get a printout of your hospital bill to ensure that the charges match the estimate you were given. Of course, hospital bills are notoriously difficult to audit. It may be hard for you to determine whether each line item is correctly charged. In general, it's better to focus on the bottom line. Is the total price equal to, close to, or less than the price quoted? If so, rest easy about the charges.

# Can You Get Your Money Back?

For a variety of reasons, you may need to postpone or cancel your trip. Family crises, health problems, or scheduling conflicts may arise that prevent you from taking your trip on time. If there's a death in the family, if you come down with a sinus infection, or if you can't get the time off from work, you may need to reschedule your trip.

Even more important, what happens if after arriving at your destination, meeting your doctor, and seeing the hospital, you decide that you don't feel comfortable and don't want to go through with your procedure? What then?

Does that mean you'll have to forfeit your deposit or lose the money you spent on airfare? Always ask about cancellation and rescheduling policies before you go abroad. Be sure to inquire about guarantees in case you decide to opt out of your procedure if the medical facility or doctor doesn't live up to your expectations.

> **Doctor's Orders**
>
> To avoid losing your deposit and having to pay cancellation or postponement fees, you may want to consider booking your trip through a medical tourism agency. Full-service agencies often waive such fees.

# Can You Sue?

As mentioned in previous chapters, one of the major concerns you may have about medical tourism is whether you have any recourse if something goes wrong. Basically, can you sue your surgeon or the hospital if you have a bad outcome? According to Dale Van Demark at national law firm Epstein Becker & Green, trying to sue a medical provider overseas could be very difficult.

"Your first option," says Van Demark, "is to go back overseas and try to take advantage of the justice system there. But you'll need to figure out how the court system works, and you'll have to deal with language barriers, and more." All of this takes a lot of time and money, neither of which you probably have in abundance.

> **Code Blue!**
>
> Be aware that medical malpractice laws vary from country to country, and few are as comprehensive and patient friendly as those in the United States.

Even if you are able to file a lawsuit, the amount of recovery you can receive may be negligible. In the United States, punitive awards and compensatory damages can be sizable. In many other countries, substantial awards simply don't exist. Unfortunately, the size of your award may not even cover the costs of the lawsuit or additional medical costs you've incurred due to the doctor's or hospital's negligence.

If the prospect of suing the medical provider in the destination country—whether it be the physician or the medical facility at which treatment was provided—isn't feasible, you might consider suing that provider in the U.S. court system within your own state. But this possibility may have limitations as well, according to Van Demark. "Does the U.S. court have jurisdiction over the foreign provider?" he asks. "And what body of law applies—U.S. law or the law of the foreign provider's country?"

While U.S. courts might refuse to hear a case involving an overseas medical provider, Van Demark notes that "if the doctor or hospital has significant contacts within your state, such as advertising, having employees, or leasing office space within the state, it may help you bring a claim in the U.S."

Even if you are able to file a claim in a U.S. court, you may face other problems. "There is no case law, there are no statutes, and there is no guidance for this type of case because there haven't been any cases like this yet," says Van Demark.

> **Check-Up**
>
> Epstein Becker & Green's Dale Van Demark says that he knows of only one medical malpractice case that comes close to a medical tourism lawsuit. "There was a claim of medical malpractice on a cruise ship that had originated its voyage in Florida," he says. "The patient tried to sue in the state of Florida, but the courts said it was outside the boundaries of Florida jurisdiction. They ruled that the cruise doctor couldn't be sued in Florida courts so the patient had no recourse."

## Tips on Tipping

In the United States, it's customary to tip restaurant servers, cab drivers, airport baggage handlers, and more. In other countries, tipping doesn't necessarily follow the same rules as in the United States, and trying to figure out who to tip and how much can be tricky business.

For instance, in many Central American, South American, and European countries, gratuities often are included in restaurant bills so you don't need to leave a tip for the server. In the Middle East and Africa, tipping often isn't practiced at all. In many Southeast Asian destinations, tipping isn't common and may even be considered insulting.

Before your departure, do some research on tipping in your destination country. Find out if the practice is acceptable, which situations call for tipping, and how much you should tip in those situations. For a quick tipping guide for several popular medical destinations, check out the following chart.

Remember that the following tips on tipping are just generalities. Within each country, tipping practices may vary from city to city or may depend on the type of restaurant or hotel. For instance, in India, a 10 percent service charge often is added to the bill in fine dining establishments, so an additional tip isn't necessary. However, inexpensive local eateries in India don't usually include a service charge, and a tip of about 10 percent is appreciated.

## Guide to Tipping in Medical Tourism Destinations

| Country | Restaurants | Taxis | Baggage Handlers |
| --- | --- | --- | --- |
| Argentina | 10% | Round up fare | $1 per bag |
| Brazil | 10–15% | No, but 10% in Rio | $1 per bag |
| China | No | No | No |
| Costa Rica | Included | No | $1 per bag |
| India | Included (10% if not included) | No | $1 per bag |
| Malaysia | No | No | No |
| Mexico | 10–15% | Metered cab 10%, no if negotiated price | $1 |

*continues*

## Guide to Tipping in Medical Tourism Destinations    (continued)

| Country | Restaurants | Taxis | Baggage Handlers |
|---------|-------------|-------|------------------|
| Philippines | Included | Round up fare | 50 cents–$1 (10% if not per bag |
| Singapore | No | No | No |
| South Korea | No | No | No |
| Thailand | No | No | No |
| UAE/Dubai | No | No | No |

## The Least You Need to Know

- ◆ ATMs are a good choice for exchanging currency.

- ◆ Credit cards are the most common form of payment for overseas medical services.

- ◆ Your actual charges should be close to your estimate.

- ◆ Trying to sue a foreign medical provider will be extremely tough.

- ◆ Local tipping customs vary from country to country and from city to city.

# Part 4

## Globetrotting

When it comes time to hit the road for your health-care voyage, you have to think about both the medical and the travel aspects of your trip. In this part, you'll discover the pre-op and post-op steps you can take to ensure a successful procedure and to make your recovery more comfortable. You'll learn the ABCs of international travel so your journey will be as smooth and hassle-free as possible.

# 18

# Pre-Op Checklist

## In This Chapter

◆ Why you should tell your local doctor about your medical travel plans

◆ Why your overseas medical provider needs to know your medical history

◆ Which pre-op tests surgeons commonly recommend

◆ Which medications you need to avoid before surgery

◆ Why you must quit smoking prior to your procedure

◆ How alcohol negatively affects medical tourists

If you're like most people, you may think that your overseas surgeon is the only person responsible for ensuring a safe and successful surgery. Wrong! You may be surprised to discover that you also play an important role in making sure that your procedure and recovery go smoothly. In fact, you can and should do a number of things before your departure to help improve your chances of a good outcome. In this chapter, I offer a host of pre-op steps that are commonly recommended by surgeons worldwide.

# Buddy Up to Your Doctor at Home

If you're contemplating medical travel, you may be afraid to discuss the possibility with your doctor or with a surgeon at home. What will your doctor think? Will he or she try to dissuade you from going abroad? Will your doctor look down on you for seeking medical care overseas? Will he or she refuse to treat you if you need follow-up care when you return? Similarly, what if you're going overseas because you want treatment or a procedure that your local doctor can't or won't provide? Should you write them off entirely?

The answer is a resounding no. "When you're going abroad for treatment, it's incredibly important to maintain a positive and professional relationship with your local doctor and to try to make them part of your team," says Dr. Steven Tucker, an American oncologist who practiced for many years in the Los Angeles area before moving to Singapore, where he is founder and director of the Pacific Cancer Center and president of the International Medical Travel Association. Dr. Tucker treats a large percentage of international patients from a number of neighboring countries and the United States. He says that he works in concert with many U.S. medical providers, sharing information to provide the best treatment both abroad and at home.

> **Code Blue!**
>
> "If you have health insurance, be sure to read your policy closely," advises Dr. Steven Tucker, president of the International Medical Travel Association and founder and director of the Pacific Cancer Center in Singapore. "Make sure that going 'out-of-network' or abroad for treatment doesn't void your domestic insurance or that subsequent follow-up treatment or procedures will be excluded from coverage."

Your best move is to discuss your plans with your local doctor or surgeon and to enlist their help to treat you, if necessary, when you return. In most cases, they aren't going to refuse to treat you because you went abroad for surgery.

# Time to Tell All—Your Medical History

Before you head overseas, be sure to provide your foreign physician or dentist with your medical history. This detailed look at your overall health should include information on past surgeries, past or present medical conditions or diseases, allergies, and medications you're currently taking. In addition, you should offer any pertinent information on your mental health, including any medications you might be taking for depression or anxiety.

The information you provide your foreign surgeon is extremely important for your safety and wellbeing, so it's imperative that you be completely truthful. Certain medical conditions and allergies can be a cause for concern when you're having surgery with anesthesia. Based on your medical history, your surgeon or dentist may have to alter the way your procedure is performed to ensure your safety.

Certain medical conditions may require your surgeon or dentist to take additional precautions. Here are a few examples:

- If you have a heart condition, your surgeon may want to have a cardiologist provide additional monitoring during the procedure.

- If you have a heart murmur and you're having dental work, you may need to take antibiotics prior to your appointment.

- If you have any implants, such as breast or cheek implants, you may have to take antibiotics prior to dental appointments.

- If you're allergic to latex, your surgeon or dentist may need to use gloves made from another material to avoid an allergic reaction.

- If you're allergic to eggs, which are commonly found in some anesthetics, your surgeon can make sure the anesthesiologist uses a type of anesthesia that doesn't contain any egg products.

Be aware that any changes or adjustments to your procedure may involve additional fees or costs.

On occasion, your medical history may actually prevent you from being considered a candidate for medical travel. If you have serious health issues, your doctor may decide that you simply aren't well enough to travel for surgery. Remember that this is for your own safety.

## CASE STUDY

| | |
|---|---|
| Name: | Suzie |
| Age at time of surgery: | 53 |
| Residence: | Florida |
| Procedure: | Hysterectomy and tumor removal |
| Destination country: | Southeast Asia |
| Cost in United States: | $50,000 |
| Total cost abroad (travel included): | Would have been about $13,000 |

Life was good for Suzie until one night when the longtime recovery room nurse felt excruciating pain in her lower abdomen. "I thought my appendix was rupturing," recalls Suzie, who rushed to the emergency room. A litany of tests showed that Suzie's appendix was just fine, but they revealed something far more ominous—a 10-pound tumor that wrapped back and forth between her ovaries.

What the tests didn't show was whether the tumor was cancerous or benign. That couldn't be determined until surgery to remove it was performed. Suzie could have stayed in the hospital and had surgery immediately, but she wanted to tie up some loose ends at home and prepare her children for the ordeal. With prescriptions for strong medications to control her pain, she headed back home.

As if learning that she had a potentially cancerous 10-pound tumor wasn't enough, Suzie had to deal with another problem—how was she going to pay for the surgery? Although she'd been a nurse for many years, Suzie worked independently rather than for a particular hospital, and therefore didn't have any health insurance. One of the surgeons she worked for understood her situation and mentioned seeing something about medical tourism on a TV show. That was all Suzie needed to hear.

"I started researching and decided that it was the most practical thing for me to do financially," she says. Suzie found a medical tourism agency and asked them to put her on a fast track because she needed surgery sooner rather than later. The whole process was quick, and her surgery was scheduled for several weeks later. "I needed to get a passport, which takes time," Suzie says. "Plus, my best friend, a registered nurse, was going to come with me, and she had to coordinate her vacation time at work, and that took some time."

Finally, everything was in place. "The doctor's credentials were amazing, so I felt very safe and secure about my decision," she says. "I was all set to go on a Friday, but the Monday before, the pain hit me so hard that I had to go back to the hospital to have a morphine drip. The prescription pills just weren't enough to control the pain anymore."

The doctors decided that Suzie's condition was such that surgery just couldn't wait anymore. "They ended up doing the tumor removal and a total hysterectomy on me, and I walked out of there with close to a $50,000 bill," she sighs. "If I had gone abroad, it would have only cost about $13,000. And in addition to the tumor removal and total hysterectomy, I was also going to have some gallstones removed at no extra cost. Plus, I would have been staying in the ICU, which would never happen here, and I would have had a private nurse."

The unexpected change in plans meant that Suzie had to seek refunds for her plane tickets and deposits. Getting her money back was a breeze thanks to the medical tourism agency. Unfortunately, paying off the $50,000 hospital bill hasn't been so easy. "Every month, I make payments to the hospital, the radiology department, the anesthesiologist, and more. I will be paying for this for a very, very long time. Considering the tumor turned out to be benign, I guess I should just be happy that I'm still alive to be here to pay all these bills."

Even though Suzie's medical trip didn't work out, she's become a firm believer in the concept. "Now, I tell anybody who'll listen that if they need heart surgery, hip replacement, or whatever, and they have to pay for it, they have options."

To evaluate your health, your overseas doctor or the international hospital may send you a medical history form that you must fill out and return prior to your departure. If you're using a medical travel agency, you might receive a form from the agency. After the form has been completed and returned to the agency, your agent will forward it to your physician.

If you aren't provided with a medical history form, that doesn't mean you shouldn't make your surgeon aware of any health issues. Remember, your safety is at stake; it's up to you to inform your physician or dentist about any medical conditions or concerns. Take a look at the following sample medical history form to get an idea of the kinds of things you should bring to your medical provider's attention. You also can find downloadable medical history forms on the International Medical Travel Association website (www.intlmta.org).

## Sample Medical History Form

| Desired Procedure(s) | |
|---|---|
| **1.** | 4. |
| **2.** | 5. |
| **3.** | 6. |

| Physical Info | Your Answers | Additional Information (If Required) |
|---|---|---|
| Gender | | |
| Date of birth | | |
| Height | | |
| Weight | | |

| Medical History and Information | Your Answers | Additional Information (If Required) |
|---|---|---|
| What is your blood type? | | |
| What is your average blood pressure? | | |
| Date of last blood pressure reading: | | |
| Have you ever had surgery? When? | | |
| If yes, what surgery was performed? | | |
| Any surgical complications? | | |

| Mental Condition | Your Answers | Additional Information (If Required) |
|---|---|---|
| Why are you considering this procedure? | | |

| Mental Condition | Your Answers | Additional Information (If Required) |
|---|---|---|
| Are you currently consulting a psychiatrist or psychologist? | | |
| Have you discussed your intentions of having the above-mentioned surgery? | | |
| Have you ever been treated for a psychiatric illness? (This includes depression.) | | |
| If so, what medications (such as anti-depressants, sleeping pills, or anxiolytics) have you taken to treat psychiatric illness? | | |
| How long have you been taking this/ these medication(s)? | | |
| Can your physician provide a comprehensive report of your condition? | | |

| Please Respond *Yes* or *No* | Your Answers | Additional Information (If Required) |
|---|---|---|
| AIDS or HIV positive | | |
| Allergies | | To what: |
| Anemia | | |
| Arthritis | | |
| Asthma | | |

*continues*

## Sample Medical History Form     (continued)

| Please Respond *Yes* or *No* | Your Answers | Additional Information (If Required) |
|---|---|---|
| Back problems | | |
| Blood clots | | |
| Blood disorders | | |
| Bleeding problems | | |
| Breathing problems | | |
| Cancer | | |
| Chest pains | | |
| Colitis | | |
| Depression | | |
| Diabetes | | |
| Dry eyes | | |
| Ear problems | | |
| Eye problems | | |
| Epilepsy | | |
| Heart problems | | |
| Heart murmur | | |
| Hepatitis | | |
| High blood pressure | | |
| Irregular heartbeat | | |
| Kidney problems | | |
| Migraine headaches | | |
| Nervous breakdown | | |
| Nose/throat problems | | |
| Osteoporosis | | |
| Pneumonia | | |

| Please Respond *Yes* or *No* | Your Answers | Additional Information (If Required) |
|---|---|---|
| Psychiatric condition | | |
| Rheumatic fever | | |
| Seizures | | |
| Shortness of breath | | |
| Skin cancer | | |
| Stomach problems | | |
| Stroke | | |
| Thyroid problems | | |
| Tuberculosis | | |
| Transfusion | | |
| Are you pregnant? If yes, what is your estimated due date? | | |
| Have you ever smoked? | | |
| Do you currently smoke? | | |
| If yes, how many years? | | |
| If yes, how many cigarettes per day? | | |
| Do you drink alcohol? | | |
| If yes, how many drinks per day? | | |
| Have you ever abused drugs? | | |
| If so, which drugs and for how long? | | |

*continues*

## Sample Medical History Form  (continued)

| Medications | Your Answers | Additional Information (If Required) |
|---|---|---|
| Are you allergic to any medications? | | |
| If yes, which medications? | | |
| If yes, describe allergic reaction. | | |
| Are you currently taking any medications? | | |
| If so, which medications? (Include dosages.) | | |
| Have you ever had problems with anesthesia? | | |
| If so, please describe. | | |
| Please describe any other issues that may need attention. | | |

# Schedule Necessary Pre-Op Tests

Depending on the kind of surgical procedure you're having, your age, your medical history, and your doctor's personal preferences, certain pre-op tests may be required. These tests will give your physician a better idea of your overall health and whether you're fit for travel. In this section, I detail some of the more commonly required lab tests.

Based on your individual situation, you may be required to have some, all, or none of these tests. Even if your overseas medical provider doesn't require you to have any of these tests, Dr. Tucker suggests that you may want to be proactive and get a pre-op evaluation anyway. "It can provide you with a baseline or snapshot of your current health status," he says.

In most cases, it's a good idea to have any required tests at home prior to your departure. Yes, it will cost you a bit more money to undergo a series of tests in the United States rather than in your destination country, but it can be worth it. If your tests reveal any abnormalities, you may need further testing or treatment before you can travel abroad. In some instances, your test results may reveal that you aren't healthy enough for travel. In either of these cases, you may need to postpone or cancel your travel plans.

If you wait until you've arrived in your destination to have your pre-op tests, and abnormalities are discovered, what then? If your procedure has to be postponed, will you be able to afford to extend your stay to allow for the extra time required to treat the problem? If you're now considered a high-risk patient, and your procedure costs are higher, will you have the funds to cover the additional charges? In the worst-case scenario, if you discover that you can't have your procedure as planned, you'll have wasted your money on airfare and accommodations. Ultimately, this will cost you a whole lot more than the price of a few tests.

## Complete Blood Count

To measure standard blood levels, a complete blood count (CBC) is performed. A small amount of blood is drawn, usually from your arm. This can be done in a doctor's office or a clinical laboratory. A lab technician will analyze your blood to look for any abnormalities. Common disorders that can be detected with a CBC are *anemia* and infection. Typically both are conditions that must be treated and corrected before you can have surgery.

A CBC also can reveal blood disorders that could impact your procedure or could negatively affect your recovery. Following is a chart that details various blood deficiencies and how they can affect your procedure.

## def•i•ni•tion

**Anemia** is a blood disorder in which the body's red blood cell count is decreased. It can take several weeks or even months of treatment before blood levels return to normal.

## Blood Disorders and How They Can Affect Your Procedure

| Blood Disorder | Possible Problems |
| --- | --- |
| Low white blood cell count | Increases the risk for infection |
| Low platelet levels | Increases bleeding and bruising |
| Low hemoglobin levels | Slows the healing process |

Any blood disorders or deficiencies may need to be treated before you get the green light to go overseas.

## Chemistry Panel

A chemistry screen is a single comprehensive blood test that evaluates the function of your liver and kidneys and measures levels of electrolytes, blood sugar, and more. A chemistry panel can screen for conditions, such as diabetes, liver disease, and kidney disease. For this simple test, you may be asked to fast for up to 12 hours prior to having your blood drawn.

> **Doctor's Orders**
>
> If you don't have a local doctor to visit for blood tests, you can instead go directly to the lab where the blood is analyzed. Quest Diagnostics, the nation's leading provider of diagnostic laboratory testing, has almost 2,000 Patient Service Centers nationwide where you can have blood drawn. You can find a center near you on their website at www. questdiagnostics.com.

## Electrocardiogram

An electrocardiogram (ECG, or EKG) is a test that measures your heart's electrical activity. An ECG can reveal a variety of important information about your heart, including whether your heartbeat is normal, slow, fast, or irregular. Having an abnormal heartbeat could require further testing or could mean that extra precautions will need to be taken during your overseas procedure.

Performed in your doctor's office, an ECG is painless and involves attaching small stickers called electrodes to your chest and possibly to your legs and arms. The stickers are connected to a machine that prints out a graph of your heart's electrical activity. Your doctor will interpret the graph to determine whether there are any abnormalities.

## Chest X-Ray

A simple chest x-ray takes images of the chest, lungs, heart, diaphragm, blood vessels, ribs, and spine. The most common x-ray performed, a chest x-ray, can show signs of heart problems, lung disorders, and more. For a chest x-ray, you'll be asked to remove any jewelry, belts with buckles, eyeglasses, and any other metal objects. You also may be asked to remove some of your clothing and to put on an examination gown. You may be asked to stand or lie down while the x-ray is taken. Usually, the technician takes one x-ray from the back and one from the side. The entire process takes only a few moments.

## Mammogram

A mammogram is an x-ray of the breasts that is used to help diagnose a variety of breast diseases, including cancer. To take the x-rays of your breasts, a technician will place each breast between two plates and compress them. The compression can cause some discomfort, but it usually only lasts for a few seconds.

The American Cancer Society recommends annual screening mammograms for all women over the age of 40. If you're having cosmetic breast surgery, such as breast augmentation, you may want to have a mammogram prior to your procedure regardless of your age. This mammogram can be used as a baseline for comparison with future mammograms.

# Medications To Avoid

No matter what procedure you're going to have—cosmetic surgery, medically necessary surgery, or major dental work—you'll be asked to refrain from taking certain prescription and over-the-counter (OTC) medications, as well as many vitamins, herbs, and supplements. Typically, you'll need to avoid these medications for at least two full weeks prior to your procedure and for another two weeks after your treatment.

What makes these medications a no-no? Some of them can thin the blood, which may prevent it from clotting normally and may result in excessive bleeding during or after surgery. Some drugs contain stimulants that can cause a dangerous reaction during surgery. Other drugs may pose a risk when combined with the effects of anesthesia.

Your medical provider or medical travel agency may provide you with a list of medications to avoid. You also can check the list of prescription and OTC medications to avoid in Appendix D. Be aware that this list isn't comprehensive, and shouldn't be used as a replacement for your doctor's recommendations. If you're taking something that isn't on the list, don't assume it's okay to continue taking it. It is imperative that you notify your overseas doctor of all your prescribed and OTC medications and ask for his or her guidance regarding medications you should stop taking prior to your procedure.

## Prescription Pills You May Need to Stop Popping

A number of prescription medications should be discontinued before your surgery. If you take any kind of blood-thinning medication, such as Coumadin (warfarin), you may be advised to discontinue its use before your procedure. It's very important, however, that you discuss this with both your U.S. physician and your overseas surgeon before you stop taking this drug.

Certain medications that are prescribed to treat depression also may pose a risk during surgery. For example, monoamine oxidase (MAO) inhibitors can cause a serious drop in blood pressure when combined with anesthesia. In some cases, you may need to stop taking or wean off of certain anti-depressants and other medications several weeks prior to surgery because it can take that long for the drugs to get out of your system.

## Just Say No to These Over-the-Counter Meds

Many common OTC pain relievers, fever reducers, and cold and cough remedies contain aspirin or ibuprofen, both of which can thin the blood. It's best to avoid any OTC items containing these elements. If you need a pain reliever in the weeks leading up to your surgery, many physicians recommend Tylenol, which isn't made with aspirin or ibuprofen. Ask your physician what he recommends for pre-op pain relief.

## Give Vitamins the Heave-Ho

Although vitamins generally are accepted to provide health benefits, they may pose risks when you're having surgery. For example, Vitamins E and K have blood-thinning properties that can increase your tendency to bleed during or after surgery. Other vitamins also may have negative effects, which is why many physicians recommend avoiding all vitamins prior to surgery.

## Stop Taking Herbs and Supplements

Don't assume that just because something is natural or herbal it is safe to take before surgery. Many herbs and supplements can pose a health hazard when combined with the effects of surgery and anesthesia. For example, did you know that garlic, fish oil, ginseng, and gingko can all thin the blood? Did you know that popular supplements like kava kava and St. John's wort can intensify the effects of sedation?

Herbs and supplements can lead to other problems, too. Take ephedra, for example. Commonly used in diet supplements, ephedra acts as a stimulant that can increase your heartbeat, can lead to changes in the rhythm of your heartbeat, and can cause your blood pressure to spike. All of these possible effects can be very dangerous while you're on the operating table.

Be aware that even some herbal teas or green tea can have negative effects when you're having surgery. If you're a tea drinker, ask your doctor whether you need to stop for a while.

Check the following chart for a list of herbs and supplements and the possible problems they can cause. Take note that this is not a comprehensive list. If you're taking some form of herb or supplement that isn't on this list, ask your doctor whether you should stop taking it.

| Herbs and Supplements That Can Cause Excessive Bleeding | |
| --- | --- |
| Alfalfa | Gingko biloba |
| Bilberry | Ginseng |
| Cayenne | Goldenseal |
| Chamomile | Guarana |
| Dong quai root | Horse chestnut |
| Feverfew | Papaya |
| Garlic | Selenium |
| Ginger | Willow bark |

| **Herbs and Supplements That Can Cause a Rapid Heartbeat, High Blood Pressure, or Irregular Heartbeat** | |
|---|---|
| Ephedra | |
| Ginseng | |
| Gotu Kola | |

| **Herbs and Supplements That Can Cause Low Blood Pressure, Decreased Heart Rate, or Decreased Breathing Rate** | |
|---|---|
| Kava kava | Muwort |
| Hawthorn | St. John's wort |
| Lavender | Valerian root |
| Lemon verbena | Yohimbe |

# Kick the Smoking Habit

If you're a smoker, you'll need to stop smoking for at least two to four weeks before and two or more weeks after your surgery. In addition to avoiding cigarettes, you also must cut out all other forms of nicotine, including patches, gum, chewing tobacco, pipes, and cigars. Why is smoking so bad? Smoking and nicotine interfere with the post-operative healing process and can cause cardiovascular and respiratory problems during surgery.

**Doctor's Orders**

"I strongly advise anyone who smokes and is going to have surgery to stop smoking now," says Dr. Steven Tucker, president of the International Medical Travel Association and founder and director of the Pacific Cancer Center in Singapore. "Smoking increases the chances of wound infection even for simple procedures. It is well-known that smokers experience delayed healing compared to people who have never smoked. Quitting smoking for four weeks is highly recommended, and if you can go four weeks without smoking, why not drop it altogether?"

Oxygen is essential to the healing process. In a healthy nonsmoker, blood vessels beneath the skin carry oxygen to the surface of the skin to heal surgical incisions. In smokers, however, nicotine constricts those blood vessels, preventing them from supplying an adequate amount of oxygen to the skin. The decrease in oxygen can result in delayed wound healing, poor wound healing, skin death requiring skin grafts, and an increased risk for infection.

### Check-Up

Did you know that according to medical studies …

◆ Smoking doubles the complication rate following a face lift.

◆ Smokers are twice as likely to experience wound-healing or cardiopulmonary complications following orthopedic surgery.

◆ Smokers are nearly six times as likely to experience post-anesthesia pulmonary complications as nonsmokers.

When undergoing surgery, smokers also are at increased risk for respiratory and cardiovascular complications, which can be life-threatening in some instances. Evidence shows that by quitting smoking for a prescribed time period before undergoing surgery, these risks are reduced.

# Put Down That Glass of Wine

Like some medications, alcohol has blood-thinning properties that can lead to unnecessary bleeding during or following an operation. In addition, alcohol has a sedative effect that can be dangerous when combined with anesthetics or other medications used during surgery. This same effect can pose a hazard if you drink alcohol while taking narcotic pain relievers following your procedure. In general, you should eliminate all types of alcohol from your diet for at least a few days before and after your procedure.

Alcohol presents additional risks for medical travelers taking long overseas flights to and from their destination countries. The low atmospheric pressure in airplane cabins causes your body to lose fluids, which can cause the blood to thicken. This can increase the risk of developing blood clots (see more on blood clots in a later chapter). Because alcohol also causes dehydration, it intensifies this risk. Thus, drinking alcohol before or during your flight to or from your destination is discouraged.

## The Least You Need to Know

- ◆ Maintaining a positive relationship with local doctors can pay off.

- ◆ Your medical history needs to be as complete as possible.

- ◆ A pre-op evaluation is very beneficial.

- ◆ Some medications should be avoided before surgery.

- ◆ Quitting smoking can help speed your recovery.

- ◆ Drinking alcohol before your procedure is not recommended.

Chapter **19**

# Trip Basics

## In This Chapter

- When to schedule your tourist activities
- What you need to know about passports and international visas
- What vaccinations you might need
- Ways to prevent a dangerous condition associated with air travel after surgery
- Why destinations at high altitudes aren't right for all medical tourists
- How to avoid the most common traveler's ailment

Wherever you go for your medical treatment, you'll need to keep a few travel basics in mind. In this chapter, you'll learn the ins and outs of applying for passports and international visas. You'll also find out which vaccinations and immunizations you might want to get to prevent coming home with the wrong kind of souvenir.

In addition to the basics that apply to all tourists, you'll also discover how a host of travel issues specifically affect you as a medical tourist. For example, you'll find out why surgery doesn't always mix well with air travel or high altitudes.

# Leisure Time: Before or After Treatment?

If you'd like to include some vacation activities in your medical journey, think about whether you should do them before or after your procedure. Depending on the treatment you're having, you may or may not feel up to vigorous activities following your procedure.

For example, if you're having nonsurgical dental work, it may not make any difference whether you schedule activities before or after your treatments. With many dental procedures, only local anesthetics are used, and pain is usually manageable. In general, dental procedures won't affect your mobility, prevent you from swimming in the ocean, or keep you from basking in the sunshine.

Cosmetic and medically necessary surgical procedures typically require more in the way of recuperation. Your movement may be restricted, and you may need to refrain from any heart-pounding activities to prevent excessive bleeding or swelling. In addition, swimming in the ocean and sunbathing often are discouraged. That doesn't leave you with many exciting vacation opportunities.

Because of this, if you're hoping to hit the trail for a jungle trek, to brave the waves with some surfing, or to sit for hours on a bumpy road for a safari, you may want to think about doing those activities before you go under the knife rather than after.

---

### CASE STUDY

| | |
|---|---|
| Name: | Johnny |
| Age at time of surgery: | 50s |
| Residence: | New York City |
| Procedure: | Cosmetic surgery, dental crowns, and buttocks augmentation |
| Destination country: | South Africa, Brazil |
| Cost in United States: | about $20,000 |
| Total cost abroad (travel included): | about $10,000 |

No newcomer to the world of cosmetic surgery, Johnny has enough money to routinely visit one of New York City's top plastic surgeons for a variety of nip/tuck procedures. In the United States, he's had a face lift (which cost him $25,000), a hair transplant, and numerous other procedures. So why would someone like him try medical travel? An experienced world traveler,

*continues*

*continued*

Johnny says, "I just thought that for the price I would pay for surgery in the U.S., I could get a vacation, too." After doing some serious homework—"I wouldn't go to just anybody," he says—Johnny booked a trip to South Africa for cosmetic surgery (he can't recall the exact procedure he had there) and a safari. Most medical tourists have surgery first and then go on safari a week or so later, but not Johnny. "After plastic surgery, I know that I don't feel so great," he explains. "I definitely don't want to be doing much or lugging suitcases around. The idea of having surgery and doing tourist stuff a week later isn't realistic for me. That's why I did the safari first and then had my surgery."

The New Yorker's medical travel exploits also have taken him to Brazil on several occasions. "I had my butt filled three times with an injectable filler that isn't available in the U.S. It probably would have cost me $10,000 or $12,000 in the U.S., but I only paid $2,000 in Brazil." In the South American country, he also opted for some work on his smile with five crowns, which cost about $400 compared to more than $1,000 in New York City. In Brazil, Johnny quickly learned some of the reasons why prices are so much lower abroad. He explains, "Doctors abroad may not have a reception area. You ring a buzzer, and the doctor comes out. He does the consultation, he does the procedure, and he collects the money. It's like a one-man band. There aren't so many paper shufflers."

Lower prices weren't the only thing about medical travel that attracted Johnny. "For my crowns, I had an appointment every day and never waited more than five minutes," he recalls. "I had all the preliminary stuff done in about a week and then only had to wait a couple of days for the actual crowns. In the U.S., it probably would have been months before I got the crowns. "That's not all. According to Johnny, the Brazilian dentist used better technology than what's available in the U.S. "He took me to the lab to match the color of my teeth, and he put a lighted wand in my mouth, and a number came up to indicate the perfect color match. In the U.S., they would have held a color chart up to my teeth to try to match the color."

Remember that even if you schedule active vacation time prior to your procedure, you'll still need to spend adequate time recuperating in your destination after your procedure. This will increase the total number of days you'll be spending abroad, which ultimately will add to the cost of your trip. If you're on a tight budget or a strict time schedule, you may not be able to afford those extra "tourism" days before your procedure.

If you're the kind of person who shies away from sweat-inducing tourist activities in favor of leisurely strolls or sightseeing, then it's probably okay to wait until after your procedure to take in the local sights. As always, check with your overseas doctor before engaging in any post-operative activities.

# Don't Overschedule Activities

When you're traveling abroad to an exotic location, it's tempting to try to see and do as much as possible. After all, how likely is it that you'll ever be returning to this destination? Your medical trip could be your only chance to check out some unforgettable sights, whether it's the Taj Mahal in India, Iguazu Falls National Park in Brazil, or the rainforest in Costa Rica. It's no wonder you may want to book some sightseeing tours or museum visits before you leave home.

There's nothing wrong with wanting to see some of the world's biggest tourist attractions, but jamming your post-op schedule with outings can backfire on you. As explained earlier, you probably won't have tons of energy following surgery. The idea of being on your feet for a few hours in a museum or trudging around a major tourist attraction amid throngs of tourists may no longer be appealing to you.

In this case, if you've booked and pre-paid for tourist activities, you may not be able to get your money back. Or worse, if you feel compelled to go on an outing because you've already paid for it even though you don't feel up to it, you could set yourself up for a serious setback in terms of your recovery. Overdoing it after a major medical procedure is one of the quickest ways to delay the healing process and increase your risk for complications.

A much smarter approach is to leave your post-op schedule open. That way, you can see how you feel before signing up for any activities. In most cases, if you're feeling well enough, your hotel or medical travel agency can help you make arrangements for any sightseeing you might want to do within a day's notice.

# The ABCs of Passports and Visas

As explained in Chapter 8, you must have a valid passport for international travel. If you're applying for a passport for the first time, you'll need to appear in person at one of more than 9,000 locations throughout the United States. To apply for a new U.S. passport, you'll need the following:

◆ A completed application form

◆ Two 2" × 2" color photos

◆ Proof of U.S. citizenship

◆ A valid form of identification

To find a passport acceptance facility near you or to download an application form, check the U.S. Department of State website at www.travel.state.gov/passport/passport_1738.html. Your photos must have been taken within the last six months, must show a front view of your face, and must be taken against a white background. Documentation accepted as proof of citizenship includes a certified birth certificate, a certificate of citizenship, a naturalization certificate, or a consular report of birth abroad. To prove your identity, you'll need documentation, such as a valid driver's license, a government ID, or a military ID.

It can take several weeks or even more than a month to process your passport application, so be sure to apply several months in advance of your trip. Even if you aren't sure whether you're going to follow through with your medical trip, there's no harm in applying for a valid passport just in case.

A visa may be required in addition to a passport to visit certain medical tourism destinations. Destinations that currently require a visa include the following countries:

- Brazil
- India
- China
- Philippines
- United Arab Emirates (UAE)

You can find out more information about visas and how to apply for them at the U.S. Department of State website at travel.state.gov/travel/cis_pa_tw/cis/cis_1765.html. To ensure that you receive it in time, apply for your visa at least one month prior to your departure date.

# Do You Need to Get Vaccinations or Immunizations?

In general, most medical tourism destinations are located in major metropolitan settings where vaccinations aren't required or even recommended. However, if you're planning on going jungle trekking or visiting out-of-the-way backwoods villages in certain destinations, you could pick up some souvenirs you definitely don't want—diseases such as hepatitis A, hepatitis B, typhoid fever, yellow fever, and malaria. To minimize your risk of contracting a nasty disease if you're traveling in these areas, the Centers for Disease Control (CDC) may recommend vaccinations or preventive medications.

**Hepatitis A** is a liver disease that can be transmitted through food and water. The risk is highest for travelers visiting rural areas of developing countries, and the risk is much lower for travelers who stay in major cities and tourist areas.

**Hepatitis B** is a liver disease that can be transmitted through exposure to blood or bodily fluids or through contaminated medical equipment—the kind you might find in some unaccredited back alley facility. Most medical tourism health-care facilities meet stringent standards for cleanliness and safety so the risk is minimal.

**Typhoid fever** is a disease caused by bacteria that is usually transmitted through food and water. Eating in rural villages or buying food from street vendors puts you at greater risk, and may merit vaccination. Restricting your dining to major hotels and restaurants greatly reduces your risk.

**Yellow fever** is a virus that is transmitted by the bites of infected mosquitoes. If you'll be traveling to specific areas within your destination country where yellow fever is present, you may want to immunize yourself against yellow fever. In general, travelers are at low-risk for yellow fever in most metropolitan areas.

**Malaria** is a disease that is contracted via mosquito bites. Most of the urban areas within medical tourism destinations aren't considered malaria-risk zones. India, including the major city of Mumbai, is an exception and does pose a risk. When traveling to India, it's recommended to take antimalarial drugs as a precaution.

Vaccinations aren't used to prevent or treat malaria. Instead, it's recommended that you take the antimalarial drug chloroquine as a precaution when traveling to malaria-risk areas. Purchase these drugs in the United States before your departure and take them with you. Using insecticides to prevent mosquito bites also can reduce the risk of contracting malaria.

The following chart shows the current vaccination requirements and recommendations for several popular medical tourism destinations, according to the CDC's recommendations. Take note that requirements can change as world health issues evolve so be sure to check the CDC website (www.cdc.gov) for the latest information on vaccinations for travelers. Similarly, the CDC website can give you the most up-to-date recommendations on malaria-risk areas.

## Required and Recommended Vaccinations for Destination Countries

| Destinations | Vaccinations Required | Vaccinations Recommended | Notes |
|---|---|---|---|
| Argentina | None | Hepatitis A | |
| | | Hepatitis B | |
| | | Typhoid | Only if dining outside major hotels/ restaurants |
| | | Yellow Fever | Only certain areas |
| | | Malaria | Only certain areas |
| Brazil | None | Hepatitis A | |
| | | Hepatitis B | |
| | | Typhoid | Only if dining outside major hotels/ restaurants |
| | | Yellow Fever | Only certain areas |
| | | Malaria | Only certain areas |
| China | None | Hepatitis A | |
| | | Hepatitis B | |
| | | Typhoid | Only if dining outside major hotels/ restaurants |
| | | Malaria | Only certain areas |
| Costa Rica | None | Hepatitis A | |
| | | Hepatitis B | |
| | | Typhoid | Only if dining outside major hotels/ restaurants |
| | | Malaria | Only certain areas |

*continues*

## Required and Recommended Vaccinations for Destination Countries    (continued)

| Destinations | Vaccinations Required | Vaccinations Recommended | Notes |
|---|---|---|---|
| India | None | Hepatitis A Hepatitis B Typhoid | Only if dining outside major hotels/ restaurants |
| | | Malaria | Urban areas included |
| Malaysia | None | Hepatitis A Hepatitis B Typhoid | Only if dining outside major hotels/ restaurants |
| Mexico | None | Hepatitis A Typhoid | Only if dining outside major hotels/ restaurants |
| Philippines | None | Hepatitis A Hepatitis B Typhoid | Only if dining outside major hotels/ restaurants |

| Destinations | Vaccinations Required | Vaccinations Recommended | Notes |
|---|---|---|---|
| Singapore | None | Hepatitis A Hepatitis B Typhoid | Only if dining outside major hotels/ restaurants |
| South Korea | None | Hepatitis A Hepatitis B Typhoid | Only if dining outside major hotels/ restaurants |
| Thailand | None | Hepatitis A Hepatitis B Typhoid | Only if dining outside major hotels/ restaurants |
| UAE | None | Hepatitis A Hepatitis B Typhoid | Only if dining outside major hotels/ restaurant |

When traveling abroad, you also should make sure that you're up-to-date on routine vaccinations, such as tetanus and measles/mumps/rubella. These vaccinations protect against diseases that may still be common in developing nations even though they are rare in the United States. Visit the CDC website for more information on routine vaccinations you may need.

If you do need any vaccinations, make an appointment with your doctor at least four to six weeks in advance of your trip. Why so early? Some vaccinations must be given as a series of injections over a matter or days or over a series of weeks while other vaccinations take time to become effective.

# Air Travel Concerns

Flying long distances can be a real pain. Cramped quarters in coach can leave your legs and back feeling stiff, and the low humidity levels in the cabin can lead to dry skin and dehydration. If you're prone to motion sickness, a long flight can make your tummy do flip-flops. Of course, there's the jet lag to deal with. Here's some advice to help you avoid these common problems ...

- ◆ Move around the cabin to stretch your legs.

- ◆ Drink plenty of water and juice to stay hydrated (this helps fight jet lag, too).

- ◆ Avoid caffeinated beverages and alcohol, which add to dehydration and can worsen the effects of jet lag.

- ◆ Consider taking medication to prevent air sickness, but check with your doctor before taking anything new (especially prior to surgery).

While these air travel concerns can be an annoyance, others pose more serious health risks. Two potentially serious conditions you need to be aware of are *deep vein thrombosis (DVT)* and *pulmonary embolism.*

## def•i•ni•tion

**Deep vein thrombosis (DVT)** is a blood clot that develops in the body, usually in the legs or calf area.

When a blood clot breaks off and travels to the lungs, it causes a **pulmonary embolism,** which can be a life-threatening condition.

## Deep Vein Thrombosis

When a blood clot forms within the veins, it's called deep vein thrombosis (DVT). Considered to be a relatively uncommon condition, DVT is most likely to occur in veins within the legs—especially in the calf area—or pelvis. DVT isn't always dangerous, but in some cases, it can be very serious—even fatal.

As a medical tourist, you may be more at risk for developing DVT than the general population. Why? DVT can be brought on by long periods of inactivity—think long-haul flights and post-op bed rest. Plus, the act of having surgery itself or having anesthesia also can lead to blood clot formation. Considering that a medical tourism trip typically combines surgery, anesthesia, bed rest, and long plane rides, it's a formula that increases your risk.

Blood clots can occur without causing any symptoms, or they may cause some of the following symptoms:

- Leg pain
- Swelling in the affected leg
- Tenderness in the affected leg
- Skin in the affected area may feel warm to the touch
- Skin in the affected are may appear red

 **Check-Up**

Certain surgeries are more likely to lead to blood clot formation:

- Orthopedic hip procedures
- Orthopedic knee procedures
- Pelvic and gynecologic procedures

Note that ankle swelling is common on long flights; if both of your ankles appear swollen, it probably isn't cause for alarm.

Doing the following can help prevent blood clots during your post-op flight home:

- Try to reserve a seat with additional leg room, such as a bulkhead seat.
- Periodically flex and point your toes to exercise your lower calf muscles.
- Don't sit with your legs crossed for long periods.
- Get up and walk around the plane as often as possible.
- Don't wear tight or restrictive clothing.
- Don't take sleeping pills that leave you motionless for hours.
- Ask your doctor whether you might benefit from wearing support hose.

By taking these precautions, you may be able to reduce your risk of developing blood clots.

If you do develop a blood clot, you may need medical treatment. In some cases, blood clots dissolve on their own. If not, some form of blood-thinning medication may be administered to help dissolve the clot. In the event of a blood clot, you may need close monitoring or even additional hospitalization.

## Pulmonary Embolism

Although it's considered unusual, a blood clot that forms in your legs or other area of your body can break off and travel through your veins to your lungs. This is called a pulmonary embolism, and, in some cases, it can create a life-threatening situation. Here are some of the most common signs of pulmonary embolism:

- Chest pain that gets worse when you breathe deeply or cough
- Rapid heartbeat
- Sudden shortness of breath
- Coughing up blood

If you experience any of these symptoms, immediately contact your doctor.

# Avoid Long Car and Train Rides

As a rule, it's best to avoid spending hours traveling by car or train in your final destination. For example, if your medical provider isn't centrally located, it might take you a few hours to go from the airport to the hospital. After you've already spent 8, 10, or 18 hours in a plane, you definitely won't want to have to hit the highway or railway.

Similarly, if you're staying in a hotel or resort that's miles away from the medical facility, you may have to endure a number of long rides back and forth for appointments. That may not be such a concern before your procedure, but it may be more bothersome after your surgery when you aren't feeling so great.

After having your procedure, you also may want to nix the idea of going to any far-off tourist sites. Being stuck in a vehicle for hours on end can leave you feeling stiff and fatigued. Even worse, sitting for long time periods in a car or train can increase the chances of developing blood clots, just like on an airplane.

# High Altitudes and Your Health

If you decide to visit a destination that's at high altitude, it may have some affects on your health. At altitudes that are high above sea level, there's less oxygen in the air, which can sometimes cause problems for people who normally live at lower altitudes. Usually referred to as altitude sickness, common symptoms may include the following:

♦ Headache

♦ Lightheadedness

♦ Nausea

♦ Difficulty sleeping

♦ Weakness

Symptoms associated with altitude sickness can range from mild to severe, with the most severe cases also involving difficulty breathing and confusion.

Altitude sickness is most likely to occur at altitudes over 8,000 feet. It's possible, however, to feel the effects at lower altitudes as well. You may want to keep this in mind if you're traveling to any of the following medical tourism destinations:

♦ Mexico City, Mexico—7,400 feet above sea level

♦ Bangalore, India—3,000 feet above sea level

♦ São Paulo, Brazil—2,500 feet above sea level

♦ San José, Costa Rica—3,800 feet above sea level

If you have any chronic health issues, such as severe heart disease or pulmonary disease, traveling to high altitudes can be dangerous for your health. If you have any chronic conditions, it's best to check with a physician to determine whether it's safe for you to travel to high altitudes.

If you're concerned about the possibility of altitude sickness on your medical voyage, visit a doctor before your departure to ask about medications used for prevention. By all means, to help prevent or lessen the effects of altitude sickness, drink lots of water and avoid excessive exercise, alcohol, and smoking.

# Foreign Foods and Water: Protecting Your Tummy

One of the best things about traveling is sampling the local cuisine. One of the worst things about traveling is sampling the local cuisine—and what it can do to you. Exotic spices, different flavors, and unfamiliar ingredients can really do a number on your tummy. Even worse, in many developing nations, food and water can become contaminated due to preparation practices that don't meet the usual American standards. If you gulp down contaminated food or water, you're going to pay for it.

Traveler's diarrhea, the trots, Montezuma's revenge—whatever you want to call it, it's the most common ailment affecting international travelers. In fact, according to the CDC, 20 to 50 percent of all international voyagers will get hit with a case of the runs, along with a host of other nasty symptoms, such as nausea, vomiting, abdominal cramping, bloating, and fever.

As if that isn't bad enough, imagine getting hit with a bout of this when you're already feeling low from having surgery. Not a pretty picture, is it? To help keep you from becoming a victim …

- Don't eat food from street vendors.
- Don't eat raw or undercooked seafood or meat.
- Don't eat fresh fruits unless you peel them yourself.
- Don't drink the tap water.
- Don't order any drinks with ice.
- Don't order fountain drinks.

By sticking to major hotels and restaurants for your meals, you'll reduce the chances of coming down with traveler's diarrhea.

If you do get sick while you're abroad, immediately contact your overseas surgeon. Your doctor may be able to prescribe medication or recommend over-the-counter drugs that can relieve your symptoms.

**Code Blue!**

As a rule, beware of any dining establishment or food vendor that doesn't accept credit cards. If a restaurant isn't technologically advanced enough to process credit card payments, its food preparation processes may not be up to snuff either. If you can pay only with cash, don't eat there. Your tummy will thank you.

## The Least You Need to Know

◆ It's best to schedule intense activities for before your surgery.

◆ When to apply for passports and visas.

◆ Areas where vaccinations and immunizations are recommended.

◆ Preventive measures can help you avoid blood clots.

◆ High-altitude destinations and surgery don't always mix.

◆ Stick to eating in major hotels and restaurants.

# Chapter 20

# What To Take With You

## In This Chapter

- How to decide whether to bring a companion with you
- Why you need to take copies of all your medical info
- Which over-the-counter remedies to put on your packing list
- What clothing do's and don'ts for medical tourists
- What snacks, sundries, and other supplies to pack in your suitcase
- How to pack like a medical travel pro

Planning what to take with you for a medical travel excursion can be a real challenge. Not only do you have to think about all the routine items international travelers need to take, but you need to also factor in all the medical necessities. For first-time international travelers, it's enough to make your head spin.

In this chapter, you'll get the inside scoop on medical travel must-haves that can make your health-care adventure a far more enjoyable and stress-free experience. Plus, I offer tips and advice on what to leave behind so you aren't lugging around a lot of stuff you don't need. With the helpful packing checklists provided in this chapter, you can pack like a seasoned medical tourist.

# Should You Bring a Caregiving Companion?

Bringing along a companion on your medical voyage has numerous benefits. A companion can provide you with physical, emotional, and communications support throughout the entire surgery process.

After your procedure, your companion can help you with a variety of chores. Whether it's running errands to pick up prescriptions or over-the-counter (OTC) drugs at the nearest pharmacy, changing bandages, or helping you perform your physical therapy exercises, your companion can handle necessary caregiving duties.

In addition, your companion can be of great assistance in the communications department. For example, when you have your in-person consultation with your doctor, your companion can tag along and take notes or ask questions that you may forget to ask. Considering that you may be feeling a bit nervous at this time, your companion may do a better job of retaining important information about your procedure and your post-op instructions.

Your companion also can handle the chore of communicating with loved ones back home. Immediately following your procedure, you probably won't feel like making a bunch of phone calls. That's why it's better to have your companion call your family and friends to let them know that your surgery went well and that you're in the recovery room resting comfortably.

> **Doctor's Orders**
>
> Before leaving home, make a list of phone numbers or e-mail addresses for a few key friends and family members back home that you want your companion to contact. Then ask those key contacts to contact your other loved ones with updates on your condition. This will save you money on overseas phone calls and will prevent your companion from having to make dozens of calls repeating the same info over and over.

In addition to handling the little things, traveling companions also can offer a wealth of emotional support. A friend or spouse can cheer you up when you're feeling down and can keep you company while you're recuperating so you don't feel so alone.

It's a good idea to have a frank discussion with your traveling companion about their role in your medical journey before you leave home. For example, you may want to talk about how much help you expect from them and how much time you expect them to spend in the hospital with you. You need to also make sure that they understand that you won't be able to join them for any strenuous tourist activities after your procedure. In fact, it is important that they understand you may not even feel up to everyday activities or conversations.

### Doctor's Orders

A quick note for caregiving companions: don't forget to take care of yourself while you're playing the role of caregiver. If possible, don't stay in the hospital all day and all night. Take some time away from the patient to recharge your batteries.

By ironing things out prior to your departure, you can help avoid any disappointment or disagreements with your caregiver in your destination. After all, the last thing you need while you're recuperating from surgery overseas is to have your companion's presence turn into a stressful situation.

### CASE STUDY

Not everyone agrees that bringing a companion with you is the only way to go. Just ask Didi Carr Reuben, who had a face lift in Costa Rica and who is now the U.S. patient coordinator for the plastic surgeon who did her procedure. Reuben organizes "sleep away camp" group trips to Costa Rica for patients who want face lifts and other cosmetic procedures. Her group patients stay together at the same recovery retreat following surgery as a way to offer support to each other. Reuben sometimes accompanies patients on the trip and acts as a sort of "den mother" to the group, seeing to their needs and offering emotional support. Because there's already a built-in support network for her groups, a companion isn't necessary. In fact, based on her experiences, she actually discourages patients from bringing a companion with them.

"It turns out to be a liability," explains Reuben. "The patient ends up worrying about their loved one, worrying that they must be bored. But it isn't good for the patient to be worrying about someone else after surgery—the patient just needs to rest, rest, rest. Plus, face lift patients in particular aren't supposed to talk a lot after surgery. You can really jeopardize your results by lifting your head, talking, and laughing. But when a spouse or loved one is with them, they feel bad if they don't engage in conversation so they end up talking more than they should. I've also seen patients prematurely go out on tours with their companion because they feel bad that the person is sitting around doing nothing. And then the patient comes back from the tour feeling miserable."

# Take Hard Copies of All Medical Documents

To ensure that everything relating to your upcoming medical procedure goes on without a hitch, take copies of any and all medical documents with you. Having your files at your fingertips while overseas can come in handy. Although it isn't common, overseas medical providers—just like U.S. doctors and hospitals—can lose or misplace files. Plus, if you run into any discrepancies regarding the price or the surgical procedure being recommended, you can refer to your files for clarification.

At home, as soon as you begin contemplating medical tourism, start a file where you can place copies of all your medical information. By putting everything in one place, it'll be a snap for you to grab the file and take it with you.

## Medical History

If you're asked to send a completed medical history form to your overseas medical providers, make an extra copy and put it in your file. Even if your provider doesn't request this information prior to your departure, create a medical history anyway. There's always a chance that your foreign doctor or anesthesiologist will ask you about past surgeries or your experiences with anesthesia after you arrive in your destination. Trying to recall off the top of your head exactly when you had your wisdom teeth removed or whether you had general anesthesia or sedation for the procedure can be difficult. It's better to have all this information written down and available for easy reference.

## Medical Reports

You should include in the medical file you take your U.S. doctors' or dentists' reports regarding your current condition. These reports may include diagnostic information, recommendations for treatment, and any results from nonsurgical treatments you've tried. For example, if you've tried physical therapy for orthopedic problems, or if you've taken hormonal medication to deal with gynecologic troubles, you may have paperwork that details how you responded to those treatments.

## Lab Test Results

Take copies of the results from any lab tests performed prior to your departure, such as blood tests, chemistry panels, ECGs, urine tests, and pap smears. Even if your overseas physician wants to perform some of these tests again, it can be beneficial to have the results of the previous tests available for comparison.

## X-Rays and Other Imaging Reports

Be sure to take copies of any x-rays, magnetic resonance images (MRIs), computed tomography (CT) scans, positron emission tomography (PET) scans, ultrasound scans, and any other medical images. Even though you may have already sent these imaging reports to your overseas physician, it's a good idea to have your own copies for reference.

## All Correspondence with Overseas Medical Providers

In addition to filling your medical file with reports, lab test results, and imaging reports, also include copies of all correspondence regarding your medical voyage. For example, print out and save each and every e-mail to and from your overseas physician, foreign medical facility, or medical travel agency. Having a printed record of these communications can be critical in the event that the prices being quoted after you reach your destination don't match the original estimates or that the procedures or surgical techniques being recommended differ from what was initially proposed.

# Take Medications You Might Need

No matter what country you'll be visiting, it's a good idea to take some medications with you. There's no guarantee that the drugs you take on a regular basis will be available overseas, so it's better to take what you need.

## Prescription Drugs

Of course, you should have an adequate supply of any prescription medications you need to take. If you're like a lot of people who want to save suitcase space by putting loose pills in a plastic bag, in a 7-day or 14-day pill organizer, or in any other unmarked container, you may run afoul of airport security or customs. Although it may not be the most efficient packing system, leave your medications in the pharmacy containers that show your name, your doctor's name, and the name of the medication.

To avoid running into trouble, carry copies of your prescriptions with you. In addition, obtain a letter from your doctor explaining that you're going abroad for medical treatment, describing your condition, and detailing why you need the medications. Be sure to keep the letter in an easily accessible spot as you go through airport security and customs.

## Over-the-Counter Remedies

At home, you're used to heading to the local drug store for whatever ails you. Of all the available OTC medications, you probably have your favorites that work best for you—maybe it's Tylenol for aches and pains, Pepcid for heartburn, and Benadryl for allergies. Unfortunately for the medical tourist, you may not find your favorite remedies if you try heading to the nearest pharmacy in your destination country.

In some countries, they may not offer the same brand or the same formulas that you're used to. For example, in Singapore, you can't buy antacids like Pepcid, Tagamet, or Nexium. They're sold under different names. In addition, some OTC drugs that are sold in the United States require a doctor's prescription abroad. In Singapore, common drugs such as Benadryl, Advil, and Tylenol may need a prescription.

Because they may be unavailable in your destination country, take a supply of the OTC remedies you routinely use. Don't forget to include OTC drugs for minor ailments you might experience abroad, such as diarrhea, nausea, or headache. If you're having a procedure that may require post-op narcotic painkillers, take a stool softener with you as well. Narcotic pain medications are known to cause constipation.

In general, it's much better to have a supply of these items on hand just in case you need them. If you don't stock up prior to your departure and you do end up needing an OTC medication, you'll have to rush around a foreign location trying to find the right drug when you aren't feeling up to snuff. Not a good idea.

# Bring Your Legal Documents

Nobody likes to think about the possibility of complications before a surgical procedure, but complications can happen whether you're in a local medical facility or in a hospital thousands of miles away. To add to your peace of mind, you may want to have certain health-care legal documents drawn up, such as an *advance health-care directive* and a *power of attorney* document. An advance health-care directive spells out your wishes for treatment should you be unable to communicate your desires, and a power of attorney document appoints another person to make decisions for you.

When you're traveling abroad for medical care, you should take copies of these documents with you and give them to your medical providers. You should understand that these documents may or may not be respected depending on the country and your individual situation. In general, you'll find that most international medical providers will be amenable to following your wishes as stated in your documents. In unique situations, however, your documents may not be enforceable due to cultural differences.

## def•i•ni•tion

An **advance health-care directive** is a legal document that details your preferences for treatment, surgical procedures, and resuscitation. It also may designate the person of your choice to make health-care decisions for you in the event you aren't able to make those decisions yourself.

A **power of attorney** document gives authorization to another person to act on your behalf.

# What to Pack

Packing for any kind of overseas excursion can be a real challenge. What kind of clothing should you take? How many pairs of shoes do you need? Which toiletries can you live without? What should you bring to make the flight more enjoyable? Which items are best left behind? And of course, after you stuff everything on your must-have list into your suitcase and it doesn't come close to closing, what do you take out? All of these are typical packing dilemmas. The task only gets tougher when you're packing for an international health-care trip.

When a medical procedure is the primary reason for your trip, you need to think differently about things like clothing options, toiletries, and sundries. Plus, you have to make room for any post-op medical supplies you may need.

## Choosing the Right Clothing

When packing your clothing, you may be tempted to fill your suitcase with your favorite jeans and t-shirts. But these common fashion staples may not translate into the best options for your post-op recovery. Think about it. Depending on the kind of surgery you're having, you may have significant swelling, or you may have trouble bending, stretching, or lifting your arms as you recover. Tight jeans may cause discomfort and may not fit at all for some time after surgery. It may be painful for you to lift your arms to put on a t-shirt or to pull it down over your face if you've had some kind of facial procedure.

A far better plan is to opt for loose, comfortable clothing. Choose sweatpants, pants, or flowing skirts with elastic waistbands that you can easily pull up. Take shirts and sweaters (if needed) with buttons or zippers in the front so you don't need to pull them on over your head. If you won't be able to bend over for a few days, take slip-on shoes or flip-flops so you don't have struggle to tie your shoes.

Don't forget that if you're having a facial cosmetic procedure, you'll probably be instructed to stay out of the sun following surgery. That means a wide-brimmed hat is a must-have. It's best to select a soft hat that can be folded or squished into your suitcase without damaging its shape. If you're traveling to a country with a tropical climate during the rainy season, you may want to opt for a waterproof hat. If you're having facial surgery, you may want to bring some big sunglasses and a scarf that you can tie around your head. These can help hide some of the telltale signs of cosmetic surgery.

# To Bring or Not To Bring Toiletries

If you can't survive without your favorite lotion, shampoo, conditioner, makeup, toothpaste, or hair products, then by all means, find space for them in your suitcase. You don't want to have to be hunting down personal grooming products in local stores, and you definitely don't want to be stuck in the hospital when you realize you didn't bring your toothbrush or your favorite lip balm.

However, you might discover that after surgery, you aren't as inclined to wash your hair, shave, put on makeup, or spritz yourself with perfume or cologne. You may find that you're just as comfortable going au naturel. In any case, it's better to have your usual items on hand in case you want them.

## Sundries for Your Suitcase

Sometimes, it's the little things that make all the difference. A host of miscellaneous items can greatly improve your comfort while you convalesce and can make your recovery more enjoyable. For example, a simple pair of earplugs can help you shut out the annoying beeping and whirring of all that hospital equipment so that you can sleep better. Insect repellant can protect against nasty bug bites so you don't feel itchy all over. A little handheld fan with a spritzer can help cool you down when it's hot and humid. These are only some of the many incidentals you might want to take with you. See the packing list later in this chapter for more sundries to pack.

## Pack Some Snacks

Think about packing some of your favorite snack foods when you go abroad. Sure, you can usually order room service in your hotel if you've got the munchies, but sometimes you just want a light snack—a bag of chips or some pretzels—rather than a whole meal. Even though more and more American snack foods and beverages are being exported everyday, the snacks in medical tourism destinations may not be what you're used to. For example, a few local delicacies you might find abroad include the following:

◆ Green tea bean cakes (Thailand)

◆ Deep-fried samosas filled with spicy potatoes (India)

◆ Fish-flavored bean crackers (Malaysia)

◆ Prawn crackers (Singapore)

◆ Wasabi-coated green peas (China)

Don't they sound tasty? Even if you do find some Western-style snack foods, such as chips or crackers, they may not be the same as their U.S. versions. That's why you may want to stuff your suitcase with some refreshments. If you do, make sure you pack individually packaged snacks. You don't want to attract bugs with open containers of food lying around.

## Pack Post-Op Supplies

Depending on the procedure you're having, you may need a few post-op medical supplies. Be sure to have your foreign surgeon send you a list of supplies you may need after your procedure. For many procedures, you may need to change bandages or gauze dressings after you're discharged. Sometimes, it's easier to buy these items in your nearest drug store than to search for them overseas.

Other procedures require you to wear certain garments following surgery. Take breast augmentation, for example. If you're getting breast implants, you'll be instructed to wear a sports bra day and night for several weeks after your procedure. Make sure that the bra is in your post-op size and that it zips up the front to make it easy to put on and take off. Bring more than one sports bra so you can wear one while you wash the other.

If you're having liposuction, you may need a post-op compression garment. These garments help reduce swelling and provide gentle support while you heal. Typically, you'll be required to wear your compression garment 24/7 for a specified time period. Your best action plan is to purchase compression garments stateside before your departure. Splurge on two compression garments so you won't have to go without when you wash one of them.

> **Doctor's Orders** _____
>
> Mark and Willie, who had plastic surgery in Southeast Asia, definitely recommend taking two compression garments if you're having liposuction. "They say that you can use a hair dryer for 20 minutes to dry it and then put it back on," says Mark. "But we tried that and it still wasn't dry after twice that amount of time. So then Willie had to put it back on when it was still damp and it was really uncomfortable."

Another item you may want to include in your suitcase if you're having liposuction is a supply of feminine hygiene pads. These pads are ideal for absorbing bodily fluids that leak from the small incisions made for the procedure. In many countries, you'll find a very limited selection of feminine hygiene products so it's better to pick these up at home.

Simple things such as safety pins also may come in handy if you've had a tummy tuck or some other procedure that requires post-op drains. Drains are used following certain procedures to prevent the accumulation of fluids under the skin. During surgery, drainage tubes are placed within the treated area. These drainage tubes are attached to small bulbs that capture fluids. By fastening the drains to your clothing with safety pins, you can avoid bumping or breaking the bulbs as you walk around.

## Converters and Adapters

Don't forget to take an alternating current (AC) power converter or an AC plug adapter if you're going to be schlepping any electric appliances, such as chargers for cameras or cell phones. Check the appendix for the electricity requirements in each country, and remember that some of the better hotels in destination countries provide converters and adapters for guests. Check with your hotel about availability.

# What Not to Take

When deciding what to take and what to leave at home, always keep in mind that the primary goal of your trip is medical treatment, not tourism. Fancy clothing and fine jewelry really aren't necessary. Expensive jewelry can make you a target for muggers, so leave your best pieces at home. Similarly, don't expect to be spending a lot of time fixing your hair for outings. Curling irons, flat irons, hot rollers, and the converters or adapters that they require can take up a lot of precious room in your suitcase.

Don't bring everything you normally carry in your purse or wallet. Take nonessential keys off your key ring—just keep your house key and your car key if you drove to the airport. Take out all of your local store credit cards and membership cards. You certainly aren't going to need your Costco membership card while you're abroad. Rid your wallet of all those frequent buyer cards from the local pizzeria, car wash, and ice cream shop. Basically, you want to lighten the load as much as possible.

Of course, you need to adhere to the Transportation Security Administration's guidelines. Check the organization's website (www.tsa.gov/travelers/airtravel/index.shtm) for a list of prohibited items.

# Your Packing Guide

Use the following packing list as a guide to help you plan what to take. This list includes items that have been recommended by medical tourists who have already been there, done that. Remember that everybody's situation is unique, and this list is meant only to offer suggestions. You may not need to pack all the items on this list; on the flip side, you may want to pack personal items that aren't listed.

**Packing Checklist**

**Documents**

Passport

Visa (if necessary)

List of contact information

Itinerary

Airline and hotel reservations

Medical history

Medical reports

Lab test results

X-rays and imaging reports

Copies of correspondence with doctor(s)

Copies of prescriptions

Letter from doctor

Advance health-care directive

Power of attorney document

Vaccination certificates

**Medical Supplies**

Bandages

Gauze dressings

Compression garment (2)

Feminine hygiene pads

OTC remedies for the following:
Constipation
Diarrhea
Heartburn
Aches and pains
Motion sickness/nausea
Nasal congestion
Eye dryness

Prescription medications

Sports bra with front zipper (2)

**Clothing and Accessories**

Loose pants

Loose shorts

Loose skirts

Loose dresses

Button-down/zippered shirts

Button-down/zippered sweaters

Slip-on shoes

Slippers

Flip-flops

Wide-brimmed hat

Scarf

Sunglasses

Undergarments

Light jacket/raincoat

Pajamas

Robe

Socks

Swimwear

**Toiletries**

Aftershave lotion

Antibacterial hand wipes

Brush/comb

Cologne/perfume

Contact lens equipment

Cotton balls

Dental floss

Deodorant

Eyeglasses and case

Feminine hygiene products

Hair care products

Hair elastics/scrunchies

Lip balm

Lotion

Makeup

Mirror

Mouthwash

Nail file

Razor/shaver

Shaving cream

Sunscreen

Q-tips

Talcum / baby powder

Tissues

Toothbrush and toothpaste

**General**

Calculator (solar)

Camera

Cell phone/SIM card

Converter/adapter

Earplugs

Gifts

Insect repellant

International calling card

iPod

Laptop

Money belt

Notebook (small)

Pens

Pillow (small)

Playing cards and small games

Purse/wallet

Reading material

Safety pins

Sleeping mask

Snack foods

Spray bottle with fan

Water-purifying tablets

Ziploc plastic bags

Finances

Credit/ATM card

Foreign currency

U.S. cash (small amount)

# What to Take In Your Carry-On Bags

Knowing what to pack is only half the battle. Figuring out what needs to go in your carry-on bags versus your checked baggage is just as important. Packing your carry-on bags with the right stuff can make a long flight far more comfortable and enjoyable. If you pack your carry-on like a travel guru, you can get by in case your checked baggage gets lost or stolen.

Basically, anything you can't do without on your trip needs to go in your carry-on bag. As a medical traveler, this includes all your medical documents, medications, and possible medical supplies, in addition to routine travel necessities. Check the following list for items you may want to carry with you on the plane.

**Carry-On Bag Packing List**

Anything irreplaceable

Brush/comb

Contact lens equipment

Eyeglasses and case

iPod

Laptop

Makeup

Medical documents

Medications

Tissues

Toothbrush and toothpaste

Playing cards/small games

Reading material

Snacks

## The Least You Need to Know

- ◆ Your companion should understand his or her role before your departure.

- ◆ Having copies of your medical documents and correspondence can come in handy.

- ◆ Your favorite OTC remedies may not be available in your destination country.

- ◆ Loose and comfortable clothing is ideal .

- ◆ Medical supplies should be purchased before you leave.

- ◆ Your carry-on bag is the place for all your must-have items.

Chapter **21**

# Post-Op Tips

## In This Chapter

◆ How to make your recovery more comfortable

◆ What to do to control post-op pain

◆ How to keep your recovery on track

◆ What to do if you experience complications abroad

◆ Why you need to get copies of all your medical records

◆ How to make your post-op return home a little easier

You may be completely focused on the surgery portion of your medical voyage, but you should realize that you'll spend the bulk of your time abroad recuperating from your procedure. If you're like most people, you're probably worried that you'll be in pain after surgery or that you'll feel miserable. Rest assured that your surgeon will make every effort to keep any post-op pain under control and will give you detailed instructions to help keep you on the road to recovery.

In this chapter, I examine the recovery process and what you can do to make your post-op time abroad as comfortable as possible. By taking the proper steps, you can minimize discomfort, help your body heal, and get back to normal faster.

# Hospital, Hotel, or Recovery Center

Following your procedure, you'll stay in a hospital, a hotel, or a recovery center. You may need to stay in the hospital for a certain time period before going to a hotel or recovery center. If your procedure takes place in an outpatient clinic, you'll head straight to a hotel or recovery center after your operation.

## Get the Most Out of Your Hospital Stay

A post-op hospital stay will provide you with the highest level of care. Your doctor and the nurses will see to your every need. Take advantage of that care while you're in the hospital, and use the time to rest, relax, and focus on recuperation. Be sure to communicate to your caretakers how you're feeling and don't be afraid to ask questions. Also, make sure the nurses demonstrate how to change bandages, empty drains, or anything else you might need to do on your own after you're discharged.

## How to Recover in Comfort in Your Hotel

If you head to a hotel immediately following an outpatient procedure, you can do a number of things to make your recovery more comfortable. Make sure you have some bland snacks available, such as crackers. They can help fight nausea, a common side effect of anesthesia. Have a few Gatorades or sodas available for the same reason, but be sure to let the sodas go flat before you drink them, because carbonation can irritate the stomach and cause painful gas. So that you don't have to go out, take advantage of hotel room service to order a light meal—items such as soup can be a good choice after surgery.

**Doctor's Orders** _____

Hotel or recovery center pillows may not be your cup of tea—they may be too firm, too squishy, too puffy, or too small. Using a new pillow can disrupt your sleep pattern even if you're in the best of health. After surgery, it can be even more uncomfortable. To combat this problem, consider bringing your own pillow with you. Of course, this works best if you have a rather small pillow that can be folded or squished into your suitcase. If you've got a mammoth-sized pillow, leave it at home.

You also may want to ask your hotel to provide you with a few extra pillows. That's because many procedures will require you to keep your head, knees, or arms raised while you're sleeping or resting. Extra pillows also come in handy for cardiac patients. If you've had a cardiac procedure, clutch a pillow to your chest when you cough or take a deep breath to minimize pain. If you've had an orthopedic procedure, ask whether the hotel has a potty chair available to make it easier to get on and off the toilet.

If you're going straight to your hotel after outpatient surgery, you might be doing so with a handful of prescription medications. Common post-op prescriptions include antibiotics, pain medications, and anti-nausea drugs, among others.

It's very important to take any prescribed medications as directed. For example, some drugs need to be taken with food, while others must be taken without food. Some you must take at scheduled times; others you can take on an as-needed basis. Unfortunately, it can get a little confusing, especially when you're feeling disoriented and fatigued after surgery. If you're in a foreign country, the instructions on the pill bottle may be written in a different language.

This is why a clear-headed companion is so important. To avoid confusion, your traveling companion should be responsible for administering your medications. Here are a few tips to help you keep track of your prescriptions:

- ♦ Write the name of the drug on the top of the cap.

- ♦ Write what the drug is for—nausea, pain, and so on—on the side of the bottle.

- ♦ Write special instructions such as "with food" or "without food" somewhere on the bottle.

By doing so, it will be much easier to take the medications as directed and to avoid any mistakes.

## Recovery Center Tips

Because recovery centers specialize in caring for patients, they usually offer many of the post-op amenities you might find in the hospital. For example, they may offer special meals for sensitive post-op tummies. Be sure to inform your recovery center coordinator or host of any special food requests before you go in for surgery. You may want to also have your own supply of crackers in the recovery center in case you can't stomach anything else just yet.

Recovery centers might also have bathrooms equipped with handrails and potty chairs to make it easier for patients with mobility issues. They often have staff nurses who can administer medications and assist you in getting around if your mobility is restricted.

# Keeping Post-Op Pain in Check

Following any surgery, you can expect to feel some discomfort. The amount of pain you experience depends in part on the procedure. Some procedures, such as face lifts and nose jobs, aren't typically associated with a lot of pain. On the other end of the spectrum, tummy tucks, which tighten underlying abdominal muscles and involve lengthy incisions, tend to cause a higher level of pain. Your individual tolerance for pain also comes into play; the exact same procedure may cause virtually no pain at all in one person and severe pain in another.

In the United States, doctors and nurses will ask you to rate your post-op pain on a scale of 0 to 10, with 0 being no pain and 10 being excruciating pain. Many hospitals around the world also use this pain scale. To keep your pain under control, it's best to take pain medications when your pain is on the lower end of that scale rather than waiting for it to reach the higher level. You should reach for the pain reliever when your pain feels like a 3 or 4 out of 10. In part, this is because it can take up to about 45 minutes for some pain relievers to start working. In addition, the worse your pain is, the more pain medication you'll need to get it under control.

### Code Blue!

Don't try to prove how tough you are by enduring post-op pain. Refusing pain relief can actually slow the healing process and increase your risk for developing complications.

Controlling your pain is a major priority following surgery. It not only makes you feel better, but it also helps you heal faster and helps prevent certain complications after surgery. With proper pain management, you can reduce your chances of developing blood clots or contracting pneumonia. You're more likely to be able to walk around and take deep breaths, things that help prevent blood clots and pneumonia.

Fortunately, when it comes to pain relief, you've got a lot of medicinal options. Pain relief you may receive during your overseas health-care excursion include narcotic and non-narcotic medications. Pain medications may be administered in numerous forms, such as *patient-controlled analgesia*, injections, or pills. Be sure to discuss your post-op pain relief options with your overseas surgeon before your procedure so you understand how your pain will be managed.

# def•i•ni•tion

**Patient-controlled analgesia** is a pain management option that puts you in control of administering your own pain relief. Typically administered through an intravenous (IV) site in your arm, you simply press a button to deliver a pre-determined dose of medication. Limits are pre-programmed so you can't overdose on the medication.

## Narcotic Pain Relievers

In the United States, narcotic pain medications such as Vicodin, Percocet, and Tylenol with codeine are commonly prescribed to alleviate moderate to severe post-op pain. Narcotic pain relievers work by blocking pain signals in the body from reaching the brain. Although these drugs can become habit-forming, they are generally considered safe when taken as directed for a short time period.

Prescription pain medications may cause a number of side effects, including drowsiness, nausea, vomiting, and constipation. Whether you experience side effects is highly individual and can differ depending on which narcotic pain reliever you're taking. If the drug prescribed makes you vomit or produces strong nausea, inform your doctor. He or she may be able to prescribe another drug that you will tolerate better.

Be aware that in foreign countries, post-op narcotic pain relievers aren't prescribed as often as in the United States. In many foreign countries, doctors are concerned about over-medicating their patients. Therefore, they might initially prescribe milder pain relievers for you. They may prescribe something stronger only if you complain that your pain isn't being adequately alleviated. That's why it's very important to communicate with your doctor and your nurses if your pain isn't being controlled.

**Check-Up**

In many Southeast Asian countries, the people are generally much smaller than the average American. Thus, the most commonly used pain relievers and dosages in these countries may not be adequate for Americans. If the pain relievers you're given aren't doing the job, by all means, speak up and tell your doctor.

## Non-Narcotic Pain Relievers

Non-narcotic pain relievers include drugs containing acetaminophen (Tylenol), ibu-profen (Advil and Motrin), and naproxen (Aleve). These drugs are designed to relieve mild to moderate pain. In the United States, these drugs are sold over the counter, but in foreign countries, they may require a prescription from your doctor. Take note that medications containing aspirin or ibuprofen may not be recommended following surgery because they can thin the blood and cause excessive bleeding.

# Follow Your Post-Op Instructions

No matter what procedure you have overseas, your doctor will likely give you post-op instructions that you'll need to follow. These instructions are intended to keep you on the road to recovery by reducing your chances of developing complications. They're also designed to help make you more comfortable during your recuperation. So, it's a good idea to follow them to the letter.

Your overseas surgeon may give you written post-op instructions or may simply tell you what you need to do. If your doctor takes the verbal route, be sure to write down the information so that you don't forget. Make sure that your companion is with you when your doctor discusses any post-op instructions because he or she will likely be assisting you during the recovery period.

Post-op instructions vary based on the surgery you're having, your individual situation, and your doctor's personal preference. For example, the instructions for an abdominal hysterectomy may be quite different from those associated with laparoscopic proce-dures. To give you an idea of what to expect after your surgery, we've put together the following lists of common post-op instructions for some of the most popular medical travel procedures.

## General Post-Op Instructions for any Procedure

◆ Protect the treated areas from injury or impact.

◆ Place ice bags on affected areas to reduce swelling.

◆ Don't smoke.

◆ Refrain from drinking alcohol.

◆ Drink plenty of water.

- Eat a soft, bland diet at first and then gradually introduce other foods as tolerated.

- Change bandages as directed.

- Keep incisions dry.

- Use a topical antibacterial ointment to clean your incisions.

- Walk as often as possible.

- Do deep-breathing exercises once an hour while awake.

# Hip Replacement Post-Op Instructions

- Do not bend your hip beyond a 90-degree angle for 6 weeks.

- Keep your legs and knees apart for 6 weeks.

- Place a pillow between your legs when you sleep or rest to keep them apart.

- Move your body as a whole and keep your legs apart as you get out of bed.

- Do not rotate the affected leg inward.

- Do not bend over to pick up anything.

- Use a walker or cane as needed.

- Do not drive for 6 weeks.

- Use only the back seat of a car and keep your leg straight as you get into and out of it.

- Use chairs with armrests and keep your leg out straight as you sit down.

- Do not lean forward when sitting down into or getting up from a chair.

- Do not lean forward while sitting in a chair.

- Keep your legs and knees apart while sitting.

- Place a few pillows on chairs to prevent bending your hip too much when sitting down.

- Do not cross your legs.

- Use an elevated toilet for 6 weeks.

- Do not soak in the bathtub, a pool, or the ocean for 6 weeks.
- Use assistive devices to help you dress for 6 weeks.

# Spinal Fusion Post-Op Instructions

- Keep your spine properly aligned at all times.
- While lying in bed, turn frequently using a "log rolling" technique.
- When riding in a car, do so in a reclining or lying-down position.
- Wear a back brace as recommended.

# Hysterectomy (Abdominal) Post-Op Instructions

- Have a supply of sanitary pads on hand for bleeding and discharge, which can last several days.
- Avoid lifting anything over 5 pounds for about 6 weeks.
- Avoid soaking in water—such as in a bathtub, a pool, or the ocean—for about 6 weeks.
- Avoid intercourse, douching, and tampons for about 6 weeks.
- Avoid strenuous activities for about 6 weeks.
- Gentle walking is okay.

# Face Lift Post-Op Instructions

- Use pillows to keep your head elevated while resting or sleeping.
- Sleep on your back for the first few days.
- Use ice bags as directed to reduce swelling.
- Keep laughing, talking, smiling, and yawning to a minimum.
- Don't chew gum or eat foods that require a lot of chewing.
- Don't bend over to pick up anything.
- Don't lift anything over 5 pounds for about 3 weeks.

- Avoid aerobic exercise and strenuous activities for about 3 weeks.

- Avoid sunbathing for at least 3 weeks. Wear a wide-brimmed hat and sunscreen when outdoors.

- Avoid coughing and blowing your nose.

- Don't wash your hair for about 3 days.

- Be gentle when washing your hair for the first time and very carefully comb it out.

- Wait about 1 week before washing your face or using facial moisturizer.

- Don't wear any makeup for about 1 week.

- Don't get your hair dyed for about 3 to 4 weeks.

# Rhinoplasty Post-Op Instructions

- Don't let your eyeglasses or sunglasses rest on the bridge of your nose for up to 4 weeks. If necessary, your surgeon can help you devise an alternate way to wear your eyeglasses, for instance, taping them to your forehead.

- Avoid rubbing or touching your nose.

- Try not to smile too much because it makes your nose move.

- Don't chew gum or eat foods that require a lot of chewing.

- Avoid caffeinated beverages.

- Don't blow your nose for about 10 days.

- Use saline spray to keep your nostrils moist.

- Sneeze with your mouth open.

- Sleep on your back with your head elevated.

- Avoid bending over for about 2 weeks.

- Don't lift anything over 5 pounds for about 2 weeks.

- Avoid contact sports and vigorous activities for up to 6 weeks.

## Breast Augmentation Post-Op Instructions

- Wear a sports bra 24/7 until instructed otherwise. You may remove the bra to shower.

- Sleep on your back for at least 1 week.

- Put pillows under your upper body while resting in bed.

- Avoid bending over for 1 week.

- Avoid activities and exercise that involve the upper body for about 6 weeks.

- Avoid aerobic exercise for about 3 weeks.

- Avoid wearing an underwire bra for about 6 weeks.

## Liposuction Post-Op Instructions

- Wear your compression garment 24/7 until instructed otherwise. You may remove it to take a shower or to wash it.

- Avoid soaking in the bathtub, a pool, or the ocean for up to 2 weeks.

- Avoid aerobic activities and strenuous exercise for about 3 weeks.

- Don't lift anything over 5 pounds for about 2 weeks.

    - Gently massage the treated areas after they are no longer tender.

## Tummy Tuck Post-Op Instructions

- Sleep on your back with your upper body raised at an angle for a few weeks.

- While lying in bed, keep your knees propped up with a pillow.

- Try sleeping in a recliner if that's more comfortable for you.

- Avoid lying on your stomach for at least 6 weeks.

- For a week or 2, lean forward and bend slightly at the hips while walking.

- Wear the compression garment as instructed for up to a couple of months. You may remove it to shower or to wash it.

- Empty drainage tubes as instructed and record how much fluid is drained each time.

- Do not lift anything over 5 pounds for about 4 weeks.

- Do not bend over to pick up anything.

- Avoid strenuous activities and aerobic exercise for at least 6 weeks.

- Walk as often as possible to help prevent blood clots.

- Don't soak in the bathtub, a pool, or the ocean for several weeks.

# Take It Easy

No matter where you stay or what procedure you have, do yourself a favor and take it easy while you recover. Overdoing it can lead to all sorts of problems, including increased swelling and excessive bleeding. In extreme cases, your incision could separate, or if you're a hip replacement patient, the artificial ball could pop out of the socket, requiring additional treatment.

By kicking back and relaxing, you allow your body to focus on healing. Treat yourself right during the recuperation period, and you'll probably be back to normal a lot sooner than if you try to rush your recovery. Take advantage of having a companion with you to run errands and to help you get around. You'll be glad you did.

# Side Effects and Complications While Overseas

Side effects such as swelling, bruising, and pain are common after any surgical procedure. These side effects are only temporary and typically resolve on their own. You can expect to experience some side effects following your procedure.

Complications, on the other hand, are causes for concern. They may delay healing and may require some form of treatment. Your surgeon will inform you of the possible risks associated with your procedure and will let you know the warning signs that might indicate post-op complications. Each individual procedure carries a certain set of risks. Some complications can occur after just about any type of surgical procedure. These include the following:

- **Infection:** A fever and redness at the incision site may indicate an infection. Take heart that numerous safety precautions are in place to minimize the risk of infection in foreign hospitals. Antibiotics generally are used to treat infections.

- **Excessive bleeding:** It's normal to have a small amount of bleeding after surgery, but excessive bleeding should be immediately reported to your surgeon. Your surgeon will determine whether treatment is necessary.

- **Incision problems:** Incisions can separate, which may delay healing and may necessitate additional treatment.

- **Scar problems:** Some people can develop scars that are thick and raised. A number of topical treatments are available to soften and smooth abnormal scarring.

- **Seroma:** Fluid that pools under the skin is called a seroma. Small seromas may resolve on their own, but large ones may require drainage.

- **Hematoma:** Blood that collects beneath the skin is called a hematoma. If a hematoma doesn't dissolve on its own, your surgeon may need to drain it.

- **Blood clots:** Blood clots can develop due to surgery or immobility and are potentially life-threatening if they break off and travel to the lungs. Blood thinning medication or other treatment may be necessary to dissolve blood clots.

- **Pneumonia:** Sometimes it hurts to take a deep breath after surgery, so a patient may choose to take only shallow breaths. This can lead to pneumonia, which can be a serious complication that requires additional treatment. Surgeons usually recommend that patients do deep-breathing exercises to help prevent pneumonia.

You may be comforted to know that a majority of patients don't experience any complications following surgical procedures either in the United States or abroad. In addition, it's important to understand that minor complications are the most common, and serious complications are the least common. In fact, life-threatening complications are considered rare.

If you think you're experiencing a complication after your procedure, don't hesitate to contact your overseas surgeon. In some cases, your surgeon may be able to calm your fears and reassure you that what you're experiencing is completely normal. In the event that you actually do have a complication, your doctor can take quick action to treat you if needed.

# Get Copies of Your Paperwork from the Medical Facility

When your procedure is over and you're ready to leave the hospital, outpatient clinic, or dentist's office, be sure to get copies of everything in your file. Your medical records are very important, and you should add all of your overseas records to your own personal health record.

## Prescriptions

Obtain copies of any prescriptions your overseas doctor gives you. This can be helpful for a few reasons. First, if you're taking any of the prescribed medications back home with you, you may need to present them to airport security or customs. In addition, it's always a good idea to have a record of any medications you've taken and how you responded to them. For example, if you experienced severe side effects, such as nausea and vomiting, from a pain medication, you may want to remember the name of the drug so you can avoid it in the future.

## Medical Reports, Lab Test Results, and Imaging Reports

Ask your surgeon to provide you with copies of all your medical reports and lab test results, as well as any x-rays, magnetic resonance images (MRIs), or other imaging reports. Having these documents in your file can come in handy if you ever need to see another doctor for follow-up. Even if you don't require any follow-up treatment, it's still important to have these items in your medical file.

## Physical Therapy Recommendations

If you're having a procedure that requires a lot of physical therapy, such as knee or hip replacement, secure a copy of your doctor's physical therapy instructions. After you return home, it'll be up to you to continue with your physical therapy. Sometimes it can be confusing to remember exactly what you're supposed to do, so having the instructions in writing helps ensure that you'll do the exercises correctly.

## Get a Receipt

Never leave the medical facility without getting a copy of your bill or at least a receipt for what you've paid. Compare the amount on this receipt with the amount charged to your credit card when you receive your credit card bill. This is yet another way to ensure that you've paid the proper amount for your treatment.

# Non-Medical Post-Op Advice

When you're on the mend, and you're ready to head back home, it's time to start thinking about the travel portion of your return trip. Unfortunately, if you've had major surgery, your flight home may be very uncomfortable, especially if you're taking a long trans-Pacific flight.

Here's a quick checklist of post-op travel tips:

❏ Double check flight times the day before you're scheduled to leave because departure times can change.

❏ Arrange for transportation from your hotel to the airport.

❏ Arrange for transportation from the airport to your home.

❏ Pack a few snacks for the flight.

❏ Keep your most important things in your carry-on bag.

❏ Get to the airport at least two hours before departure.

❏ If necessary, contact your airline to arrange for a wheelchair. Be sure to let them know that you have a doctor's note.

❏ Ask to be seated in a bulkhead or exit row for more legroom.

❏ Ask for an aisle seat so you don't have to climb over people to get in and out of your seat.

❏ Be sure to walk around the cabin as often as possible.

❏ Do in-flight leg exercises to help prevent blood clots.

By taking these steps, you can make your return trip a more comfortable and stress-free experience.

## The Least You Need to Know

◆ Planning for your recovery can prevent post-op misery.

◆ A variety of pain control options are available.

◆ Post-op instructions are designed to keep your recovery on track.

◆ If you have post-op concerns, you can contact your surgeon.

◆ You should be given copies of your medical records.

◆ A little preparation can make your flight home more comfortable.

# Chapter 22

# Recovering At Home

## In This Chapter

- ◆ Why you'll need help around the house at first
- ◆ How to prepare your home to improve your comfort
- ◆ Where you can go for post-op treatment if you need it
- ◆ Why you can't slack off on your physical therapy
- ◆ When you can return to work and your normal routine

One of the benefits of recuperating in a foreign country is that you're far away from the stresses of everyday life, which allows you to concentrate solely on getting better. But when you get back home, you'll be faced with all of those routine responsibilities—work, grocery shopping, cooking dinner, washing the dishes, getting the kids ready for school, and more. If you're like many patients, you may feel compelled to dive right back into your normal schedule. Don't!

Depending on the procedure you've had, you may need some additional time to recuperate at home. Even if you've healed well from your surgery, you may have a serious case of jet lag. Plan on taking it easy around the house for a while and slowly easing back into your usual activities.

# Get Some Help at Home

Usually, by the time you return home, you'll be well on your way to feeling like you're back to normal. Even so, you may want to enlist a little help with some routine household chores for the first few days or weeks while you continue to heal. Think about it: even if you've healed well from your surgery, do you really want to be out mowing the lawn or doing major housework right after you return home from an overseas trip? Probably not.

Jet lag, in addition to your surgery, can cause fatigue, irritability, a lack of concentration, and an inability to perform simple everyday functions. Basically, it can leave you feeling out of it. Add that to any post-op symptoms you're still experiencing, and you can see that you may not be able to tackle your usual chores.

**Check-Up**

Jet lag affects more than 90 percent of passengers on long-haul flights. In general, it's said that for every hour of time zone difference between your home and your destination, you'll need approximately one full day to recover. For a trip to South America, recovery might take four or five days, but for a voyage to Southeast Asia, it could take more than a couple of weeks.

Based on my own experiences and those of my clients, jet lag seems worse after the trip home. Perhaps there's so much excitement involved in arriving in an exotic destination and anticipating your surgical procedure that you don't feel the jet lag. When you return home, however, you're more likely to be exhausted from the whole ordeal.

If you've had orthopedic surgery, a spinal procedure, or some other procedure that requires a lengthier recuperation, you'll definitely need some assistance around the house. Ask your traveling companion, a friend, or a family member to pitch in with things like yard work, housecleaning, and grocery shopping. Or use some of your savings from your medical travel excursion and splurge on a maid or gardening service for a few weeks.

Sometimes after major surgical procedures, or if you've come home after just a few days abroad, you might need more than just household help. If you feel like you would benefit from having a nurse or a nurse's aide assist you with your return home, you can hire a trained professional. A nurse can help you get settled and can train your family members to properly assist you. You can hire a nurse for a single day or for as many days as you feel it's necessary. Sure, this will add to the total cost of your trip, but it could be worth the extra expense. Hiring a professional, even for a short time period, can ensure that you and your family understand exactly what's necessary for you to make a speedy recovery at home.

# Make Sure Your House Is Prepared

Coming home to a house that's prepped for your arrival can do wonders for your recovery and your mood. By preparing your home before your departure, or by having your family get the house ready while you're gone, you can concentrate on recovering rather than worrying about the little things. In this section, I detail some of the things you and your family can do to make your home more comfortable.

## Get Equipped

If you're going to need any medical equipment or devices—such as a cane or a toilet extender—when you return home, get them beforehand or have your family buy them before you get back. By anticipating these needs and securing this equipment in advance, you can save yourself a lot of discomfort upon your return.

Nonmedical gear can be just as useful. For instance, make sure you have several extra pillows available. You may need to place these under your back, knees, or arms as per your doctor's orders. As previously mentioned, after certain procedures, holding a pillow to your chest can minimize the pain you might otherwise feel when you cough or take a deep breath.

You also may need something to protect your bed and your furniture from draining bodily fluids. After some cosmetic surgery, such as liposuction, bodily fluids drain from the incisions for anywhere from a few days to a few weeks. When you're resting at home, these fluids can leak onto couches, chairs, and beds. A simple solution is to head to the nearest pet store where you can buy "piddle pads," absorbent pads designed to protect carpets and rugs while puppies are being housetrained. They also work extremely well to keep furniture from being ruined by post-surgical drainage.

## Stock Up on Food Staples

If you load up the kitchen cupboards with basics, fill the refrigerator shelves with your favorite beverages, and stock the freezer with frozen dinners or other pre-cooked meals before you leave for your trip, it'll make your homecoming that much sweeter.

After a long flight home, you probably won't want to head right back out to go grocery shopping or to grab a bite to eat in a local restaurant. Having something at home that you can just pop in the microwave can give you time to decompress and relax after your long voyage.

## CASE STUDY

| | |
|---|---|
| Name: | Georgia |
| Age at time of surgery: | 46 |
| Residence: | Alaska |
| Procedure: | Tummy tuck, liposuction, and a lower blepharoplasty |
| Destination country: | Malaysia |
| Cost in United States: | $39,000 |
| Total cost abroad (travel included): | $13,000 |

Georgia had worked as a cop and in the medical industry before she hurt her back and had to go on disability. The back injury severely limited the exercises she could do and that resulted in weight gain. Discouraged, she started thinking about a tummy tuck and liposuction to help her regain her figure.

One day, she ran into a friend who for more than 10 years had been bent over due to agonizing knee pain. The woman was now standing upright and walking without any trouble. Her secret? A medical travel voyage to Southeast Asia where she had a knee replacement operation.

This chance encounter got Georgia thinking about medical tourism as an option for her own cosmetic procedures. She contacted the medical travel agency the other woman had used, and started doing some serious research on the plastic surgeon being recommended. "I liked the fact that he was board-certified in the U.S. and had practiced in the U.S. for more than 20 years," she says.

After she met with the surgeon overseas, Georgia asked about a few other possible procedures—lower eyelid surgery and a face lift. What really impressed Georgia is that the surgeon didn't jump at the chance to pad his wallet with the additional procedures. "He had me lie down and hold a mirror up to my face, and asked me if I liked what I saw in the mirror better than what I saw when I was standing up. I told him I didn't really see that much difference. That's when he told me, 'Then you aren't ready for a face lift,'" she explains. "He could have just said, 'Yes, let's do the face lift,' and he would have earned more money, but he didn't." That really impressed her.

Over the next two days, she had a tummy tuck, the lower eyelid procedure, and liposuction on her inner and outer thighs, hips, love handles, bra bulge, and inner knees. She spent three days in the hospital wearing a compression garment that went from her armpits to her ankles. Yes, it was painful and she was uncomfortable, but she had five nurses attending to her needs.

Because Georgia spent 22 days recovering overseas, she was feeling fine by the time she returned home. Sure, she needed time to get reacclimated and catch up on her sleep, but she feels like she could have gone back to an office job within a week of her homecoming. Even though she felt pretty good, Georgia treated herself and tried to take it easy, which was hard for her considering she's a real go-getter. Instead of cooking during that first week or so, she ordered meals from a caterer's gourmet meal service.

The whole experience, from the planning stages to the recovery, turned out positive for Georgia, who's very happy with her results. "I went from a size 16 to a size 8 skirt," she says. "I lost five inches around my waist, 4.5 inches from my hips, and my thighs went from 26 inches to 22. I even bought my first bikini in more than 20 years."

Of course, it doesn't make any sense to stock up on perishables, such as milk, fruits, or vegetables, prior to your departure because they'll probably go bad before you return home. You may want to have family members at home pick up these staples a day or two before you come back, or you can wait a day or so after your return to shop for these items.

When food shopping, remember to abide by any special dietary restrictions set by your physician. If you've had facial plastic surgery, you may need to stick to a soft diet for a certain time period. After cardiac procedures, you may be required to follow a strict regimen. Similarly, after bariatric procedures, you may have lifelong eating restrictions. By being aware of these dietary needs ahead of time, you can plan accordingly by purchasing the appropriate foods for your recovery at home.

> **Doctor's Orders**
>
> Even if you don't feel hungry after having surgery, it's important to include some protein in your post-op diet. Protein is essential for tissue repair and often is recommended following surgery because it promotes healing. That means that eating protein during your recovery can help you heal faster.

## Have Books, Magazines, and DVDs on Hand

If you're still required to take it easy for a while after you get back from your medical voyage, be aware that boredom can quickly set in when you're just hanging around the house recuperating. To keep from going stir crazy, make sure you have a good supply of entertainment on hand. Set your DVR to record your favorite television shows while you're away, and have some books, magazines, and DVDs ready for you when you get back home.

# Coordinate Post-Op Care With a Local Medical Provider

As mentioned earlier, your best course of action is to consult with your local doctor, if you have one, before your departure to ensure that he or she will be willing to continue to care for you when you return. If you're one of the many Americans who don't have a regular doctor, you still have options if you require follow-up care after you get back home.

**Check-Up**

Did you know that there are about 9,000 urgent care centers located throughout the United States? To find an urgent care center in your area, visit the Urgent Care Association of America website at http://www.ucaoa.org/buyers/ucaoa_orgs.php.

In the event that you need minor follow-up treatment—say, removing a few stitches or removing a drain—and you don't have a regular doctor, consider going to the nearest urgent care facility. Urgent care centers are open evenings and weekends and see patients on a walk-in basis—no appointment necessary. Visits to these facilities typically cost less than emergency room visits. Of course, if you're experiencing a true medical emergency, don't hesitate to call 911 or go to the nearest emergency room.

# Keep Doing Your Physical Therapy

Just because you're back home doesn't mean you can slack off on your physical therapy. If your overseas surgeon recommends that you do some form of post-op physical therapy, by all means, continue doing the exercises for the prescribed time period. In some cases, this will include doing the prescribed exercises on your own after you've returned home. Following through with your physician's recommendations can make a world of difference in the overall success of your procedure, so stick with the program.

# What To Do When Complications Occur

In general, the most common post-op complications occur within the first week or so after surgery. This is one of the main reasons why foreign physicians recommend that international patients spend one or more weeks recuperating in the destination country. Overseas physicians want to ensure that they can treat you in the event of a complication. If you spend the recommended time length abroad, your risk of developing a complication after you return home will be diminished.

In the event that you do experience complications after your return, contact your overseas physician, your medical travel agency, or the international hospital. They may be able to advise you about treatment options. In some instances, they may suggest that you visit a local physician for treatment. If you don't have a regular doctor, you can visit an urgent care center. For life-threatening emergencies, call 911 immediately or go to the nearest emergency room.

# Returning to Everyday Activities

Your surgeon will let you know when you can resume normal activities such as driving and exercise. For minor procedures, including many forms of dental work, you may be able to get behind the wheel or hit the gym soon after your return.

With cosmetic procedures, the area of the body that has been treated will likely determine when you'll be able to maneuver a car safely and without pain. For instance, after a nose job, you can usually drive after just a few days. However, you won't be able to do any strenuous exercise for about six weeks after having your nose reshaped.

Having cosmetic breast surgery, such as augmentation, can make driving a painful proposition. It may take a few weeks before you feel comfortable using your arms to steer the car. If you've had a tummy tuck, you'll probably need several weeks before you get behind the wheel.

> **Doctor's Orders**
>
> If you've had any kind of abdominal surgery, make driving or riding in a car more comfortable by placing a small pillow over your abdomen and putting the seatbelt over the pillow to protect the surgical area.

For major procedures that are medically necessary, including hip replacement, you'll probably be instructed to avoid driving for about six weeks. In the meantime, you'll need to have friends or family chauffeur you wherever you need to go. Getting back to any kind of strenuous exercise after joint replacement surgery or spinal procedures will be a slow process. Follow your doctor's orders regarding returning to various activities.

# Going Back to Work

One of the most common questions we hear is, "When will I be able to go back to work?" Unfortunately, there's no easy answer. Your ability to return to work will depend on the kind of work you do, the type of procedure you're having, your individual situation, and how quickly you recuperate. Some medical travelers are back to work a few days after returning home. Others need a week or more before getting back on the job.

**Code Blue!**

Coordinate with your supervisors and co-workers before your departure to ensure that your workload will be covered in your absence. The last thing you need when you aren't feeling 100 percent is to be faced with a huge backlog of tasks when you return to work.

Even if you're anxious to get back to work because you need the income, don't schedule your return for the day after you get back home. You'll probably be too exhausted from the surgical experience and the international travel to bounce back the very next day. Give yourself a few days to get adjusted before heading back to the office.

You may even want to consider initially going back to work part-time or half-days. Many medical tourists find that they get fatigued quickly and can't make it through an entire eight-hour day. If you initially schedule half-days, you can help yourself ease back into your job without wearing yourself out.

# Getting Back to Normal

There's no doubt that the medical travel process is a lengthy and trying endeavor. However, as the weeks and months pass after your procedure, you'll find yourself getting back in the swing of things. Eventually, the bruising, swelling, and other telltale signs of your surgical experience—along with the jet lag—will fade away, and you'll simply be able to enjoy the results of your procedure.

Whether you've had cosmetic surgery, a smile makeover, or a medically necessary procedure, you'll love the fact that you're looking better and feeling better. Like the many satisfied medical tourists profiled in this book, you may want to spread the news about your overseas medical trip. Who knows? Your story just might inspire somebody else to go globetrotting for a safe, successful, and affordable medical procedure overseas.

## The Least You Need To Know

- ◆ You may need assistance with everyday chores.
- ◆ Hiring a nurse for a day or so can be helpful.
- ◆ Having your home prepared in advance will make your return more pleasant.
- ◆ If you need medical treatment, you have a number of options.
- ◆ Sticking with your physical therapy program is a must.
- ◆ You don't have to immediately return to work full-time.

# A

# Destination Countries

## Argentina (Buenos Aires)

Argentina emerged as an attractive medical tourism destination in 2002 following the collapse of the Argentinian peso. This resulted in favorable exchange rates for American tourists visiting Argentina for cosmetic surgery, dentistry, or other medical procedures. Argentina offers some of the lowest prices for dental work, but its prices for plastic surgery and other medical procedures tend to be on the higher end of the spectrum.

Buenos Aires, the nation's largest city and capital, is considered the Paris of Latin America. This cosmopolitan city also is known for its advanced health-care system and highly skilled doctors. In particular, it's earned a reputation among medical tourists for dentistry and plastic surgery. It's estimated that 1 in 30 Argentineans have had at least one plastic surgery procedure.

Cosmetic surgery's popularity in Argentina has sparked a boom in plastic surgery outpatient clinics, with many clinics located in Buenos Aires. If you're considering traveling to Argentina, be aware that English isn't commonly spoken, so you may need a translator.

# Travel Notes

**Languages spoken:** Spanish, some English

**People:** European, Mestizo, and Indian

**Personality:** Warm and friendly

**Infrastructure:** First World

**Currency:** Peso

**Time zone:** GMT–3

**Country phone code:** 54

**Electricity:** 220V, 50Hz

**Weights and measures:** Metric system

**Elevation concerns:** None

**Climate:** Located south of the equator, summer is from December to February, and winter is from June to September. Temperatures in Buenos Aires range from about 50 degrees Fahrenheit in the winter to about 94 degrees in the summer.

**Clothing:** In the summer, shorts are a must. Evenings can be chilly, so it is wise to bring a jacket. In the winter, a light jacket is usually warm enough.

**Getting online:** Fax, Internet, and e-mail services typically are available in all major hotels and in cybercafés.

**Visa required:** No

**Immunizations required:** None

**Public health considerations:** Avoid drinking tap water.

# Cultural Do's and Don'ts

- Do use professional titles with last names (for example, Dr. Baum).
- Do make eye contact when communicating.
- Do learn a little Spanish when going to Argentina.
- Don't use first names until you are asked to do so.

◆ Don't make unflattering comparisons between North America and South America.

◆ Don't ask personal questions until you've established a good relationship.

## Hospitals

Despite the influx of medical travelers from the United States, Argentina's hospitals have not made great strides to earn international accreditation. Plastic surgery clinics in Argentina don't require accreditation, so I am hesitant to recommend any specific clinics. I can, however, recommend a dental clinic that offers very low prices and high quality.

Clinica Dental Dentistry (CDD)
Virrey Olaguer y Feliu 2462 #4 B
Ciudad Autónoma de Buenos Aires
Argentina C1426EBB
www.dentistry.com.ar/en_index.html
Telephone number: 011-54-11-4788-5226
Specialties: Dental implants, cosmetic
dentistry

At CDD, you'll find the same advanced technology you would find in the top dental clinics in the United States, Canada, and Europe. The U.S. Embassy, the Australian Embassy, and many leading American corporations located in Buenos Aires entrust their smiles to this clinic. CDD houses four dental offices, an operating room, and an on-site dental lab in which crowns, bridges, and other dental devices can be fabricated.

## Average Procedure Costs in Argentina

| Procedures | Average Prices |
| --- | --- |
| *Cosmetic* | |
| Face/neck lift | $3,900 |
| Blepharoplasty (upper/lower eyelids) | $2,100 |
| Rhinoplasty | $2,800 |
| Brow/forehead lift | $2,000 |
| Otoplasty | $1,600 |

*continues*

## Average Procedure Costs in Argentina   (continued)

| Procedures | Average Prices |
| --- | --- |
| Liposuction (per area) | $1,300 |
| Tummy tuck | $5,600 |
| Breast augmentation | $5,000 |
| Breast lift | $3,700 |
| Inner thigh lift | $2,900 |
| Outer thigh lift | $3,900 |
| Buttock lift | $2,700 |
| Lower body lift (inner/outer thighs, buttock) | $8,300 |

*Medical*

### Orthopedics

| | |
| --- | --- |
| Hip replacement (per hip) | $13,000 |
| Hip resurfacing | $13,000 |
| Knee replacement (per knee) | $11,000 |
| Knee replacement (both knees) | $18,000 |

### Spinal Procedures

| | |
| --- | --- |
| Spinal fusion | $14,000 |
| Spinal disc replacement | $16,000 |

### Cardiology

| | |
| --- | --- |
| Angiogram | $1,700 |
| CT angiography scan | $600 |
| Aortic aneurysm surgery | $18,000 |
| Bypass Surgery CAB | $14,000 |
| Coronary angioplasty (one stent and one balloon) | $7,000 |

### Obstetrics and Gynecology

| | |
| --- | --- |
| Hysterectomy | $6,000 |

### General Surgery

| | |
| --- | --- |
| Diagnostic laparoscopy | $1,900 |
| Gallbladder removal | $3,900 |
| Hernia repair | $1,900 |

| Procedures | Average Prices |
|---|:---:|
| **Dentistry** | |
| Crowns | $250 |
| Veneers | $150 |
| Implants | $550 |
| Bridges | $200 |
| Bone grafts | $300 |
| Root canal | $160 |
| Extractions | $80 |

# Brazil (São Paulo, Porto Alegre, and Rio de Janeiro)

Beauty and the beach—that's what you can find in Brazil, which has been hailed as the "plastic surgery capital of the world." The Brazilian Society of Plastic Surgery (SBCP) boasts approximately 4,000 members, giving Brazil the world's highest number of plastic surgeons per capita. The country has earned worldwide renown as a leader and innovator in the aesthetic plastic surgery field. In fact, one of Brazil's most renowned plastic surgeons, Dr. Ivo Pitanguy, has been called the "father of modern cosmetic surgery."

Brazil's prowess in body contouring and other beautification treatments has attracted hordes of international patients. But don't expect rock-bottom prices when traveling to Brazil for cosmetic procedures. Some of the nation's most successful surgeons command prices that near those in the United States, although it is possible to achieve prices that are about one-third to one-half lower than in the United States.

Thousands of outpatient plastic surgery clinics and day hospitals are scattered throughout Brazil, especially in its largest cities, São Paulo and Rio de Janeiro. Prices may be slightly lower in smaller, charming cities such as Porto Alegre.

There is a significant language barrier in Brazil. Although some doctors speak some English, many nurses and medical personnel do not. On top of that, most hospital websites aren't written in English. Few plastic surgeons have personal websites, so it can be difficult to track down qualified doctors.

# Travel Notes

**Languages spoken:** Portuguese, some English

**People:** Native Indians, Africans, and Europeans

**Personality:** Warm and friendly

**Infrastructure:** First World

**Currency:** Real

**Time zone:** GMT–3

**Country phone code:** 55

**Electricity:** 110V or 220V, 60Hz

**Weights and measures:** Metric system

**Elevation concerns:** None

**Climate:** São Paulo has a mild climate with an average temperature of 66 degrees Fahrenheit. A subtropical climate in Porto Alegre includes freezing temperatures in winter. In Rio de Janeiro, you can expect warm weather most of the year. Remember, Brazil is in the southern hemisphere, so winter is from June to August and summer is from December to February.

**Clothing:** Depending on the time of year and the location, you may need light summer clothing or warmer options. Casual clothing is usually acceptable.

**Getting online:** Fax, Internet, and e-mail services typically are available in all major hotels and in cybercafés.

**Visa required:** Yes (approximately $130 fee)

**Immunizations required:** None; a yellow fever vaccination is recommended if you're traveling to certain areas of Brazil

**Public health considerations:** Yellow fever is a concern in some areas, but not in most coastal areas. Avoid drinking tap water.

# Cultural Do's and Don'ts

- Do use professional titles with last names (for example, Dr. Baum).
- Do make eye contact when communicating.
- Do learn a little Portuguese (remember, Brazil is not Spanish speaking).

- ◆ Do use taxis instead of buses.

- ◆ Do know where you are going at all times.

- ◆ Don't walk alone outside after dark.

- ◆ Don't bring valuables on your trip.

- ◆ Don't drink excessive amounts of alcohol.

# Hospitals

In Brazil, most plastic surgeons operate out of clinics or day hospitals, which aren't accredited by the same organizations that offer hospital accreditation. This makes it difficult to judge whether these facilities meet international standards for quality and safety. In addition, I must caution that these outpatient clinics may not be equipped to handle major complications that can occur during surgery. Because of this concern, I recommend having surgery in an accredited hospital rather than in a clinic. A few hospitals meet the high standards required for Joint Commission International (JCI) accreditation.

Hospital Moinhos de Vento
Rua Tiradentes 333
Bairro Moinhos de Vento
Porto Alegre, RS, Brazil
www.hmv.org.br/content/home/Default01.aspx (in Portuguese)
Telephone number: 011-55-51-3314-3434

Accreditation/certification: JCI

Specialties: Breast center, cardiology, neurology and neurosurgery, orthopedics, and oncology

Considered one of the top hospitals in all of Latin America, Moinhos de Vento Hospital was established in 1927. The facility has made a commitment to modernization and technological advances. A major expansion was completed in 2004 that included building additional facilities and making significant technological updates.

Albert Einstein Jewish Hospital (AEJH)
Av. Albert Einstein, 627/701
Morumbi, São Paulo, SP, CEP
Brazil 05651-901
www.einstein.br/ingles/ (in English)
Telephone number: 011-55-11-3747-1233

Accreditation/certification: JCI (first hospital outside the United States to earn JCI accreditation in 1999), International Organization of Standards (ISO) 9001:2000, and ISO 14001:1996

Inaugurated in 1971, AEJH now contracts with nearly 4,500 registered physicians, 500 of whom are staff employees. It offers international patient support services, including translation, appointment scheduling, and more. Recognized for its cutting-edge technology, its surgeons perform the most liver transplants in all of Latin America. To alleviate some of the anxiety that comes with a hospital stay, the hospital strives to be as welcoming as a five-star hotel and to make patients feel at home.

Specialties: Among more than 30 specialties are cardiology, neurology, oncology, and transplants

Ivo Pitanguy Clinic
Rua Dona Mariana, 65
Botafogo, Rio de Janeiro, RJ
Brazil 22280-020
www.pitanguy.com.br/en/clinica/clinica.htm
Telephone number: 011-55-21-2266-9500

Dr. Ivo Pitanguy is widely recognized as the world's leading pioneer in plastic surgery. Originally trained in plastic surgery in the United States during the 1940s, he returned to Brazil where he founded his own clinic as well as the Pitanguy Institute in 1963. The Pitanguy Institute, which offers training in plastic surgery techniques, has since awarded diplomas to more than 500 students from 40 countries. More than 50,000 patients have had some form of plastic surgery in the clinic, which has four fully equipped operating rooms.

Specialties: All types of plastic and reconstructive surgery, and hair transplants

# Average Procedure Costs in Brazil

| Procedures | Average Prices |
| --- | --- |
| *Cosmetic* | |
| Face/neck lift | $3,900 |
| Blepharoplasty (upper/lower eyelids) | $2,100 |
| Rhinoplasty | $2,800 |
| Brow/forehead lift | $2,000 |

| Procedures | Average Prices |
| --- | --- |
| Otoplasty | $1,600 |
| Liposuction (per area) | $1,300 |
| Tummy tuck | $5,600 |
| Breast augmentation | $5,000 |
| Breast lift | $3,700 |
| Inner thigh lift | $2,900 |
| Outer thigh lift | $3,900 |
| Buttock lift | $2,700 |
| Lower body lift (inner/outer thighs, buttock) | $8,300 |

### *Medical*

### Orthopedics

| | |
| --- | --- |
| Hip replacement (per hip) | $13,000 |
| Hip resurfacing | $13,000 |
| Knee replacement (per knee) | $11,000 |
| Knee replacement (both knees) | $18,000 |

### Spinal Procedures

| | |
| --- | --- |
| Spinal fusion | $14,000 |
| Spinal disc replacement | $16,000 |

### Cardiology

| | |
| --- | --- |
| Angiogram | $1,700 |
| CT angiography scan | $600 |
| Aortic aneurysm surgery | $18,000 |
| Bypass surgery CAB | $14,000 |
| Coronary Angioplasty (one stent and one balloon) | $7,000 |

### Obstetrics and Gynecology

| | |
| --- | --- |
| Hysterectomy | $6,000 |

### General Surgery

| | |
| --- | --- |
| Diagnostic laparoscopy | $1,900 |
| Gallbladder removal | $3,900 |
| Hernia repair | $1,900 |

*continues*

## Average Procedure Costs in Brazil   (continued)

| Procedures | Average Prices |
| --- | --- |
| **Dentistry** | |
| Crowns | $225–$1,000 |
| Veneers | $60–$350 |
| Implants | $650–$3,000 |
| Bridges | $250 |
| Bone grafts | $400–$750 |
| Root canal | $165–$250 |
| Extractions | $120–$150 |

# China (Beijing and Hong Kong)

Some Westerners are intrigued by China's stem cell treatments, which are still considered experimental in the United States. But to date, China hasn't captured much of the medical tourism market. Why not? "The infrastructure just isn't there yet," according to Dr. Steven Tucker, president of the International Medical Travel Association and founder and director of the Pacific Cancer Center in Singapore. However, China's health industry is hoping to change that.

The 2008 Olympics in Beijing pushed the world's most populous nation into the limelight. The country's health officials are hoping to use that world stage to generate interest in China as a medical tourism destination. With the 2008 Olympics, China focused on improving its health-care facilities and processes to appeal to foreign patients. In addition, Beijing doctors treating foreign patients were required to speak and write in English.

In the former British colony of Hong Kong, English is more widely spoken than in Beijing. This cosmopolitan spot has long been a hub for tourists, and is beginning to promote its private hospitals as destinations for medical tourists.

## Travel Notes

**Languages spoken:** Mandarin, Cantonese, and English (in Hong Kong)

**People:** Han Chinese (the largest ethnic group)

**Personality:** Polite and efficient

**Infrastructure:** First World in Beijing and Hong Kong

**Currency:** Yuan Renminbi in mainland China; Hong Kong dollar in Hong Kong

**Time zone:** GMT+8

**Country phone code:** 86 in mainland China; 852 in Hong Kong

**Electricity:** 220V, 50Hz

**Weights and measures:** Metric system

**Elevation concerns:** None in Beijing

**Climate:** Beijing and Hong Kong summers are rainy and hot, hot, hot, with highs over 100 degrees Fahrenheit. Winters in Beijing are freezing with temps below 0 degrees. Hong Kong winters are mild. Fall offers some of the best weather in both locations.

**Clothing:** American-style clothing is acceptable.

**Getting online:** Fax, Internet, and e-mail services typically are available in all major hotels and in cybercafés.

**Visa required:** Yes, for mainland China; no, for Hong Kong

**Immunizations required:** None

**Public health considerations:** Air pollution can be a concern. Avoid drinking the tap water.

# Cultural Do's and Don'ts

- ◆ Do avoid conflict.

- ◆ Do avoid embarrassment.

- ◆ Do remember that names are in reverse order from English; for example, Dr. Wu Chuan is Dr. Wu.

- ◆ Don't rush to fill silences in conversations.

- ◆ Don't bring up politics.

- ◆ Don't bow; the Chinese have largely dropped this habit.

# Hospitals

Because Hong Kong was a British colony, its numerous private hospitals have long adhered to British standards for quality control and safety. Now, many also are seeking JCI accreditation to increase their appeal to Western medical tourists. Private hospitals in Beijing also are jumping on the JCI accreditation bandwagon in an effort to woo foreign patients.

Beijing United Family Hospital
#2 Jiangtai Lu
Chaoyang District
Beijing, China 100016
www.unitedfamilyhospitals.com/en 11.asp?id=6&sid=63&rights=1
Telephone number: 011-86-10-5927-7000

Accreditation/certification: JCI

Specialties: Dermatology, eye clinic, general surgery, gynecology, and dentistry

A pioneering health-care organization, United Family Hospitals and Clinics provides comprehensive integrated health-care services. The international group's first Western-style health-care facility in China, Beijing United Family Hospital, opened its doors in 1997. In 2004, the group opened the Shanghai United Family Hospital, and plans are in the works to expand into other locations throughout China. Many of the medical providers at these hospitals have international training and experience. English is widely spoken in the Beijing facility, which offers concierge services to assist foreign patients with transportation and lodging.

Hong Kong Adventist Hospital
40 Stubbs Road
Hong Kong
www.hkah.org.hk/new/eng/index.htm
Telephone number: 011-852-3651-8888

Accreditation/certification: JCI, Trent

Specialties: CyberKnife center, cardiac, and general surgery

Part of a global network of more than 160 hospitals, this private, not-for-profit hospital has long been catering to international patients. One of the hospital's main attractions is its CyberKnife Center, which opened in 2006. CyberKnife is a highly advance radiosurgical system that is used to destroy tumors.

## Average Procedure Costs in China

| Procedures | Average Prices |
|---|---|
| *Cosmetic* | |
| Face/Neck lift | $3,600 |
| Blepharoplasty (upper/lower eyelids) | $2,000 |
| Rhinoplasty | $2,600 |
| Brow/forehead lift | $1,900 |
| Otoplasty | $1,500 |
| Liposuction (per area) | $1,200 |
| Tummy tuck | $5,200 |
| Breast augmentation | $4,100 |
| Breast lift | $3,500 |
| Inner thigh lift | $3,600 |
| Outer thigh lift | $3,600 |
| Buttock lift | $2,500 |
| Lower body lift (inner/outer thighs, buttock) | $7,800 |
| *Medical* | |
| **Orthopedics** | |
| Hip replacement (per hip) | $12,500 |
| Hip resurfacing | $12,500 |
| Knee replacement (per knee) | $10,200 |
| Knee replacement (both knees) | $17,400 |
| **Spinal Procedures** | |
| Spinal fusion | $13,400 |
| Spinal disc replacement | $15,300 |
| **Cardiology** | |
| Angiogram | $1,600 |
| CT angiography scan | $600 |
| Aortic aneurysm surgery | $17,200 |
| Bypass surgery CAB | $13,200 |
| Coronary angioplasty (one stent and one balloon) | $6,700 |

*continues*

## Average Procedure Costs in China    (continued)

| Procedures | Average Prices |
|---|---|
| **Obstetrics and Gynecology** | |
| Hysterectomy | $5,500 |
| **General Surgery** | |
| Diagnostic laparoscopy | $1,600 |
| Gallbladder removal | $3,600 |
| Hernia repair | $1,700 |
| **Dentistry** | |
| Crowns | $200–$900 |
| Veneers | $60–$350 |
| Implants | $600–$2,750 |
| Bridges | $250 |
| Bone grafts | $350–$700 |
| Root canal | $125–$250 |
| Extractions | $125–$200 |

# Costa Rica (San José)

Considered the jewel of Central America, Costa Rica is an oasis of serenity. With its lush rainforests and pristine beaches, it is a perennial favorite among the ecotourism crowd. Costa Rica also is earning a reputation as an excellent destination for medical tourism thanks to its proximity to the United States; its affordable prices; and its world-class hospitals, plastic surgery clinics, and dental clinics. A host of recovery retreats featuring 24/7 nursing care and homey rooms add to the attraction.

Cosmetic surgery and cosmetic dentistry definitely are the main draws, although bariatric, orthopedic, and eye procedures are being sought at an increasing rate. The small Central American nation boasts a cadre of internationally trained and board-certified surgeons, many of whom are bilingual. Many of its hospitals and clinics are state-of-the-art facilities that use the latest medical equipment and technology.

Medical providers in Costa Rica actively are catering to U.S. medical tourists. Many hospitals, surgeons, dental clinics, and recovery retreats have created websites in English to entice U.S. patients. Additionally, international patient centers are common in the major hospitals and can assist you with planning.

# Travel Notes

**Languages spoken:** Spanish (official language), but English is widely spoken

**People:** European, mestizo, African, and indigenous; Costa Ricans call themselves "ticos"

**Personality:** Courteous and gregarious

**Infrastructure:** First World

**Currency:** Colón

**Time zone:** GMT–6

**Country phone code:** 506

**Electricity:** 110V, 60Hz

**Weights and measures:** Metric system

**Elevation concerns:** None

**Climate:** The climate in Costa Rica is tropical and subtropical, with a dry season (December to April) and a rainy season (May to November). The temperature in San José ranges from a high of 73 to 78 degrees Fahrenheit, to a low of 59 to 62 degrees. The hottest months are March, April, and May.

**Clothing:** Casual clothing is acceptable, but conservative dress is customary in big cities. Shorts are acceptable only in beach areas.

**Getting online:** Fax, Internet, and e-mail services typically are available in all major hotels and in cybercafés.

**Visa required:** No

**Immunizations required:** None

**Public health considerations:** Avoid drinking tap water, and avoid raw fruits and vegetables unless you peel them.

# Cultural Do's and Don'ts

- ◆ Do learn some basic Spanish phrases.
- ◆ Do your exploring with a friend or companion, not alone.
- ◆ Do make a copy of your passport to carry with you (picture page and entry stamp).

- Do your research so you know what to expect.

- Do bring mosquito repellant.

- Don't litter or take things away from the rainforests and beaches.

- Don't expect flawless and swift service.

- Don't get in a taxi without agreeing on the fare prior to accepting a ride.

- Don't bring expensive jewelry.

- Don't travel to Costa Rica during Semana Santa (Easter week), when most businesses close.

# Hospitals

Costa Rica is home to two international hospitals that cater to foreigners seeking high-quality, affordable medical care. These medical facilities—which are staffed with bilingual, board-certified surgeons—treat thousands of foreign patients each year. Costa Rica also is renowned for superior dental work.

Hospital Center for International Medicine Advanced (CIMA) San José
San José, Costa Rica
www.cimahospital.com/
Telephone number: 011-506-2208-1000

Accreditation/certification: JCI accreditation in process

Specialties: Cosmetic surgery, orthopedics, and ophthalmology

With approximately 160 internationally trained physicians in more than 50 medical specialties, CIMA offers cutting-edge, multidisciplinary treatments. The hospital includes a complete imaging department, a full-service lab, and a 24-hour pharmacy. CIMA currently is in the process of receiving JCI accreditation; but, in the meantime, the hospital already meets exacting requirements that are comparable to North American standards. Foreigners represent more than 25 percent of the patients at CIMA, which has a special international insurance claims department to assist Americans. The modern facility is affiliated with Baylor University Medical Center in Texas and is one of the organization's teaching hospitals.

Clinica Biblica
1st & 2nd Street, 14th & 16th Avenue
San José, Costa Rica
http://hospitalbiblicamedicaltourism.com/index.html

Telephone number: 011-506-2522-1000

Accreditation/certification: JCI

Specialties: Cosmetic surgery, bariatric surgery, orthopedics, dentistry, and ophthalmology

Founded in 1929, Hospital Clinica Biblica has earned a reputation for providing excellent medical care and superior service. The hospital's $50 million infrastructure and new $35 million building rival facilities in the United States. In addition, many of its approximately 200 highly skilled physicians have been trained at the most renowned medical schools in Europe and the United States. More than 15 percent of the hospital's patients come from other countries. An International Patient Center houses English-speaking coordinators and staff who are in place to assist foreign patients. In fact, international patients are assigned a health-care assistant who coordinates care and handles travel arrangements and other VIP services. The hospital is affiliated with several U.S. institutions, including Mount Sinai Medical Center in Florida and New Orleans's Tulane Medical Center and Oschner Clinic.

# Dental Clinics

Prisma Dental
Rohrmoser Blvd.
Prisma Building, 3rd Floor
San José, Costa Rica
www.cosmetics-dentistry.com/
Telephone numbers: 1-866-741-8194 (call toll-free from the United States) and 011-506-2291-5151

Specialties: Cosmetic dentistry, dental implants, crowns, bridges, root canals, whitening

The dentists at Prisma are internationally trained, hold advanced-training certificates in implant dentistry, and are members of the International Congress of Oral Implantologists. Prisma offers all forms of cosmetic dentistry as well as implants, crowns, bridges, root canals, whitening, and more. Prisma uses the highest standards of sterilization in accordance with the American Dental Association and imports equipment from Europe and the United States. It also boasts its own in-house lab. Americans, Canadians, and Europeans make up about 50 percent of the clinic's clientele.

Instituto Flikier de Rehabilitación Oral
P.O. Box 80-6155 Forum Santa Ana
Rohrmoser from President Óscar Arias house
50 meters West #36
San Jose, Costa Rica
www.dentalinstitutecr.com/flikier.html
Telephone number: 011-506-232-1626

The Instituto Flikier de Rehabilitación Oral is one of Costa Rica's leading cosmetic and restorative dental spas. Offering the most advanced dental procedures available, the office adheres to the American Dental Association's highest standards. Dr. Flikier was educated and trained at Boston University, where he also taught and practiced dentistry. Several members of his team also have received training in the United States. The clinic performs cosmetic dentistry and offers crowns, bridges, teeth whitening, implants, root canals, gum surgery, and more.

## Average Procedure Costs in Costa Rica

| Procedures | Average Prices |
| --- | --- |
| *Cosmetic* | |
| Face/neck lift | $3,900 |
| Blepharoplasty (upper/lower eyelids) | $2,100 |
| Rhinoplasty | $2,800 |
| Brow/forehead lift | $2,000 |
| Otoplasty | $1,600 |
| Liposuction (per area) | $1,300 |
| Tummy tuck | $5,600 |
| Breast augmentation | $5,000 |
| Breast lift | $3,700 |
| Inner thigh lift | $2,900 |
| Outer thigh lift | $3,900 |
| Buttock lift | $2,700 |
| Lower body lift (inner/outer thighs, buttock) | $8,300 |

| Procedures | Average Prices |
|---|---|
| *Medical* | |
| **Orthopedics** | |
| Hip replacement (per hip) | $13,000 |
| Hip resurfacing | $13,000 |
| Knee replacement (per knee) | $11,000 |
| Knee replacement (both knees) | $18,000 |
| **Spinal Procedures** | |
| Spinal fusion | $14,000 |
| Spinal disc replacement | $16,000 |
| **Cardiology** | |
| Angiogram | $1,700 |
| CT angiography scan | $600 |
| Aortic aneurysm surgery | $18,000 |
| Bypass surgery CAB | $14,000 |
| Coronary angioplasty (one stent and one balloon) | $7,000 |
| **Obstetrics and Gynecology** | |
| Hysterectomy | $6,000 |
| **General Surgery** | |
| Diagnostic laparoscopy | $1,900 |
| Gallbladder removal | $3,900 |
| Hernia repair | $1,900 |
| **Dentistry** | |
| Crowns | $225–$1,000 |
| Veneers | $60–$350 |
| Implants | $650–$3,000 |
| Bridges | $250 |
| Bone grafts | $400–$750 |
| Root canal | $165–$250 |
| Extractions | $120–$150 |

# India (Mumbai, Bangalore, Delhi, and Chennai)

India, which offers some of the lowest prices for medical treatments, is determined to become the world leader in medical tourism. According to an article in *Medical Tourism* magazine, an estimated 150,000 Westerners travel to India each year for high-quality, low-cost health care. In recent years, a number of first-rate, technologically advanced private hospitals have been erected to attract international patients.

Indian physicians are world-renowned as highly educated and trained medical providers. Nearly 60,000 Indian physicians practice in the United States, Great Britain, Canada, and Australia. A growing number of these internationally trained doctors and surgeons are returning to India to treat the influx of medical travelers. With its world-class physicians, high-tech hospitals, and rock-bottom prices, India has emerged as an excellent destination for medical treatment.

On the downside, some of India's thoroughly modern medical facilities are located in close proximity to slums where the nation's wide-scale poverty is evidenced. This may be disturbing or unsettling to you and could affect your overall experience. You also should be prepared for hectic traffic and overcrowding in the nation's large cities. Although India's procedure prices may be as low as one-tenth of the U.S. costs, hotel prices often are higher than those in other destinations.

## Travel Notes

**Languages spoken:** Hindi (official language), about 20 other languages are spoken; as a former British colony, English is widely spoken

**People:** India is a veritable cocktail of cultures and ethnic groups

**Personality:** Warm and inviting

**Infrastructure:** Third World

**Currency:** Rupee

**Time zone:** GMT+5

**Country phone code:** 91

**Electricity:** 230V to 240V, 50Hz

**Weights and measures:** Metric system

**Elevation concerns:** Mountainous in the north

**Climate:** The climate varies depending on the geographic region; you'll find desert conditions in the west, glaciers in the north, and tropical weather in the islands. Check the city where your hospital is located for regional climate information.

**Clothing:** The varied climate means that a wide variety of clothing styles is appropriate.

**Getting online:** Fax, Internet, and e-mail services typically are available in all major, top-tier hotels and in cybercafés.

**Visa required:** Travelers must obtain a medical (M) visa, which is now available and is valid for up to one year. In conjunction with this visa, up to two accompanying family members may obtain an MX visa.

**Immunizations required:** None

**Public health considerations:** Anti-malaria drugs are recommended because the risk of malaria is present even in urban areas, such as Mumbai and Delhi.

## Cultural Do's and Don'ts

♦ In public, women should dress to cover legs and shoulders.

♦ Don't kiss or show intimacy in public.

♦ Don't raise your voice in public.

♦ Women must initiate a handshake first.

## Hospitals

Many of the top hospitals already have earned JCI accreditation, and the vast majority of private hospitals catering to medical tourists have begun the application process. India is especially renowned for cardiac care, joint replacement, and hip resurfacing, but the country is not as well known for cosmetic surgery. One of the central beliefs of Indian culture is "Athithi devo bhava," which means "guest is God." This translates into an outstanding level of customer service in the nation's hospitals.

Hiranandani Hospital
Hill Side Avenue,
Hiranandani Gardens Powai
Mumbai 400 076
India
www.hiranandanihospital.org
Telephone number: 011-91-22-2576-3300

Accreditation/certification: ISO 9001:2000, German Accreditation Council (DAR), National Accreditation Board for Certification Bodies (NABCB), and National Accreditation Board for Hospital & Healthcare Providers (NABH); one of only 10 hospitals in the country to receive the prestigious NABH accreditation, an initiative of the Quality Council of India

Specialties: Cardiology, ophthalmology, joint replacement, hip resurfacing, general surgery, bariatric surgery, dental surgery, reproduction, and aesthetics

Opened in 2004, this 130-bed hospital was built in honor of a renowned physician, Dr. L. H. Hiranandani. The state-of-the-art facility houses all medical and diagnostic services under a single roof and blends advanced technology with personalized care. The hospital is staffed with internationally trained physicians and nurses, and offers residential facilities for patients' family members. Its Overseas Patient Care Centre offers a wide range of services to facilitate the medical travel process.

Max Healthcare
Max Super Specialty Hospital
1 Press Enclave Road, Saket
New Delhi, India 110017
www.maxhealthcare.in/corporate/index.asp
Telephone number: 011-91-11-2651-5050

Accreditation/certification: NABH

Specialties: Orthopedics and joint replacement, neurosurgery and neurology, gynecology, and pediatrics; cardiac care is available in the adjacent facility

Dedicated to total patient care, this family of facilities combines high-quality medical treatment with superior service and care for your overall wellness. Max also provides a variety of international patient services to meet the needs of overseas travelers. Max Super Specialty Hospital, with 200 beds, boasts a team of highly experienced surgeons and nurses who go the extra mile to enhance the patient experience. Next door is Max Devki Devi Heart and Vascular Institute, which offers a vast array of cardiac services.

Wockhardt Hospitals (Mumbai and Bangalore)
Wockhardt Hospitals, Mumbai
Mulund Goregaon Link Road
Mumbai, India 400078
Telephone number: 011-91-22-6799-4444

Wockhardt Super Specialty Hospitals
154/9 Bannerghatta Road
Opp. IIM-B
Bangalore, India 560076
Telephone number: 011-91-80-6621-4444

Wockhardt Hospital and Heart Institute, Bangalore
14, Cunningham Road,
Bangalore, India 560052
Telephone number: 011-91-80-2226-1037
www.wockhardthospitals.net/

Accreditation/certification: JCI, ISO 9002; Wockhardt earned the distinction of being India's first heart hospital to achieve ISO 9002 certification

Specialties: The Mumbai location is dedicated to cardiology, neurology, orthopedics (hip resurfacing and joint replacement), ophthalmology, bariatric surgery, and minimally invasive surgery; heart hospitals are located in Mumbai, Bangalore, and several other cities

Wockhardt Hospitals boast an exclusive Indian association with Harvard Medical International, the global arm of the Harvard Medical School. The Wockhardt group operates 12 hospitals in 7 cities throughout India and has several new facilities in the works. Many of the hospitals' surgeons have international training, and all of the doctors and nurses speak English. Wockhardt Hospital and Heart Institute in Bangalore has pioneered several life-saving, innovative cardiac surgery techniques. The Mumbai location is one of the few hospitals in India to offer hip resurfacing in addition to more traditional joint replacement. Private rooms are equipped with computers, Internet connections, and sofa beds for traveling companions. An international patient services division sees to the needs of medical tourists.

Apollo Hospitals (Bangalore, Chennai, and Delhi)
Apollo Hospitals Chennai
No. 21, Greams Lane
Off. Greams Road
Chennai, India 600006
www.apollohospitals.com/Chennai.asp?PgeuId=1066
Telephone number: 011-91-44-2829-0200

Accreditation/certification: JCI, ISO 9002

Specialties: Joint replacement, hip resurfacing, angioplasty, organ transplants, stereotactic radiotherapy and radiosurgery;

Indraprastha Apollo Hospital (Delhi)
Sarita Vihar
Delhi Mathura Road
New Delhi, India 110076
www.apollohospitals.com/Delhi.asp
Telephone number: 011-91-11-2692-5858

Accreditation/certification: JCI, ISO 9001:2000, ISO 14001:1996

Specialties: Cardiology, neurology and neurosurgery, oncology, orthopedics, pediatrics, organ transplants, and minimally invasive surgery;

I.I.M.
Bannerghatta Road
Bangalore, India 500069
www.apollohospitals.com/Bangalore.asp
Telephone number: 011-91-80-4030-4050

Accreditation/certification: Information not available

Specialties: Thirteen specialties, including cardiology, neurology and neurosurgery, orthopedics, gynecology, pediatrics, and plastic surgery

The largest hospital group in India, and the third largest in the world, Apollo Hospitals Group manages more than 40 hospitals with more than 8,000 beds. The group provides a wealth of services for medical travelers through its International Patients Division. The group's first hospital was established in 1983 in Chennai. The facility boasts more than 27,000 heart surgeries with an impressive success rate of 99.6 percent. The largest hospital in the group, Indraprastha Apollo Hospital, is located in Delhi. This 560-bed facility treats about 12,000 international patients each year. The newest and most technologically advanced facility added to the Apollo roster is located in Bangalore. This facility boasts some of the most highly advanced equipment available, and most of its physicians and surgeons have trained or worked abroad in highly respected institutions.

## Average Procedure Costs in India

| Procedures | Average Prices |
|---|---|
| *Cosmetic* | |
| Face/neck lift | $2,600 |
| Blepharoplasty (upper/lower eyclids) | $1,400 |

| Procedures | Average Prices |
| --- | --- |
| Rhinoplasty | $1,900 |
| Brow/forehead lift | $1,300 |
| Otoplasty | $1,100 |
| Liposuction (per area) | $900 |
| Tummy tuck | $3,800 |
| Breast augmentation | $3,400 |
| Breast lift | $2,500 |
| Inner thigh lift | $2,600 |
| Outer thigh lift | $2,600 |
| Buttock lift | $1,800 |
| Lower body lift (inner/outer thighs, buttock) | $5,600 |

*Medical*

**Orthopedics**

| | |
| --- | --- |
| Hip replacement (per hip) | $9,000 |
| Hip resurfacing | $9,000 |
| Knee replacement (per knee) | $7,600 |
| Knee replacement (both knees) | $12,500 |

**Spinal Procedures**

| | |
| --- | --- |
| Spinal fusion | $9,600 |
| Spinal disc replacement | $11,000 |

**Cardiology**

| | |
| --- | --- |
| Angiogram | $1,100 |
| CT angiography scan | $400 |
| Aortic aneurysm surgery | $12,300 |
| Bypass surgery CAB | $9,500 |
| Coronary angioplasty (one stent and one balloon) | $4,800 |

**Obstetrics and Gynecology**

| | |
| --- | --- |
| Hysterectomy | $3,900 |

*continues*

## Average Procedure Costs in India (continued)

| Procedures | Average Prices |
|---|---|
| **General Surgery** | |
| Diagnostic laparoscopy | $1,200 |
| Gallbladder removal | $2,600 |
| Hernia repair | $1,200 |
| **Dentistry** | |
| Crowns | $150–$600 |
| Veneers | $40–$200 |
| Implants | $450–$2,000 |
| Bridges | $150 |
| Bone grafts | $250–$500 |
| Root canal | $75–$175 |
| Extractions | $75–$125 |

# Malaysia (Kuala Lumpur and Penang)

Malaysia is an excellent choice for health-care travelers and is considered to be a hidden gem within the medical tourism industry. The Malaysian government has established a national goal to become the future hub for medical tourists from around the world. To meet this goal, Malaysian hospitals and health-care providers go out of their way to pamper international patients.

Medical tourists who visit Malaysia routinely rave about how friendly and nice the people are. Travelers also appreciate the fact that it's a hassle-free destination. Transportation is readily available, and it's very easy to navigate around Malaysia. The country's unique culture is derived from a charming mix of ethnicities, cultures, and customs.

In some of Malaysia's major cities, you may feel comfortly at home thanks to the Western-style industrial development. Contrasting the modern and sophisticated city structures, serene beaches and national parks offer a peaceful backdrop for your recuperation. Many of my clients have been so thrilled with their experience in Malaysia that they're considering buying second homes there.

## Travel Notes

**Languages spoken:** Malay (official language); as a former British colony, English is widely spoken

**People:** Malay (the majority group), Chinese, and Indian

**Personality:** Very warm and friendly

**Infrastructure:** First World

**Currency:** Malaysian Ringitt (RM)

**Time zone:** GMT+8

**Country phone code:** 60

**Electricity:** 220V to 240V, 50Hz

**Weights and measures:** Metric system

**Elevation concerns:** No

**Climate:** The climate in Malaysia is tropical. Expect sunshine with warm to hot temperatures and humid conditions for the majority of the year. The rainy season runs from November to January.

**Clothing:** Light clothing is recommended. Note that fine dining establishments require appropriate attire.

**Getting online:** Fax, Internet, and e-mail services typically are available in all major hotels. You also can find many cybercafés in major tourist destinations.

**Visa required:** No

**Immunizations required**: None

**Public health considerations:** Mosquitoes tend to be present year-round, although the risk for malaria is insignificant in Kuala Lumpur and Penang. Drink only bottled or boiled water. Don't drink tap water, fountain drinks, or drinks with ice cubes. Avoid eating food from street vendors.

## Cultural Do's and Don'ts

- Do smile when you greet people.

- Do dress neatly when entering places of worship. Women should wear long sleeves and loose pants.

◆ Don't touch an adult's head.

◆ Don't point the bottom of your feet at any individual.

◆ Don't shake hands with women unless they offer to do so first.

◆ Don't point using your index finger. Instead, use your thumb with your four fingers folded into the palm of your hand.

# Hospitals

The Association of Private Hospitals of Malaysia lists 35 hospitals in operation. Although many of the private hospitals in Malaysia have opened their doors to international patients, I have chosen to highlight only hospitals that I have personally worked with and that I can recommend. These hospitals are either in their final stages of receiving JCI accreditation, are American managed, or are sponsored by some of the largest American companies. You can find every type of cosmetic, elective, medically necessary, or dental procedure in Malaysia.

Gleneagles Intan Medical Centre KL
282 & 286, Jalan Ampang
Kuala Lumpur, Malaysia 50450
www.gimc.com.my
Telephone number: 011-60-3-4257-2775

Accreditation/certification: ISO 9002, Malaysian Society for Quality in Health, JCI accreditation in process

Specialties: Specialty centers include a cardiac lab, stem cell therapy, fertility and in vitro fertilization (IVF), dermatology, oncology, women's wellness, and executive screening

A subsidiary of Parkway Group Healthcare, this 330-bed private hospital has been in operation since 1996. Because Malaysia was a British colony until 1957, many surgeons and specialists were trained and educated in the United Kingdom. The hospital caters to international patients and offers a broad range of assistance to foreign patients, including language assistance services, accommodations booking, airport transfer arrangements, and post-treatment sightseeing arrangements.

Gleneagles Medical Centre Penang
1, Jalan Pangkor
Penang, Malaysia 10050
www.gleneagles-penang.com/index.htm
Telephone number: 011-60-4220-2103

Accreditation/certification: Malaysian Society for Quality in Health

Specialties: Among more than 30 specialties are cardiology, gynecology, orthopedics, spinal surgery, general surgery, neurosurgery, ophthalmology, oncology, and pediatric surgery

Established in 1973, Gleneagles Medical Centre Penang was the first private hospital on the island of Penang. Commonly referred to as the "Pearl of the Orient," Penang boasts a wide range of specialist services and facilities. A subsidiary of Parkway Group Healthcare, the hospital underwent a four-year renovation project that was completed in 2000. There also are plans for another expansion in 2009. Now, it is recognized as one of the most technologically advanced hospitals in the country. You may want to take advantage of the hospital's comprehensive Executive Health Screening Program, which includes a wide array of screening tests.

Penang Adventist Hospital
465, Burma Road
Pulau Penang, Malaysia 10350
www.pah.com.my
Telephone number: 011-60-4222-7200

Accreditation/certification: Malaysian Society for Quality in Health, Adventist Health Services Asia, JCI accreditation in process

Specialties: Among more than 20 specialties are cardiology, dentistry, gynecology, ophthalmology, orthopedics, pediatrics, sports medicine, and plastic surgery

Penang Adventist Hospital is one of more than 500 international hospitals and health-care institutions operated by the Adventist Health Network. Penang Adventist Hospital earned a reputation as the first private hospital in Northern Malaysia to perform a number of advanced heart procedures, including coronary bypass, trans-myocardial laser revascularization (TMR), microvascular surgery, and open-heart surgery. Add value to your medical trip with health screenings offered in the hospital's Wellness Centre.

# Average Procedure Costs in Malaysia

| Procedures | Average Prices |
| --- | --- |
| *Cosmetic* | |
| Face/neck lift | $2,900 |
| Blepharoplasty (upper/lower eyelids) | $1,600 |

*continues*

## Average Procedure Costs in Malaysia  (continued)

| Procedures | Average Prices |
|---|---|
| Rhinoplasty | $2,100 |
| Brow/forehead lift | $1,500 |
| Otoplasty | $1,200 |
| Liposuction (per area) | $1,000 |
| Tummy tuck | $4,200 |
| Breast augmentation | $3,750 |
| Breast lift | $2,800 |
| Inner thigh lift | $2,900 |
| Outer thigh lift | $2,900 |
| Buttock lift | $2,000 |
| Lower body lift (inner/outer thighs, buttock) | $6,250 |

*Medical*

**Orthopedics**

| | |
|---|---|
| Hip replacement (per hip) | $9,900 |
| Hip resurfacing | $10,000 |
| Knee replacement (per knee) | $8,200 |
| Knee replacement (both knees) | $13,900 |

**Spinal Procedures**

| | |
|---|---|
| Spinal fusion | $10,700 |
| Spinal disc replacement | $12,250 |

**Cardiology**

| | |
|---|---|
| Angiogram | $1,250 |
| CT angiography scan | $450 |
| Aortic aneurysm surgery | $13,750 |
| Bypass surgery CAB | $10,600 |
| Coronary angioplasty (one stent and one balloon) | $5,400 |

**Obstetrics and Gynecology**

| | |
|---|---|
| Hysterectomy | $4,400 |

| Procedures | Average Prices |
|---|:---:|
| **General Surgery** | |
| Diagnostic Laparoscopy | $1,400 |
| Gallbladder removal | $2,900 |
| Hernia repair | $1,400 |
| **Dentistry** | |
| Crowns | $170–$700 |
| Veneers | $50–$250 |
| Implants | $500–$2,200 |
| Bridges | $200 |
| Bone grafts | $300–$550 |
| Root canal | $100–$200 |
| Extractions | $100–$150 |

# Mexico

For U.S. residents who like the idea of cutting health-care costs, but don't fancy the notion of taking a 20-hour flight overseas, Mexico may be the ideal destination. Mexico offers significant savings on a variety of procedures, including weight-loss surgery, cosmetic dentistry, orthopedics, laser eye surgery, cosmetic surgery, dermatology, cardiology, and stem cell treatments.

This long list of procedures is offered in one of the world's most popular tourist destinations. Mexico's mélange of sophisticated cities, inviting beaches, and archeological sites make it an alluring option for the medical traveler. You should be aware, however, that some of the country's border towns may not possess the same charm as resort areas.

Mexico has one of the highest concentrations of dental clinics in the world. Unfortunately, it may be difficult to determine which clinics are the best and which dentists are the most qualified. For your own peace of mind, you may want to rely on references from people you trust.

## Travel Notes

**Languages spoken:** Spanish (official language), but English is widely spoken

**People:** Mestizo, Amerindian, and European

**Personality:** Warm and hospitable

**Infrastructure:** First World

**Currency:** Peso

**Time zone:** GMT–6/7/8

**Country phone code:** 52

**Electricity:** 120V, 60Hz

**Weights and measures:** Metric system

**Elevation concerns:** Some regions of Mexico are at a high altitude, and it may take a few days to become acclimated.

**Climate:** Average temperatures range from about 77 to 86 degrees Fahrenheit, although it can get cold at night in areas of higher elevations.

**Clothing:** Casual clothing is acceptable in most areas.

**Getting online:** Fax, Internet, and e-mail services typically are available in all major hotels and in cybercafés.

**Visa required:** No

**Immunizations required:** None

**Public health considerations:** Avoid drinking tap water and don't eat food from street vendors.

## Cultural Do's and Don'ts

- ◆ Do use "señor" and "señora," (Mr. and Ms./Mrs.) as a display of respect.
- ◆ Do learn the name of the Mexican president.
- ◆ Do stand closely to individuals when engaging in conversation (closer than is customary in the United States). Standing back or moving away from a Mexican is considered rude.
- ◆ Do use the phrase "psst, psst" to catch someone's attention.

- Don't be shy about attempting to speak Spanish. You will not be judged or criticized for even the smallest efforts.

- Don't back away from an embrace or kiss; it is considered very rude and is read as a rejection of a Mexican's friendship.

- Typical greetings for Mexicans include an embrace, "abrazo," or a gentle kiss on the cheek.

- Don't tell Mexicans that you are American or even North American because they also are American/North American. It's best to say that you are from the United States, or simply note your state of residence.

- Don't maintain eye contact for more than a few seconds.

# Hospitals

Due to their proximity to the United States, Mexican hospitals have been welcoming U.S. patients for many years. Because of increased interest in medical tourism, these hospitals have taken steps to improve and simplify the medical care process for U.S. and Canadian medical travelers. Many also have started the process of becoming JCI-accredited in an effort to appeal to medical tourists.

Hospital Angeles Tijuana
Av. Paseo de los Héroes #10999
Zona Río, Tijuana, C.P.
Mexico 22010
www.hospitalangelestijuana.com.mx/ingles/ (in English)
Telephone number: 011 52 664 635 1800

Accreditation/certification: JCI accreditation in process

Specialties: Bariatrics, orthopedics, cardiology, and stem cell treatments, among others

Hospital Angeles is the largest private hospital chain in Mexico, with 20 general hospitals currently in operation throughout the country. Another four facilities are under construction, and 12 more locations are expected to be added in the next five years. The group boasts more than 8,500 specialists, and treats about one million patients each year. Four Hospital Angeles locations are especially noteworthy for medical tourists: the facilities in the border towns of Tijuana and Juarez, and those in the retirement communities of Guadalajara and Léon. Medical tourists interested in going to any of the Hospital Angeles facilities are requested to contact the Tijuana facility as a first point of communication.

Opened in 2005, Hospital Angeles Tijuana is one of the most modern and technologically advanced hospitals in Mexico. Most of the surgeons who treat U.S. medical tourists speak English and have an international education. Note that English isn't as widely spoken among the nursing staff. The Tijuana location treats about 3,000 U.S. bariatric patients each year, making it one of the world's leading medical tourism centers for weight-loss surgery. The hospital also is expected to launch a stem cell treatment center in 2008.

Christus Muguerza International
www.christusmuguerza.com.mx/cm/modules/xfsection/article.php?articleid=451&
hospital=Eng
Telephone number: 011-52-86-6558-6070

Christus Muguerza Alta Especialidad
Av. Hidalgo Poniente 2525
Col. Obispado, Monterrey
Neuvo Leon 64060 Mexico
Telephone number: 011-52-81-8399-3400

Christus Muguerza Sur
Carretera Nacional 6501
Col. La Estanzuela, Monterrey
Neuvo Leon 64988 Mexico
Telephone number: 011-52-81-8155-5000

Accreditation/certification: JCI

Specialties: Cardiology, orthopedics, oncology, gynecology, neurology, transplants, plastic surgery, bariatrics, and dentistry

Located within driving distance of many U.S. border areas, Christus Muguerza International is affiliated with U.S.-based Christus Health and operates three facilities—one highly specialized and two general hospitals. Christus Muguerza has invested more than $100 million in recent years to modernize its facilities and technology. A free web-based portal has been developed to simplify communications between international patients and the hospital.

# Average Procedure Costs in Mexico

| Procedures | Average Prices |
| --- | --- |
| *Cosmetic* | |
| Face/neck lift | $3,900 |
| Blepharoplasty (upper/lower eyelids) | $2,100 |
| Rhinoplasty | $2,800 |
| Brow/forehead lift | $2,000 |
| Otoplasty | $1,600 |
| Liposuction (per area) | $1,300 |
| Tummy tuck | $5,600 |
| Breast augmentation | $5,000 |
| Breast lift | $3,700 |
| Inner thigh lift | $2,900 |
| Outer thigh lift | $3,900 |
| Buttock lift | $2,700 |
| Lower body lift (inner/outer thighs, buttock) | $8,300 |
| *Medical* | |
| **Orthopedics** | |
| Hip replacement (per hip) | $13,000 |
| Hip resurfacing | $13,000 |
| Knee replacement (per knee) | $11,000 |
| Knee replacement (both knees) | $18,000 |
| **Spinal Procedures** | |
| Spinal fusion | $14,000 |
| Spinal disc replacement | $16,000 |
| **Cardiology** | |
| Angiogram | $1,700 |
| CT angiography scan | $600 |
| Aortic aneurysm surgery | $18,000 |
| Bypass surgery CAB | $14,000 |

*continues*

## Average Procedure Costs in Mexico     (continued)

| Procedures | Average Prices |
| --- | --- |
| Coronary angioplasty (one stent and one balloon) | $7,000 |
| **Obstetrics and Gynecology** | |
| Hysterectomy | $6,000 |
| **General Surgery** | |
| Diagnostic laparoscopy | $1,900 |
| Gallbladder removal | $3,900 |
| Hernia repair | $1,900 |
| **Dentistry** | |
| Crowns | $225–$1,000 |
| Veneers | $60–$350 |
| Implants | $650–$3,000 |
| Bridges | $250 |
| Bone grafts | $400–$750 |
| Root canal | $165–$250 |
| Extractions | $120–$150 |

# Philippines (Manila)

The Philippines is an archipelago comprised of thousands of islands. An American colony from 1898 to 1935, the Philippines have strongly embraced American culture. An official language in the Philippines, English is spoken American-style, with American slang and idioms heavily used. The American influence affects the nation's health-care system as well. For example, many Filipino physicians have received education and training or have practiced in the United States before returning to their homeland. "That makes the Philippines even more ideal as a medical tourism destination for Americans," says Dr. Constantino Amores, a Filipino who went to the United States in 1963 for medical training. Dr. Amores is clinical director of neuro/ortho/trauma at the Charleston Area Medical Center in West Virginia and also is co-founder of the Mactan Community Hospital in the Philippines.

The country already treats an estimated 150,000 foreign patients each year—most of them Filipinos living abroad who return home for treatment. But "as word-of-mouth grows about the Philippines as a medical tourism destination, more non-Filipino Americans will give it a try," expects Dr. Amores. Some industry insiders have projected that the Philippines could become one of the top 10 medical tourism destinations in the next five years.

For now, the hospitals that are most appealing to medical tourists are located in Manila, the nation's capital. This vibrant metropolis is teeming with a mix of historic buildings and modern structures. With more than 10 million people living in the Metropolitan Manila area, the hustle and bustle can be overwhelming, especially if you aren't feeling your best. If you are feeling up to it, you'll find a wealth of world-class restaurants and exciting nightlife in Manila, which has been called the "city that never sleeps."

Another area in the Philippines expected to be an ideal location for medical tourism is Mactan, a tranquil island within a short drive from Cebu, the nation's second largest city. This tropical island houses several five-star resorts, an international airport, and a hospital.

# Travel Notes

**Languages spoken:** Pilipino (Tagalog) and English are the official languages

**People:** Tagalog, Chinese, Spanish, and many others

**Personality:** Caring and compassionate

**Infrastructure:** First World

**Currency:** Philippine peso

**Time zone:** GMT+8

**Country phone code:** 63

**Electricity:** 220V, 60Hz

**Weights and measures:** Metric system

**Elevation concerns:** None

**Climate:** Expect hot and humid weather regardless of the time of year.

**Clothing:** Light, cotton clothing is best.

**Getting online:** Fax, Internet, and e-mail services typically are available in all major hotels and in cybercafés.

**Visa required:** Yes, if staying more than 21 days

**Immunizations required:** None

**Public health considerations:** None

# Cultural Do's and Don'ts

- ◆ Do act, speak, and dress conservatively.

- ◆ Do negotiate prices when shopping.

- ◆ Don't discuss religion and politics.

- ◆ Don't show anger.

- ◆ Don't speak loudly.

# Hospitals

Two JCI-accredited hospitals in Manila are best suited to North American medical travelers. Many of the physicians in these facilities speak English and have trained in the United States.

St. Luke's Medical Center
279 E. Rodriguez Sr. Boulevard
Quezon City, 1102 Philippines
www.stluke.com.ph/
Telephone number: 011-63-2-723-0101

Accreditation/certification: JCI

Specialties: Cancer, cardiac care, orthopedics, eye care, neurosurgery, and liver transplants

Operating since 1903, this 650-bcd facility boasts extremely advanced medical equipment and technology. In fact, it claims to be better equipped than 95 percent of all hospitals in the United States. The hospital is affiliated with a number of prestigious U.S. medical institutions, including New York Presbyterian Hospital, the Memorial Sloan-Kettering Cancer Center, Columbia University College of Physicians and Surgeons, and Weill Cornell Medical College of Cornell University. An international patient care center can schedule appointments and assist with travel plans.

The Medical City
Ortigas Avenue
Pasig City, Metro Manila
Philippines
www.themedicalcity.com/
Telephone number: 011-63-2-635-6789

Accreditation/certification: JCI

Specialties: Cardiovascular procedures, neurosurgery, orthopedics, cancer treatments, stem cell therapy, plastic surgery, and minimally invasive surgery

Some 1,000 physicians—many of them trained in the United States—treat patients here using cutting-edge equipment. Doctors, nurses, and physical therapists will make "house calls," visiting international patients in nearby hotels and resorts during the recuperation phase.

## Average Procedure Costs in the Philippines

| Procedures | Average Prices |
|---|---|
| *Cosmetic* | |
| Face/neck lift | $3,200 |
| Blepharoplasty (upper/lower eyelids) | $1,800 |
| Rhinoplasty | $2,300 |
| Brow/forehead lift | $1,700 |
| Otoplasty | $1,300 |
| Liposuction (per area) | $1,100 |
| Tummy tuck | $4,600 |
| Breast augmentation | $4,100 |
| Breast lift | $3,100 |
| Inner thigh lift | $3,200 |
| Outer thigh lift | $3,200 |
| Buttock lift | $2,200 |
| Lower body lift (inner/outer thighs, buttock) | $6,900 |

*continues*

## Average Procedure Costs in the Philippines (continued)

| Procedures | Average Prices |
|---|---|
| *Medical* | |
| **Orthopedics** | |
| Hip replacement (per hip) | $10,900 |
| Hip resurfacing | $11,000 |
| Knee replacement (per knee) | $9,000 |
| Knee replacement (both knees) | $15,300 |
| **Spinal Procedures** | |
| Spinal fusion | $11,800 |
| Spinal disc replacement | $13,500 |
| **Cardiology** | |
| Angiogram | $1,400 |
| CT angiography scan | $500 |
| Aortic aneurysm surgery | $15,000 |
| Bypass surgery CAB | $11,600 |
| Coronary angioplasty (one stent and one balloon) | $6,000 |
| **Obstetrics and Gynecology** | |
| Hysterectomy | $4,800 |
| **General Surgery** | |
| Diagnostic laparoscopy | $1,500 |
| Gallbladder removal | $3,200 |
| Hernia repair | $1,500 |
| **Dentistry** | |
| Crowns | $190–$800 |
| Veneers | $50–$300 |
| Implants | $550–$2,400 |
| Bridges | $200 |
| Bone grafts | $350–$600 |
| Root canal | $100–$250 |
| Extractions | $100–$200 |

# Singapore

Singapore has long been a popular destination for international patients. In 2006, more than 550,000 visitors from dozens of countries—including Indonesia, Russia, India, Thailand, Australia, Germany, China, the Philippines, and the United States—sought some form of health care in Singapore. By 2012, the nation hopes to increase those numbers to at least one million medical travelers.

Singapore Medicine, a multi-agency organization, has been created to help achieve that goal and to improve the nation's status as an international hub for medical tourism. Singapore also is expected to be a major destination for U.S.-based insurance companies and self-funded employers that begin offering medical tourism as an option to their beneficiaries.

It's easy to see why Singapore is so attractive to American medical tourists. With its modern skyscrapers, and with English the most commonly used language, Singapore looks and feels like an American city—only prettier, cleaner, and safer. Because Singapore is one of Asia's most affluent nations, you won't come across any of the unsettling signs of poverty that you might find in locations like India, Mexico, or South America. Other plusses include several nonstop flights from the United States to its Changi International Airport and a superb public transportation system that helps keep traffic running smoothly.

The urban nation's best calling card is its first-class health-care system, which ranked first in Asia and sixth worldwide on the World Health Organization's 2000 report. Its world-class treatments come at a significant cost savings compared to U.S. prices. Be aware, however, that the savings aren't as high as those in many other destinations. For individuals—and certainly for insurance companies—that want to offer medical travel as an option, Singapore's sophisticated infrastructure, JCI-accredited hospitals, internationally trained doctors, stable government, low crime rates, efficiency, and ease of communication make up for the more modest savings.

Singapore offers treatment in a wide spectrum of medical specialties but is perhaps best known for its advances in cancer treatments, stem cell transplants, and liver transplants. As of this writing, most American medical travelers visit Singapore in search of cardiology treatments and orthopedic surgeries, such as hip or knee replacements.

# Travel Notes

**Languages spoken:** English is the most commonly spoken language; Malay, Mandarin, and Tamil (official languages)

**People:** The diverse population includes people of Chinese, Malay, Indian, and Eurasian descent

**Personality:** Caring and extremely efficient

**Infrastructure:** First World

**Currency:** Singapore dollar (SGD)

**Time zone:** GMT+8

**Country phone code:** 65

**Electricity:** 220V to 240V, 50Hz (most hotels provide transformers for appliances that are 110V to 120V, 60Hz)

**Weights and measures:** Metric system

**Elevation concerns:** None

**Climate:** Singapore boasts a tropical climate, with average temperatures ranging from 75 to 88 degrees Fahrenheit.

**Clothing:** Light, cotton clothing is best. Casual wear is acceptable in most places.

**Getting online:** Fax, Internet, and e-mail services typically are available in all major hotels and in cybercafés.

**Visa required:** No

**Immunizations required:** None

**Public health considerations:** There are no specific public health considerations. It's perfectly safe to drink tap water in Singapore.

# Cultural Do's and Don'ts

- ◆ Do dress comfortably and informally.
- ◆ Do be punctual for appointments.
- ◆ Do remove your shoes before entering a private home or temple.
- ◆ Don't raise your voice or lose your temper.

◆ Don't litter, spit, or chew gum in public.

◆ Don't jaywalk.

# Hospitals

Singapore boasts the highest number (12) of JCI-accredited facilities in Asia. The nation's hospitals achieve very high success rates, and many of them publish these rates on their websites. Unlike most destinations where private hospitals are the only facilities promoting medical tourism, Singapore's excellent public sector hospitals also cater to international patients.

Parkway Group Healthcare
83 Clemenceau Avenue
#10-05/06/07, UE Square
Singapore 239920
www.parkwayhealth.com
Telephone number: 011-65-6735-5000

Parkway Group Healthcare, a wholly owned subsidary of Parkway Holdings Limited, is the largest private health-care organization in Singapore, operating the following three hospitals, which actively seek international patients.

Mount Elizabeth Hospital
3 Mount Elizabeth
Singapore 228510
singapore.parkwayhealth.com/hospitals/meh.asp
Telephone number: 011-65-6737-2666

Accreditation/certification: JCI

Specialties: Among more than 30 specialties are cardiology, neurosurgery, cancer treatment, and stem cell transplants

Established in 1976, this 505-bed tertiary acute-care facility offers comprehensive health-care services. Of all the private hospitals in the region, Mount Elizabeth performs the most cardiac surgeries and neurosurgeries. The hospital has earned a reputation as an innovator, being the first hospital in Singapore to perform a variety of cardiac, neurosurgical, and stem cell transplant procedures.

Gleneagles Hospital
6A Napier Road
Singapore 258500
singapore.parkwayhealth.com/hospitals/geh.asp
Telephone number: 011-65-6473-7222

Accreditation/certification: JCI

Specialties: Among more than 30 specialties are liver transplant surgery, cardiology, orthopedic surgery, and gynecology

Originally founded in 1957 as a nursing home, Gleneagles has undergone several expansions to become a 380-bed tertiary acute-care hospital with 150 medical specialists on its roster. In addition to providing a full slate of medical services, this facility strives to be the most patient-friendly hospital in the region. Glencagles earned accolades as the first hospital in the region to perform a living donor liver transplant for children.

East Shore Hospitals
321 Joo Chiat Place
Singapore 427990
singapore.parkwayhealth.com/hospitals/esh.asp
Telephone number: 011-65-6344-7588

Accreditation/certification: JCI

Specialties: Among more than two dozen specialties are general surgery, pediatrics, and gynecology

This 123-bed general private acute-care hospital was originally founded as a maternity and nursing home in the 1930s. Several modernization and expansion projects have been completed since that time. Today, it provides a wide range of medical services in a comfortable, homey atmosphere. Its trademark is personalized care, and the nurses and staff routinely go the extra mile to meet patients' needs.

Singapore Health Services (SingHealth)

SingHealth manages several public health-care facilities in Singapore, including three hospitals. Of these facilities, Singapore General Hospital is the most conducive to medical travel.

Singapore General Hospital
Outram Road
Singapore 169608
www.sgh.com.sg/
Telephone number: 011-65-6222-3322

Accreditation/certification: JCI

Specialties: Among 28 clinical specialties are plastic surgery, orthopedic surgery, gynecology, and neurosurgery

Established in 1821, Singapore General Hospital (SGH) is the nation's oldest tertiary acute-care hospital. With more than 1,500 beds and 550 specialists, it also is the largest. Nearly 100,000 surgical operations are performed at SGH each year. Managed by SingHealth, SGH is considered the public sector's flagship hospital.

## Average Procedure Costs in Singapore

| Procedures | Average Prices |
| --- | --- |
| *Cosmetic* | |
| Face/necklift | $3,900 |
| Blepharoplasty (upper/lower eyelids) | $2,100 |
| Rhinoplasty | $2,800 |
| Brow/forehead lift | $2,000 |
| Otoplasty | $1,600 |
| Liposuction (per area) | $1,300 |
| Tummy tuck | $5,600 |
| Breast augmentation | $5,000 |
| Breast lift | $3,700 |
| Inner thigh lift | $2,900 |
| Outer thigh lift | $3,900 |
| Buttock lift | $2,700 |
| Lower body lift (inner/outer thighs, buttock) | $8,300 |
| *Medical* | |
| **Orthopedics** | |
| Hip replacement (per hip) | $13,000 |
| Hip resurfacing | $13,000 |
| Knee replacement (per knee) | $11,000 |
| Knee replacement (both knees) | $18,000 |

*continues*

## Average Procedure Costs in Singapore    (continued)

| Procedures | Average Prices |
|---|---|
| **Spinal Procedures** | |
| Spinal fusion | $14,000 |
| Spinal disc replacement | $16,000 |
| **Cardiology** | |
| Angiogram | $1,700 |
| CT angiography scan | $600 |
| Aortic aneurysm surgery | $18,000 |
| Bypass surgery CAB | $14,000 |
| Coronary angioplasty (one stent and one balloon) | $7,000 |
| **Obstetrics and Gynecology** | |
| Hysterectomy | $6,000 |
| **General Surgery** | |
| Diagnostic laparoscopy | $1,900 |
| Gallbladder removal | $3,900 |
| Hernia repair | $1,900 |
| **Dentistry** | |
| Crowns | $225–$1,000 |
| Veneers | $60–$350 |
| Implants | $650–$3,000 |
| Bridges | $250 |
| Bone grafts | $400–$750 |
| Root canal | $165–$250 |
| Extractions | $120–$150 |

# South Korea (Seoul)

South Korea, the Korean culture, and Korean actors are extremely popular throughout Asia. Thanks to this popularity, South Korea has been attracting a slew of medical tourists from neighboring nations—mostly Japan and China—for some time. Only recently, however, has the Korean government begun looking into offering medical care to Westerners.

The Korean government has already invested heavily in its infrastructure, making South Korea the most wired place on earth and one of the most convenient and hassle-free Asian destinations for travelers. For instance, English-speaking travelers in South Korea can dial 1330 at any time of the day or night to reach a bilingual operator who will offer translation assistance or travel information.

Now, the country is investing in its health-care infrastructure to make medical tourism just as easy. Prices in South Korea are somewhat higher than in some of the other Southeast Asian destinations, but in many cases, you're paying for a higher level of service, sparkling cleanliness, and other amenities that can add up to more value.

## Travel Notes

**Languages spoken:** Korean (official language), but English is widely spoken

**People:** Korean

**Personality:** Warm and efficient

**Infrastructure:** First World

**Currency:** Won

**Time zone:** GMT+9

**Country phone code:** 82

**Electricity:** 220V, 60Hz

**Weights and measures:** Metric system

**Elevation concerns:** None

**Climate:** There are four distinct seasons, with cold, dry winters and hot, humid, rainy summers.

**Clothing:** Western-style clothing is acceptable. Dress according to the season.

**Getting online:** Fax, Internet, and e-mail services typically are available in all major hotels and in cybercafés.

**Visa required:** No

**Immunizations required:** None

**Public health considerations:** None

# Cultural Do's and Don'ts

◆ Do remember that Korean family names are first—for example, Dr. Kim Yong-joon is Dr. Kim to you.

◆ Do use your right hand when giving or receiving a gift.

◆ Do remove your shoes before entering a Korean home.

◆ Don't beckon a person with your palm up and curling your fingers toward you.

◆ Don't use your hands to pick up food.

# Hospitals

Several South Korean hospitals are in the process of applying for JCI accreditation to increase their appeal to Western patients. Many of the nation's doctors have trained in the United States and are fluent in English. The government is working on a program to help train hospital nurses to learn medical English. Many hospitals also have international patient centers and coordinators for foreign patients.

Yonsei Severance Hospital
250 Seongsanno (134 Sinchon-dong)
Seodaemun-gu
Seoul, Korea
www.yuhs.or.kr/en/
Telephone number: 011-82-1-2228-5810

Accreditation/certification: JCI

Specialties: Dentistry, oncology, plastic surgery, orthopedics, spinal procedures, minimally invasive procedures, and health screenings

Severance Hospital, which is part of the Yonsei University Health System, was established in 1885 and was the first in Korea to practice Western medicine. Through a partnership, Severance patients can get a second opinion from Johns Hopkins Medicine International. With state-of-the-art technology and a highly skilled team of doctors, Severance is committed to becoming one of the world's most trusted medical facilities.

Seoul National University Hospital
28 Yeongeon-Dong
Jongno-gu
Seoul, Korea 110-744
www.snuh.org/eng/ebs/sub01/
Telephone number: 011-82-2-2072-2890

Accreditation/certification: Information not available

Specialties: Orthopedics, plastic surgery, oncology, general surgery, cardiovascular, health screenings, and more

With 1,600 beds, Seoul National treats approximately 2,100 inpatients and outpatients each day, including many foreign patients. The hospital's International Healthcare Service aims to increase the convenience for medical tourists, scheduling appointments and facilitating payments. English-speaking doctors are available in every medical specialty.

Samsung Medical Center
50 Iwon-dong
Gangnam-gu
Seoul, Korea 135-710
english.samsunghospital.com
Telephone number: 011-82-2-3410-3000

Accreditation/certification: Information not available N/A

Specialties: Minimally invasive surgery, Gamma Knife procedures, cancer, cardiac, stroke, and organ transplant

Established in 1994, Samsung Medical Center (SMC) has nearly 1,300 beds, 900 doctors, 1,100 nurses, 8 specialty care centers, and 100 specialized clinics. Approximately 35,000 operations are performed each year at SMC. The English-speaking International Health Services department provides assistance with scheduling appointments, choosing the right physician, translation, cost estimation, and billing.

# Average Procedure Costs in South Korea

| Procedures | Average Prices |
| --- | --- |
| *Cosmetic* | |
| Face/neck lift | $3,900 |
| Blepharoplasty (upper/lower eyelids) | $2,100 |
| Rhinoplasty | $2,800 |
| Brow/forehead lift | $2,000 |
| Otoplasty | $1,600 |
| Liposuction (per area) | $1,300 |
| Tummy tuck | $5,600 |
| Breast augmentation | $5,000 |
| Breast lift | $3,700 |
| Inner thigh lift | $2,900 |
| Outer thigh lift | $3,900 |
| Buttock lift | $2,700 |
| Lower body lift (inner/outer thighs, buttock) | $8,300 |
| *Medical* | |
| **Orthopedics** | |
| Hip replacement (per hip) | $13,000 |
| Hip resurfacing | $13,000 |
| Knee replacement (per knee) | $11,000 |
| Knee replacement (both knees) | $18,000 |
| **Spinal Procedures** | |
| Spinal fusion | $14,000 |
| Spinal disc replacement | $16,000 |
| **Cardiology** | |
| Angiogram | $1,700 |
| CT angiography scan | $600 |
| Aortic aneurysm surgery | $18,000 |
| Bypass surgery CAB | $14,000 |
| Coronary angioplasty (one stent and one balloon) | $7,000 |

| Procedures | Average Prices |
|---|:---:|
| **Obstetrics and Gynecology** | |
| Hysterectomy | $6,000 |
| **General Surgery** | |
| Diagnostic laparoscopy | $1,900 |
| Gallbladder removal | $3,900 |
| Hernia repair | $1,900 |
| **Dentistry** | |
| Crowns | $225–$1,000 |
| Veneers | $60–$350 |
| Implants | $650–$3,000 |
| Bridges | $250 |
| Bone grafts | $400–$750 |
| Root canal | $165–$250 |
| Extractions | $120–$150 |

# Thailand (Bangkok)

Thailand often is referred to as the global leader for medical tourism. The moniker is well-earned considering that far more than a million people are said to have traveled to Thailand in search of affordable world-class medical treatment. For several decades, Thailand has been a medical destination of choice for Americans, Europeans, and its own community of expatriates.

Thailand has earned a solid reputation for providing world-class health care. The country boasts technologically advanced facilities, cutting-edge equipment, and an abundance of doctors with specialist training completed in the United States and Europe. Thailand's expertise covers both elective and medically necessary procedures. It has become renowned as the world leader for gender reassignment surgery.

The first hospital in all of Asia to receive JCI accreditation is located in Thailand. Many other Thai hospitals are following its lead and have either already earned JCI accreditation or have begun the application process. The Thai government has made a commitment to the medical tourism industry and is working closely with the country's private hospital association to maintain its reputation as an international hub for health-care travelers.

# Travel Notes

**Languages spoken:** Thai (official language), but English is widely spoken

**People:** Thai, Mon, Khmer, Laotian, Chinese, Malay, Persian, and Indian

**Personality:** Thailand is referred to as the "Land of Smiles," and the people are charming and loving

**Infrastructure:** First World

**Currency:** Thai Baht

**Time zone:** GMT+7

**Country phone code:** 66

**Electricity:** 220V (some hotels provide 110V transformers)

**Weights and measures:** Metric system

**Elevation concerns:** None

**Climate:** Thailand's climate is tropical and humid. The average annual temperature is 83 degrees Fahrenheit.

**Clothing:** Light, cool clothing is advised. Beach-style casual attire—tank tops, sleeveless shirts, and short shorts—are reserved only for the beach. They are considered inappropriate dress in a medical setting. Men may be expected to wear a jacket in fine dining establishments.

**Getting online:** Fax, Internet, and e-mail services typically are available in all major hotels. Cybercafés in major tourist destinations also offer these services.

**Visa required:** No

**Immunizations required:** None

**Public health considerations:** There is no risk for malaria in cities and major tourist resorts.

# Cultural Do's and Don'ts

- Don't ever say anything negative about the royal family.

- Do dress neatly when entering a shrine.

- Don't climb onto Buddha statues to take a photo or show any disrespect to a Buddha statue.

◆ Don't shake hands when greeting Thai people; instead press your palms together in a prayer-like gesture.

◆ Don't touch a Thai person on the top of the head.

◆ Don't engage in public displays of affection.

# Hospitals

Thailand has approximately 400 hospitals, and most of them are public, state-owned facilities. Approximately 10 to 15 hospitals within the country promote international medical care. The majority of these hospitals are located in or around Bangkok. Bumrungrad International is the most globally recognized of all hospitals catering to medical tourists.

Bumrungrad International
33 Sukhumvit 3 (Soi Nana Nua)
Wattana, Bangkok
Thailand 10110
www.bumrungrad.com/Overseas-Medical-Care/Bumrungrad-International.aspx
Telephone number: 011-66-2-667-1000

Accreditation/certification: JCI (first hospital in all of Asia to receive JCI accreditation), Hospital Accreditation Board of Thailand

Specialties: Among more than 30 specialties are cardiac, neurology, orthopedics, plastic surgery, general surgery, women's health, health screening, dental, and fertility

Bumrungrad International has been featured on NBC's *Today Show* and *60 Minutes*, as well as in the pages of *Time* and *Newsweek* magazines. With more than 550 beds, it is the largest hospital in Southeast Asia, serving more than one million patients a year, including more than 400,000 foreign patients. The international patient center serves the needs of medical travelers from nearly 200 countries.

Phyathai Hospital
Phyathai 2 Hospital
Building 1, 4th floor
943 Phaholyothin Road, Samsennai
Phyathai, Bangkok
Thailand 10400
www.phyathai.com/phyathai_english/home.php
Telephone number: 011-66-2-617-2444

Accreditation/certification: Certified with the Hospital Accreditation Board of Thailand, ISO 9001, 14001, 18001, and HACCP

Specialties: The Phyathai Heart Center was established in 1998 in cooperation with Harvard Medical International; other specialty centers and clinics are available for cosmetic surgery, joint replacement, IVF, neurology, women's health, LASIK, dental, dermatology, and more

Established in 1987, the Phyathai 2 Hospital is the second of three hospitals in the Phyathai group. Composed of two buildings, this 550-bed facility includes 76 diagnostic rooms equipped with modern medical technology and equipment. It can handle up to 2,000 outpatient cases daily. The International Relations Center has been created to assist medical tourists with a host of services. An international ward created for foreign patients boasts rooms designed in a contemporary European style with comfortable living rooms and Internet access.

Piyavate Hospital
998 Rimklongsamsen Rd.
Bangkapi, Huay-kwang,
Bangkok, Thailand 10320
www.piyavate.com
Telephone number: 011-66-2-625-6600

Accreditation/certification: ISO 9001:2000

Specialties: Specialty centers include the Perfect Heart Institute, and centers for orthopedics, plastic surgery, dental, cancer, and women's health

This 27-story facility began serving patients in 1993. It is currently expanding to 300 inpatient beds, with 50 percent of them dedicated to international patients. The medical staff is comprised of both U.S. board-certified and Thai board-certified physicians, in addition to highly qualified registered nurses, technicians, and administrative personnel. The hospital provides medical services using modern technology and state-of-the-art equipment. A "Centers of Excellence" since 2004, Piyavate Hospital provides high-quality specialty services while maintaining other medical services.

Bangkok Hospital Medical Center
2 Soi Soonvijai 7, New Petchburi Road
Bangkapi, Huay Khwang
Bangkok, Thailand 10310
www.bangkokhospital.com/eng/index.aspx
Telephone number: 011-66-2-310-3000

Accreditation/certification: All four hospitals have JCI accreditation

Specialties: 16 specialty centers, including cardiology, neurology, plastic surgery, and gynecology

This state-of-the-art medical complex comprises four hospitals that provide comprehensive medical care. The center has more than 650 physicians, many of whom are internationally trained and certified. Dedicated to providing personalized care, these hospitals offer a host of amenities and services. One of the center's hospitals, Bangkok International Hospital, is the first hospital in Thailand created exclusively for international patients. In this facility, all the doctors and nurses are fluent in English, and translators are available to assist with communications.

Samitivej Hospital (Sukhumvit)
133 Sukhumvit 49, Klongtan Nua
Vadhana, Bangkok
Thailand 10110
www.samitivej.co.th/sukhumvit/aboutus_en.aspx
Telephone number: 011-66-2-711-8000

Accreditation/certification: Hospital Accreditation Board of Thailand

Specialties: Specialty clinics include dental, dermatology, heart, bone and joint, plastic surgery, LASIK, wellness, general surgery, women's health, and an esthetics institute

Established in 1979, this hospital boasts 270 beds, 7 examination suites, and more than 1,200 caregivers. With high-tech medical equipment and a highly skilled medical staff, the hospital offers a range of services from cosmetic surgery to tertiary care. An international department offers assistance to foreign patients. The medical complex also includes familiar convenience stores and retailers, such as 7-Eleven and Starbucks.

Preecha Aesthetic Institute (PAI)
Aesthetic Plastic Surgery Center
Dermatology and Laser Center
Bangkok Mediplex, 2nd Floor, Unit 201-203
2/70 Sukhumvit 42
Phra khanong, Khlong Toie
Bangkok 10250
www.pai.co.th
Telephone number: 011-2712-1111

Specialties: In addition to a wide range of cosmetic surgery procedures, PAI is famed for male-to-female gender reassignment, female-to-male gender reassignment, facial feminization, and penile enlargement

The Preecha Aesthetic Institute was established by Dr. Preecha Tiewtranon, one of the nation's most accomplished cosmetic surgeons and the world's most renowned sex-change surgeon. Commonly referred to as Dr. Preecha, this specialist has 30 years of experience in cosmetic surgery and gender reassignment. He has performed more than 30,000 cosmetic surgeries and more than 3,500 sex-reassignment surgeries and facial feminization treatments. The surgical techniques he pioneered in this highly specialized field have become the standard for these procedures. Dr. Preecha has trained every qualified gender-reassignment surgeon in Thailand.

## Average Procedure Costs in Thailand

| Procedures | Average Prices |
| --- | --- |
| *Cosmetic* | |
| Face/neck lift | $3,900 |
| Blepharoplasty (upper/lower eyelids) | $2,100 |
| Rhinoplasty | $2,800 |
| Brow/forehead lift | $2,000 |
| Otoplasty | $1,600 |
| Liposuction (per area) | $1,300 |
| Tummy tuck | $5,600 |
| Breast augmentation | $5,000 |
| Breast lift | $3,700 |
| Inner thigh lift | $2,900 |
| Outer thigh lift | $3,900 |
| Buttock lift | $2,700 |
| Lower body lift (inner/outer thighs, buttock) | $8,300 |
| *Medical* | |
| **Orthopedics** | |
| Hip replacement (per hip) | $13,000 |
| Hip resurfacing | $13,000 |
| Knee replacement (per knee) | $11,000 |
| Knee replacement (both knees) | $18,000 |

| Procedures | Average Prices |
|---|---|
| **Spinal Procedures** | |
| Spinal fusion | $14,000 |
| Spinal disc replacement | $16,000 |
| **Cardiology** | |
| Angiogram | $1,700 |
| CT angiography scan | $600 |
| Aortic aneurysm surgery | $18,000 |
| Bypass surgery CAB | $14,000 |
| Coronary angioplasty (one stent and one balloon) | $7,000 |
| **Obstetrics and Gynecology** | |
| Hysterectomy | $6,000 |
| **General Surgery** | |
| Diagnostic laparoscopy | $1,900 |
| Gallbladder removal | $3,900 |
| Hernia repair | $1,900 |
| **Gender Reassignment** | |
| Male-to-female | $9,000–$12,000 |
| Female-to-male (four stages) | $25,000 |
| **Dentistry** | |
| Crowns | $225–$1,000 |
| Veneers | $60–$350 |
| Implants | $650–$3,000 |
| Bridges | $250 |
| Bone grafts | $400–$750 |
| Root canal | $165–$250 |
| Extractions | $120–$150 |

# United Arab Emirates (Abu Dhabi and Dubai)

Comprised of seven states called emirates, the United Arab Emirates (UAE) is rich in oil and natural gas. This has led to tremendous wealth in the region and a luxurious lifestyle for its inhabitants. Today, the UAE is a virtually crime-free land where you can enjoy world-class hotels, unbeatable shopping, and exciting entertainment. All of this, combined with year-round sunshine and beautiful beaches, explains why the UAE has become one of the world's fastest-growing tourist destinations.

Like oases in the desert, Abu Dhabi and Dubai are two of the most modern cities in the world. With lofty skyscrapers and state-of-the-art communications services, they rival the world's most cosmopolitan cities. Still, you can find traces of the region's intriguing history outside the city centers. If you're concerned about traveling to the Middle East, rest assured that Dubai and Abu Dhabi are tolerant societies where Westerners feel safe and comfortable.

# Travel Notes

**Languages spoken:** Arabic (official language), but English is widely spoken

**People:** Arab, Indian, Pakistani, Iranian, and Southeast Asian

**Personality:** Friendly

**Infrastructure:** First World

**Currency:** Emirati Dirham

**Time zone:** GMT+4

**Country phone code:** 971

**Electricity:** 220V, 50Hz

**Weights and measures:** Metric system

**Elevation concerns:** None

**Climate:** Expect a lot of sunshine. Winters are pleasant with highs in the 70s, but summers can be scorching with highs reaching nearly 120 degrees Fahrenheit.

**Clothing:** Lightweight, cotton clothing is best.

**Getting online:** Fax, Internet, and e-mail services typically are available in all major hotels and in cybercafés.

**Visa required:** Yes

**Immunizations required:** None

**Public health considerations:** None

# Cultural Do's and Don'ts

◆ Do be aware that shops close every Friday from 11:30 A.M. to 1:30 P.M. for prayers.

◆ Don't drink alcohol in the street.

◆ Don't eat, drink, or smoke in public during Ramadan.

◆ Don't tip—it's already added in the bill.

# Hospitals

Two of the world's most highly advanced hospitals currently are in the development and construction phase in Dubai and Abu Dhabi. Both hospitals have partnered with prestigious U.S. medical institutions to ensure the highest quality of care. Huge investments are being made in these facilities, which are expected to offer luxurious amenities.

University Hospital/Dubai Healthcare City (DHCC)
P.O. Box 66566
Oud Metha Road
Ibn Sina Building, Block C, Ground Floor
Dubai, UAE
www.uhdubai.com/index.html
www.dhcc.ae/EN/Pages/Default.aspx
Telephone number: 1-800-HEALTH / 971-4-324-5555

Accreditation/certification: Hospital not operational yet, but plans to pursue JCI accreditation

Specialties: Oncology, neurosciences, orthopedics, women's health, cardiovascular, and more

Currently in the process of being developed, DHCC is expected to comprise hospitals, outpatient clinics, luxury spa resorts, and more. The ultra-modern, cutting-edge University Hospital, which is scheduled for a 2011 debut, will be a 400-bed, tertiary-care facility. DHCC has partnered with Harvard Medical International to ensure the highest quality patient care. Many physicians are expected to be U.S. trained. Situated nearby is a luxurious five-star hotel dedicated to patients' families, DHCC staff, and visiting doctors.

Cleveland Clinic Abu Dhabi (CCAD)
(Address and telephone number not yet available)
my.clevelandclinic.org/departments/abudhabi/default.aspx

Accreditation/certification: Hospital not operational yet, but plans to pursue JCI accreditation

Specialties: Cardiovascular, general surgery, gynecology, orthopedics, ophthalmology, and more

Originally scheduled to be operational in 2010, it's looking like it will be 2011 before CCAD welcomes its first patients. CCAD is expected to be a landmark structure that includes a 360-bed tertiary-care hospital and clinic. The medical facility is being established using Cleveland Clinic systems, procedures, guidelines, and standards. Most of the doctors are expected to be trained and board-certified in the United States, and the Cleveland clinic will provide continuing education.

## Average Procedure Costs in United Arab Emirates

The Abu Dhabi and Dubai hospitals that will cater to international patients aren't operational yet, but are expected to have prices that are somewhat higher than those you might find in Singapore.

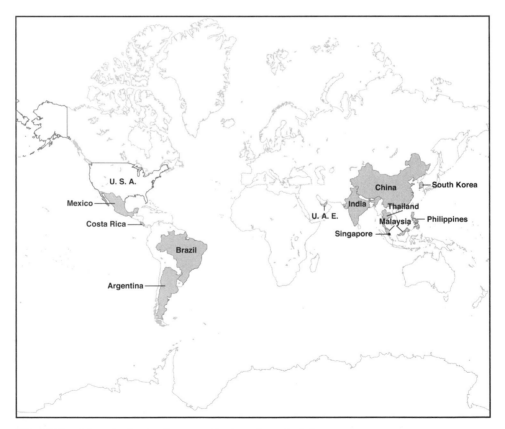

*World Map: Note the destination countries have been shaded.*

# Medicalese Made Easy

**accreditation**   A process in which a third-party agency evaluates medical facilities to ensure that they meet stringent standards.

**Adjustable gastric banding surgery**   A bariatric surgical procedure in which an adjustable band is placed around the stomach to restrict food intake.

**advance health-care directive**   A legal document that spells out your wishes for medical treatment in the event you are unable to communicate your preferences. This document also may designate the person of your choice to make health-care decisions for you.

**ambulatory care**   Any type of medical care that is provided on an outpatient basis.

**anemia**   A blood disorder in which a patient's red blood cell count is low. Anemia can cause fatigue, weakness, headaches, irregular heartbeat, and more.

**angiogram**   A diagnostic imaging test that uses x-ray technology to view a patient's blood vessels to determine if there are any blockages or other defects.

**angioplasty**   A minimally invasive cardiac procedure in which a tiny balloon and sometimes a stent are inserted into an artery to keep it open.

**anxiety**   A normal reaction to stress that can help you cope with difficult situations. When excessive, it can cause feelings of dread and also can lead to physical symptoms, such as chest pains, heart palpitations, stomachaches, and shortness of breath.

**arm lift**   A surgical procedure in which excess skin and fat are removed from the back of the upper arms.

**bariatric surgery**   A surgical procedure in which the size of the stomach is decreased and, in some cases, a portion of the intestine is bypassed to alter digestion and calorie absorption.

**blepharoplasty**   A surgical procedure in which excess skin and fat are removed from the upper and/or lower eyelids to construct a more youthful look.

**bonding**   A dental material that is affixed to the surface of damaged or discolored teeth.

**bone graft**   A dental procedure in which bone from your body or from another source is surgically implanted into your jaw.

**breast augmentation**   A surgical procedure in which implants are inserted into the breasts to increase breast size. Also called augmentation mammaplasty.

**breast lift**   A surgical procedure in which excess skin is removed from sagging breasts to restore a more uplifted bust line. Also called mastopexy.

**breast reduction**   A surgical procedure in which breast size is reduced. Also called reduction mammaplasty.

**bridge**   A dental device—consisting of two or more crowns that surround and are connected to a replica tooth—that is used to replace a missing tooth or teeth.

**brow lift**   A surgical procedure (often performed at the same time as a face lift) in which the skin of the forehead, eyebrows, and eyes is tightened. Also called a forehead lift.

**bur**   A small handheld tool with a rotational cutting device used in dentistry to prepare teeth for dental devices, such as veneers.

**buttock lift**   A surgical procedure aimed at improving the shape of sagging buttocks by removing excess skin and sometimes by augmenting the size of the buttocks using the patient's own tissues or using other materials, such as silicone implants.

**bypass surgery (CABG)**   A surgical procedure in which blood vessels from the chest or leg are used to bypass blocked coronary arteries to improve blood flow.

**cash value insurance policy**    A type of life insurance policy that not only pays a benefit upon the death of the policy holder, but also builds a cash value that can be accessed during the policy holder's lifetime.

**columella**    Referred to in plastic surgery as the narrow strip of nasal tissue that divides the nostrils.

**crown**    A dental device used to cover and repair damaged teeth. Also called caps.

**CT angiography scan**    A diagnostic procedure used to detect blockages in the coronary arteries.

**curriculum vitae (CV)** Similar to a resumé, this document typically includes a comprehensive list of a physician's education, residency, employment history, board certification, medical specialties, publications, and membership in professional associations.

**deep vein thrombosis (DVT)**    A blood clot that develops in a deep vein within the body, usually in the thigh or lower leg.

**dental implant**    A dental device used to replace a missing tooth or teeth. The device is comprised of a titanium screw (implanted into the jawbone), and a crown.

**dental pulp**    The soft tissue that is found in the center of the tooth.

**endoscopic**    A type of surgery involving the use of a miniature camera called an endoscope, which is inserted through tiny incisions in the body.

**Face lift/neck lift**    A surgical procedure in which excess skin and fat are removed and the remaining skin and underlying muscles of the face and neck are tightened to minimize the appearance of sagging. Also called rhytidectomy.

**fellowship**    A voluntary training program in a specialized field of medicine for physicians who have already completed medical school, an internship, and a residency.

**gastric bypass surgery**    A bariatric surgical procedure in which the size of the stomach is reduced and food exiting the stomach is rerouted to a more distant portion of the small intestine to reduce calorie absorption. Also called Roux-en-Y gastric bypass.

**Global ATM Alliance**    A global network of international banks that offer their customers no-fee ATM withdrawals at any of the banks within the network.

**Health Insurance Portability and Accountability Act (HIPAA)**    A set of national standards created to protect the privacy of Americans' health data.

**Health Savings Account (HSA)**    A special type of tax-advantaged savings account that can be tapped to pay for qualified medical expenses.

**heart valve replacement**   A surgical procedure in which a severely damaged heart valve is replaced with either a mechanical valve or a biological valve that comes from animal or human tissue.

**Hepatitis A**   A highly contagious liver disease that can be transmitted through contaminated food and water. A vaccine is available to help prevent this disease.

**Hepatitis B**   A serious liver infection that can be spread by contact with blood, bodily fluids, or contaminated medical equipment. A vaccine is available to help prevent this disease.

**hip replacement**   A surgical procedure in which a damaged hip joint is replaced with an artificial joint.

**hip resurfacing**   A surgical procedure that is similar to hip replacement but that preserves more of the patient's own joint. Also called BIRMINGHAM HIP Resurfacing System.

**home equity loan**   A type of loan in which your home serves as collateral.

**hysterectomy**   A surgical procedure in which the uterus, and possibly other female reproductive organs, is removed.

**in vitro fertilization (IVF)**   A process in which a woman's eggs are fertilized outside the womb and then injected into the uterus.

**informed consent form**   A document commonly used by hospitals and physicians that details the nature of a type of medical treatment or procedure, including the risks involved. Medical providers often require patients to read and sign the form prior to having a surgical procedure or medical treatment.

**informed consent**   A process in which a physician adequately informs the patient about treatment options so the patient can make an informed decision about which treatment to pursue.

**International Organization for Standardization (ISO)**   An international organization that sets commercial and industrial quality standards.

**internship**   A medical training program that takes place after the completion of medical school and that is required to become a fully licensed practicing physician.

**Joint Commission International (JCI)**   An organization that accredits international medical facilities that meet stringent safety and quality standards.

**knee replacement**   A surgical procedure in which a damaged knee joint is replaced with an artificial joint.

**LASIK surgery**   An eye procedure in which a laser is used to change the shape of the cornea with the goal of improving eyesight.

**liposuction**   A surgical procedure in which fat is suctioned from the body to produce more proportionate body contours.

**lower body lift**   A surgical procedure in which sagging skin is removed from the midsection—usually the thighs, buttocks, and abdomen.

**malaria**   An infectious disease that can be transmitted via mosquito bites.

**medical travel**   The action of traveling to a foreign country to receive some form of medical treatment.

**osseointegration**   The process in which bone within the jaw grows around a dental implant.

**otoplasty**   A surgical procedure that improves the appearance of the ears, usually bringing prominent ears closer to the head or reducing the size of large ears.

**patient-controlled analgesia**   A method of pain management that allows the patient to control the administration of pain-relieving medication.

**power of attorney**   A legal document that authorizes the person of your choice to act on your behalf in the event that you are unable to do so.

**Publication 502**   An IRS document that provides detailed information about deducting medical and dental expenses from tax returns.

**pulmonary embolism**   A life-threatening condition in which a blood clot travels to one of the lungs and blocks the blood supply to that lung.

**residency**   A hospital-based medical training program that usually follows an internship and focuses on a particular medical specialty.

**reverse mortgage**   A type of loan that allows homeowners who are 62 years old or older to convert home equity into cash.

**rhinoplasty**   A surgical procedure in which the nose is reshaped to improve its appearance.

**root canal**   A dental procedure in which the interior of an infected or decayed tooth is cleaned and filled with dental materials.

**self-funded employers**   Businesses that pay out-of-pocket for any medical treatments their employees receive, rather than paying monthly insurance premiums.

**spinal disc replacement**    A surgical procedure in which a damaged disc of the spine is removed and replaced with an artificial disc.

**spinal fusion**    A surgical procedure in which two or more vertebrae are fused or welded together.

**stent**    A tiny mesh tube commonly inserted into an artery during angioplasty procedures to keep the artery open.

**stop loss insurance**    A type of insurance that pays benefits after a self-funded employer has paid out a pre-determined amount of money for employee health-care treatment.

**subcutaneous musculoaponeurotic system (SMAS)**    The layer of facial muscles that lies beneath the skin.

**Subglandular breast augmentation**    A type of breast augmentation surgery in which the implants are placed above the chest muscle but below the breast tissue.

**Submuscular breast augmentation**    A type of breast augmentation surgery in which the implants are placed partially below the chest muscle in addition to being below the breast tissue.

**thigh lift**    A surgical procedure in which excess skin is removed from the inner and/or outer thighs to produce smoother-looking contours.

**tooth extraction**    A dental procedure in which a tooth is removed.

**tumescent fluids**    A combination of fluids, including saline, local anesthetics, and epinephrine, that are used during liposuction.

**tummy tuck**    A surgical procedure in which excess skin and fat are removed from the abdominal area and in which underlying abdominal muscles also may be tightened. Also called abdominoplasty.

**typhoid fever**    An illness caused by bacteria that is usually transmitted via contaminated food and water.

**veneers**    Thin shells of a ceramic material used to cover damaged or discolored teeth.

**visa**    A travel document that may be required when visiting some foreign countries.

**yellow fever**    A viral disease that can be transmitted when n carrier mosquito bites a human.

# Medical Tourism Directory

## Medical Tourist Organizations

**International Medical Travel Association (IMTA)**
www.intlmta.org/web/imta/home
Tourism Court 11th Floor
1 Orchard Spring Lane
Singapore 247729
011-65-6831-3505

The Singapore-based IMTA aims to improve international patient care. It has drafted an International Patient's Bill of Rights and Responsibilities to provide guidelines for patients and practitioners. The website also includes downloadable forms, such as medical history forms, for medical tourists.

**Medical Tourism Association Inc.**
www.medicaltravelauthority.com
10130 Northlake Blvd., #214-215
West Palm Beach, FL 33412

This international nonprofit association is dedicated to promoting the highest quality care for patients around the world, raising awareness about medical tourism, and providing information about hospitals worldwide.

**MedRetreat**
www.medretreat.com
2042 Laurel Valley Drive
Vernon Hills, IL 60061
1-877-876-3373

MedRetreat is the first American-owned and -operated medical tourism service agency providing a safe and affordable process for receiving health care abroad. Since January 2005, MedRetreat's worldwide network of health-care affiliates has successfully serviced more than 1,200 North American consumers.

# U.S.-Based Medical Associations and Organizations

**American College of Surgeons (ACS)**
www.facs.org/patienteducation/
633 North Saint Clair St.
Chicago, IL 60611-3211
312-202-5000/1-800-621-4111

The ACS currently has more than 70,000 members, including more than 4,000 members in foreign countries. Use the "Find a Surgeon" feature to locate members practicing in foreign countries.

**American Society for Aesthetic Plastic Surgery (ASAPS)**
www.surgery.org
11081 Winners Circle
Los Alamitos, CA 90720-2813
1-888-ASAPS-11 (1-888-272-7711)

The ASAPS is comprised of more than 2,100 plastic surgeons who are board certified by the American Board of Plastic Surgery and/or the Royal College of Physicians and Surgeons of Canada. These surgeons practice in the United States, Canada, and abroad. The website offers a wealth of patient information on various cosmetic surgery procedures, and includes a "Find-A-Surgeon" feature that lists American and international plastic surgeons.

**American Society of Plastic Surgeons (ASPS)**
www.plasticsurgery.org
444 E. Algonquin Rd.
Arlington Heights, IL 60005
847-228-9900

The ASPS is the world's largest plastic surgery specialty organization, and its website provides a vast array of information for patients considering plastic surgery. The ASPS offers referrals to member surgeons practicing outside of the United States who are board certified by the American Board of Plastic Surgery and/or the Royal College of Physicians and Surgeons of Canada. It also provides referrals to "Corresponding Members," international plastic surgeons who are not board certified in the United States or Canada but who have achieved distinction in their own countries.

**International Society of Aesthetic Plastic Surgery (ISAPS)**
www.isaps.org
3200 Downwood Circle, Suite 640
Atlanta GA 30327
404-351-0051

The membership of ISAPS includes 1,600 board-certified plastic surgeons in more than 80 countries. The website has a "Surgeon Finder" feature that lets you search for board-certified plastic surgeons around the world.

# Foreign-Based Medical Associations and Organizations

Argentine Society of Plastic, Aesthetic, and Reconstructive Surgery (in Spanish)
www.sacper.org.ar/
Av. Santa Fe 1611 P. 3
Ciudad Autónoma de Buenos Aires
Argentina

This organization's website offers information on various cosmetic and reconstructive plastic surgery procedures for prospective patients.

**Brazilian Society of Plastic Surgery (SBCP) (in English)**
www.cirurgiaplastica.org.br/english/index.cfm
Rua Funcal, 129, conjunto 21A
Vila Olímpia, São Paulo
Brazil

Enter a surgeon's name in the "Search Members" feature to ensure that the Brazilian doctor you're considering for cosmetic surgery is a member of the SBCP.

**Iberian-Latin American Federation of Plastic and Reconstructive Surgery (in Spanish)**
filacp.org/This organization's website lists the website addresses for plastic surgery societies in more than 20 Latin American countries.

**Korean Society of Plastic and Reconstructive Surgeons (in English)**
Seocho World officetel 1814
Seocho-dong 1355-3
Seocho-ku, Seoul 137-070
Korea

The "Search Member" function lets you verify whether a surgeon you're considering for plastic surgery is indeed a member of the society.

**Mexican Association of Plastic, Aesthetic, and Reconstructive Surgery (in English)**
www.plasticsurgery.org.mx
Flamencos #74, Col. San José Insurgentes
Mexico, D.F. C. P.
Mexico

This organization's website lets you find board-certified plastic surgeons throughout Mexico.

# Accreditation and Quality Standards Organizations

**Joint Commission International (JCI)**
www.jointcommissioninternational.org/23218/iortiz/
1515 West 22nd Street
Suite 1300W
Oak Brook, Illinois 60523
630-268-4800

JCI is a division of Join Commission Resources, the largest accreditation organization for health-care facilities in the United States. JCI also accredits international medical facilities that meet stringent safety and quality standards. The website offers a list of all JCI-accredited facilities around the world.

**International Organization for Standardization (ISO)**
www.iso.org/iso/home.htm
1, ch. de la Voie-Creuse
Case postale 56
CH-1211 Geneva 20, Switzerland
011-41-22-749-01-11

This website includes information about ISO standards for quality.

# General Health Background Information

### eMedTV
www.emedtv.com

With more than 100 health channels, this website offers an extensive library of articles and videos on numerous health topics.

### MayoClinic
www.mayoclinic.com

This award-winning consumer website offers articles, videos, and animations on hundreds of health-related topics.

### MedlinePlus
www.medlineplus.gov

Check out more than 750 topics on medical conditions, diseases, and wellness.

### WebMD
www.webmd.com

You'll find a wealth of health information and tools for managing your health on this consumer website.

# Travel Resources

### U.S. Department of State
travel.state.gov

Check this website for information on passports, visas, and other international travel-related information and tips for citizens of the United States.

### Centers for Disease Control and Prevention (CDC)
wwwn.cdc.gov/travel/destinationList.aspx

This is the nation's premier public health agency working to promote health and quality of life by preventing and controlling disease, injury, and disability. Use the website to check for the most up-to-date information on vaccinations, travel notices, safe food and water, and more.

### Fodor's
www.fodors.com

Get the scoop on traveling to foreign countries.

### Frommer's
www.frommers.com

Find insider info on destinations around the world.

### Lonely Planet
www.lonelyplanet.com

Get travel tips on international destinations.

### Time and Date
www.timeanddate.com/worldclock/

Check the current time and date in various cities in different time zones around the world.

### XE.com
www.xe.com

Use this handy currency converter to see how much U.S. dollars are worth abroad.

### WorldAtlas.com
www.worldatlas.com

Find world maps and a plethora of facts about international destinations.

# Publications

### Medical Tourism Magazine
www.medicaltravelauthority.com/magazine.html#Magazine-Issues

Sign up for a free subscription of this print and electronic publication that addresses important issues in the medical travel industry and that looks at health-care options in leading medical tourism destinations.

### Medical Travel Today
www.medicaltraveltoday.com

This free online newsletter keeps readers up-to-date on the latest happenings in the medical travel industry.

# Medications to Avoid Before Surgery

Although lengthy, this list isn't comprehensive. If you're taking any drugs, vitamins, herbal remedies, or supplements that aren't on this list, ask your doctor if it's okay to continue taking them prior to surgery.

**A**

Adprin-B products

Advil products

Aleve products

Alka-Seltzer products

Amigesic

Anacin products

Anaprox products

Ansaid

Argesic

Arthritis Pain Formula

Arthropan products

Asacol

Ascriptin products

Aspergum

Aspirin (ASA)

Aspirtab

Axotal

Azdone

Azulfidine products

**B**

Bayer products

BC products

Bismatrol

Bufferin products

Buffex

Buffinol

Butalbital

Butazolidin

**C**

Cama Arthritis Pain Reliever

Carisoprodol

Cataflam

Celebrex

Cheracol

Clinoril

Contac products

Coricidin products

Coumadin

**D**

Damason-P

Darvon products

Daypro

Deprenyl

Diclofenac

Diflunisal

Dimetapp products

Dipyridamole

Disalcid

Doan's products

Dolobid

Dolophine

Dristan products

Duradyne DHC

Duragesic

**E**

Easprin

Ecotrin products

Eldepryl

Emagrin

Empirin products

Endodan

Epromate-M

Equagesic

Etodolac

Excedrin products

**F**

4-Way Cold products

Feldene

Fenoprofen

Fiorinal products

Flagyl

Flurbiprofen

Furadantin

**G**

Gelpirin

Genpril

Genprin

Genasan

Goody's products

**H**

Halfprin

Haltran

Heparin

**I**

IBU

Ibuprin

Ibuprofen

Ibuprohm

Ibu-Tab

Indocin

Indomethacin

Isocarboxazid

Isollyl

**J–K–L**

Ketoprofen

Ketorolac

Lanorinal

Lodine

Lortab ASA

**M**

Magan

Magnaprin

Magsal

Marnal

Marplan

Marthritic

Meclofenamate

Meclomen

Medipren

Menadol

Meprogesic

Methocarbamol

Micrainin

Midol products

Mobidin

Mobigesic

Momentum

Mono-Gesic

Motrin products

**N**

Nabumetone

Nalfon

Naprosyn products

Nardil

Nefazodone

Norgesic products

Norwich products

Nuprin products

NyQuil products

**O**

Orphengesic products

Orudis

Oruvail

Oxycodone

**P–Q–R**

Pacaps

Pamprin products

Panalgesic

Parnate

Pentoxifylline

Pepto-Bismol

Persantine

Phenaphen

Phenelzine

Piroxicam

Ponstel

Profenal

Propoxyphene

Relafen

Rexolate

Rhinocaps

Robaxin

Robaxisal

Roxiprin

Rufen

**S**

Saleto

Salflex

Salicylamide

Salsalate

Salsitab

Serzone

Sine-Aid products

Sine-Off products

Soma Compound

St. Joseph products

Stanback Analgesic

Sudafed products

Sulindac

Supac

Synalgos products

**T–U–V**

Tolectin products

Tolmetin

Toradol

Trendar

Triaminicin

Tricosal

Trilisate

Vanquish

Voltaren

**W–X–Y–Z**

Warfarin

Zorprin

# Index